The African American History Series

Series Editors

Nina Mjagkij
Jacqueline M. Moore

D1232424

Traditionally, history books tend to fall into two categories: books academics write for each other, and books written for popular audiences. Historians often claim that many of the popular authors do not have the proper training to interpret and evaluate the historical evidence. Yet, popular audiences complain that most historical monographs are inaccessible because they are too narrow in scope or lack an engaging style. This series, which will take both chronological and thematic approaches to topics and individuals crucial to an understanding of the African American experience, is an attempt to address that problem. The books in this series, in lively prose by established scholars, are aimed primarily at nonspecialists. They focus on topics in African American history that have broad significance and place them in their historical context. While presenting sophisticated interpretations based on primary sources and the latest scholarship, the authors tell their stories in a succinct manner, avoiding jargon and obscure language. They include selected documents that allow readers to judge the evidence for themselves and to evaluate the authors' conclusions. Bridging the gap between popular and academic history, these books will bring the African American story to life.

Volumes Published

Jacqueline M. Moore
Booker T. Washington, W.E.B. Du Bois, and the Struggle for Racial Uplift (2003).
Cloth ISBN 0-8420-2994-X   Paper ISBN 0-8420-2995-8

Booker T. Washington,
W.E.B. Du Bois,
and the Struggle for
Racial Uplift

Booker T. Washington, W.E.B. Du Bois, and the Struggle for Racial Uplift

JACQUELINE M. MOORE

AFRICAN AMERICAN HISTORY SERIES

VOLUME ONE

A Scholarly Resources Inc. Imprint
Wilmington, Delaware

Scholarly Resources Inc.
104 Greenhill Avenue
Wilmington, DE 19805-1897
www.scholarly.com

Library of Congress Cataloging-in-Publication Data

Moore, Jacqueline M., 1965–
  Booker T. Washington, W.E.B. Du Bois, and the struggle for racial
uplift / by Jacqueline M. Moore.
      p. cm. — (The African American history series ; no. 1)
    Includes bibliographical references and index.
    ISBN 0-8420-2994-X (alk. paper) — ISBN 0-8420-2995-8 (pbk.)
    1. Washington, Booker T., 1865–1915—Political and social views.
2. Du Bois, W.E.B. (William Edward Burghardt), 1868–1963—
Political and social views. 3. African American intellectuals—
Biography. 4. African American political activists—Biography.
5. African Americans—Civil rights—History. 6. African Americans—
Intellectual life. 7. African Americans—Politics and government.
8. United States—Race relations. I. Title. II. Series: African American history series (Wilmington, Del.) ; no. 1.

E185.97.W4 M66 2003
370'.92—dc21   2002030927

To Gail Urban, Shelton Stromquist, Howard Allen,
and Louis Harlan, who taught me how to pronounce
the names and led me to this book

ACKNOWLEDGMENTS

My greatest debt is to Nina Mjagkij, who taught me how to talk to publishers and gave me faith in my writing abilities. She also carefully read most of the manuscript on her vacation and pointed out some obvious mistakes. My first intellectual debt is to David Levering Lewis, whom I have never personally met but without whose extraordinary biography of Du Bois this book would have been much harder to write. Not surprisingly, my other major intellectual debt is to Louis R. Harlan, whose two-volume biography of Booker T. Washington has set the standard for historians. There have been attempts to challenge his interpretation of Washington; none has succeeded. On a personal note, I also want to thank him for pinpointing documents and footnotes within seconds in the edited papers that cleared up the facts and for suggesting topics for the last chapter. I owe Dr. Harlan and his wife, Sadie, a personal debt for being so willing to listen to me babble on about my book and for welcoming me on extremely short notice.

Since I intended this book for readers with little or no background on the subject, I am especially grateful for the help of nonhistorian friends who waded through the chapters and gave me suggestions. Patrick Horne served as my number one guinea pig, and he and his father, Orion Horne, sent useful comments. Thank you for being such good sports and for your honest opinions. My stepfather, Alan Wilson, read the first chapter and made helpful suggestions, too. I am very grateful to Shelley Smith, the first student to read the manuscript as an official assignment, for being so willing to work with me on it. Thanks to Randy Leckman and Janet Imhoff for proofreading the documents with me.

Finally, thanks to Matt Hershey at Scholarly Resources for being patient on deadlines, to Emily Crockett and Barbara Salazar for the last book, and to the Austin College faculty and students for coming to hear a rather scattered talk on the most interesting things I learned about Washington and Du Bois on my summer vacation.

—Jacqueline Moore
Sherman, Texas
July 2002

ABOUT THE AUTHOR

Jacqueline M. Moore is associate professor of history at Austin College in Sherman, Texas. She is the author of *Leading the Race: The Transformation of the Black Elite in the Nation's Capital, 1880–1920*, and coeditor of the African American History Series for Scholarly Resources.

CONTENTS

NOTE ON PRONUNCIATION   xiii

INTRODUCTION   xv

CHRONOLOGY   xxi

1   Jim Crow and the Rise of Segregation   1

2   Booker T. Washington and Tuskegee Institute   15

3   W.E.B. Du Bois and Atlanta University   37

4   The Conflict   61

5   Alternatives to Washington and Du Bois   89

EPILOGUE   115

DOCUMENTS IN THE CASE   123

BIBLIOGRAPHICAL ESSAY   177

INDEX   187

NOTE ON PRONUNCIATION

The first time I heard my high school Advanced Placement history teacher pronounce Du Bois's name "Due Boys," I remember thinking to myself, "Anyone who knows anything about French should know that's wrong; it should be 'Due Bwah.' " But as she was about most things, my history teacher was correct. As his most recent and thorough biographer, David Levering Lewis, points out, Du Bois himself corrected people's pronunciation, writing that it was "Due Boys" with the stress on the second syllable. As for the "T" in Booker T. Washington, that name also has an unusual pronunciation. At the University of Maryland, I first referred to its Taliaferro Hall as "Tally-a-fair-oh," only to find to my embarrassment that it was pronounced "Tolliver." Washington's most noted biographer, Louis R. Harlan, tells us that the same was true for Booker Taliaferro Washington. Finally, "Tuskegee," which I first called "Tuska-ghee," is actually pronounced "Tuh-skee-ghee," with the emphasis on the second syllable. I make these remarks not to embarrass anyone who mispronounces the names as I did but to set the record straight so that other students can avoid embarrassment.

INTRODUCTION

It is impossible to discuss black history at the turn of the twentieth century without examining two key figures: Booker T. Washington and W.E.B. Du Bois. Both men made their presence felt in a wide variety of fields, and both men left their permanent mark on the question as to how blacks should achieve equality in America. Washington, the more conservative of the two, advocated a gradual approach toward gaining civil rights, starting with economic concerns rather than political or social issues. Du Bois, the more radical of the two, insisted on immediate and full civil rights in all areas. Their positions were not new to blacks, nor would they be the last to hold them, but their names have become symbols of the debate between the two views, largely because that debate was so public and involved almost all members of the African American community.

Not surprisingly, most earlier histories of black America in this period created an image of a community completely divided into two different camps. Recently, historians have begun to argue that there were other approaches to achieving equality, and they have unearthed a far more complex view of black life and philosophy than just the two extremes. Nonetheless, it is clear that the dissension between Washington and Du Bois went far beyond philosophical differences and permeated almost all aspects of black life. Consequently, in order to understand the black experience at the turn of the century, it is necessary to examine the debate while recognizing that it was not the only show in town.

Booker Taliaferro Washington rose to fame as the founder and principal of Tuskegee Institute, a school devoted to giving African Americans a basic education while also providing them with training in practical skills, such as carpentry, to ensure that they could earn a living. He advocated that blacks practice self-help in advancing their cause; in other words, that they should advance primarily through their own individual efforts rather than be pulled up by others, but he enlisted contributions from southern and northern white philanthropists in order to make his vision a reality. He gained a national reputation as *the* spokesman for black Americans following an address he gave at the opening ceremonies of the Atlanta Cotton States and International Exposition, a sort of world's fair held in 1895. In one of the most famous speeches ever made by an African American, he advised blacks to stay in the South and improve their lives from the bottom up through hard work, and he asked whites to help by giving blacks opportunities to show their merits. He also stated his belief that the two races could remain separate socially as long as whites included them in economic opportunities. At the time of his speech, both whites and blacks praised Washington for his fairness and his firm insistence that helping blacks was only helping to rebuild the South as a whole.

Among whites, Washington gained a national reputation as a "reasonable" black man who would not rock the boat. As such, he inspired confidence among northern white politicians who wanted to reward northern black voters through patronage without challenging existing social patterns. These men began to consult Washington on the best candidates for various positions—meaning, of course, black men who held similar accommodationist views. In this way he came to the attention of Theodore Roosevelt, governor of New York, and by 1901, when Roosevelt became president, Washington was arguably the most influential black man in the country.

William Edward Burghardt Du Bois gained notice as the first black man to graduate from Harvard with a doctoral degree in history. He had already completed postgraduate study at the University of Berlin, where he trained as a sociologist. He worked at several schools before achieving national prominence for his study *The Philadelphia Negro* (1899), still considered a classic work in what was then the new field of sociology. Following this success he took a position at historically black Atlanta University, where he conducted a series of scientific studies of race relations and conditions for African Americans. He later became one of the founders of the National Association for the

Advancement of Colored People (NAACP) and the editor of its journal, *The Crisis*.

Du Bois's wider fame before World War I, however, came through his opposition to Booker T. Washington's leadership. Du Bois objected to Washington's emphasis on industrial education as the sole method of education for blacks, because he believed that training them primarily for manual labor did not prepare them for higher learning or better opportunities. He thought it important to train a "Talented Tenth," the top 10 percent of the black population, to lead the rest of the race and to "uplift" them, or help improve their lives through education, better services, and political representation. He also objected to the idea that blacks should concentrate on economic progress to the exclusion of political or social equality. Most of all he objected to the fact that Washington seemed to have appointed himself spokesman for the race and, through somewhat underhanded methods, was opposing anyone who spoke out against that leadership. Although the two men cooperated on a variety of matters in the late nineteenth century, a series of events between 1903 and 1905 led to a complete break between them, and a very public one at that.

The break began when Du Bois published his most famous book, *The Souls of Black Folk*, in 1903, including a chapter that attacked Washington by name for his philosophies and self-imposed leadership. Following a few failed attempts to come to some agreement on issues in 1904, Du Bois decided that he needed to take more decisive action, and in 1905 he established the Niagara Movement, an organization devoted to demanding immediate civil rights and protesting any attempts to stifle differing opinions. Washington responded by stifling all coverage of the Niagara Movement's activities in the press, among other pressure tactics; as a result, in the years between 1905 and Washington's death in 1915, their bitter arguments forced most African Americans to take sides.

At first, Washington had the upper hand because he could control who got jobs and which institutions received charitable donations. But after Woodrow Wilson, a Democrat, became president in 1913, Washington, a life-long Republican, could no longer expect to give advice on political appointments. In addition, external factors such as the rise of black businesses and institutions were providing some blacks with sources of power independent of Washington's Tuskegee Institute. Moreover, race relations continued to deteriorate during this period; as segregation and discrimination increased, more blacks grew frustrated with the existing situation, and fewer had hope that a gradualist approach would work. By 1909, when Du Bois and some white reformers in New York created the organization that became the NAACP, calling for immediate challenges to segregation and to other forms of discrimination, particularly lynching, blacks were more willing to join the organization openly than they had been to join the Niagara Movement. After Washington's death in 1915 the NAACP became the major civil rights organization in America, with Du Bois as its leading spokesman.

Ultimately, objective conditions such as geography and lack of funds for effective protest restricted even the radicalism that Du Bois and Washington's other opponents espoused. Although the 1920s marked a peak of NAACP activity, the organization moved North and left the South largely untouched. The Great Migration of African Americans to the North, which intensified around 1915, allowed many to escape southern segregation, but they faced other forms of racism in the North. The Great Depression effectively ended most white philanthropy in the black community and increased racial hostilities. In the 1930s, Du Bois became a socialist, and he grew so disillusioned with American society by the end of the 1950s that he emigrated to Ghana, where he lived until his death in 1963. In the 1960s, another generation of activists would face the same issues as Du Bois and Washington did at the turn of the century, and the debate would rage again between accommodationists and radicals within the Civil Rights Movement.

Today, Washington and Du Bois continue to speak to us beyond their own historical situation. A recent Internet search discovered 77,500 references to Booker T. Washington and 55,600 to W.E.B. Du Bois. Internet bookseller Amazon.com listed 139 books on or by Washington and 179 on or by Du Bois. At one point it was fashionable to dismiss Washington as an "Uncle Tom," a black man who just said and did what white people wanted him to say and do. Scholars and activists scorned his emphasis on economic advances without regard to political rights or social equality. But many students and activists are rediscovering Washington's emphasis on self-reliance and heralding this method as the only way in which blacks can truly achieve equality. Similarly, Du Bois's *The Souls of Black Folk* remains popular reading today, and not just as a classroom assignment; readers focus less on the infamous chapter criticizing Washington and praise the other essays in the collection. Many comment on his ability to explain the fundamental dilemma of what it means to be black and also American and approve of his emphasis on setting high standards and goals for the race. In short, Du Bois and Washington, although they have already been the subjects of much study, can still teach new things about the African American struggle to achieve equality.

I do not intend this book to be the definitive explanation of the debate over racial uplift at the turn of the century, nor can I cover every aspect of black history during the period of the debate or even every part of the two men's lives. It is important to emphasize that the Washington–Du Bois conflict was only one part of the black community's search for effective ways to combat rising segregation and discrimination, even if the personal disagreements dominated much of the black political scene. What I do hope to accomplish is to explain in more detail a conflict that most textbooks only briefly outline and to place it in a broader historical context. I want to go beyond surface narration to examine the motivations of the two men and the political issues surrounding their positions. To further this goal, following the main text I have supplied a selection of contemporary documents relevant to the debate so that readers can judge the evidence themselves and draw their own conclusions.

In short, this book introduces the issues at hand and provides a basis for further discussion and exploration of black history in the late nineteenth and early twentieth centuries. In the process, the story unfolds of two of the most fascinating men and one of the most infamous disputes in American history.

CHRONOLOGY

1828

Thomas Dartmouth Rice creates "Jim Crow" character

1853

First black YMCA in United States opens in Washington, DC

1856

Booker Taliaferro Washington is born in Virginia, exact date unknown

1865

Thirteenth Amendment abolishes slavery
Washington and family move to Malden, West Virginia

1865–1872

Freedmen's Bureau provides relief to southern blacks and protects their rights

1866

Fourteenth Amendment makes blacks citizens
Fisk University and Howard University established

1867–72

Washington works for Viola Ruffner

1868

February 23   William Edward Burghardt Du Bois is born in Massachusetts

1868

Hampton Normal and Agricultural Institute established

1869

Fifteenth Amendment gives blacks voting rights

1872

Blanche K. Bruce elected to U.S. Senate from Mississippi

Amnesty Act grants general amnesty to all former Confederates

1872–1875

Washington attends Hampton Institute

1875

Washington works as waiter in upstate New York

1877

Compromise over contested 1876 election ends Reconstruction and federal protection of blacks

1878–1881

Washington teaches night school at Hampton Institute

1879

Six thousand black "Exodusters" migrate to Kansas

1880s

Bishop Henry McNeal Turner advocates emigration to Africa

1881

Washington establishes Tuskegee Normal and Industrial Institute in Alabama

1883

Supreme Court declares Civil Rights Act of 1875 unconstitutional

1885

Du Bois graduates from high school and receives scholarship to Fisk University

1887

T. Thomas Fortune founds Afro-American Council

1888

Du Bois graduates with B.A. degree from Fisk

Du Bois works as waiter in Minnesota in summer

1888–1895

Du Bois attends Harvard University

1889

Edwin McCabe proposes making Oklahoma an all-black state, which prompts wave of migration West

Edward Wilmot Blyden tours United States advocating emigration to Africa

1890s

Rise of scientific racism, lynchings, and segregation

1890

Du Bois graduates with B.A. degree from Harvard

1890 and 1891

White leaders decide at Lake Mohonk conferences that industrial training is best type of education for blacks

1891

Du Bois receives M.A. degree in history from Harvard

YMCA appoints William A. Hunton first black international secretary

1892–1894

Du Bois studies at University of Berlin

1894–1896

Du Bois teaches at Wilberforce University

1895

Du Bois receives Ph.D. degree in history from Harvard

September 18   Washington speaks at opening ceremonies of Atlanta Exposition

1896

In *Plessy v. Ferguson* the Supreme Court declares segregation constitutional

		National Association for Colored Women forms with Mary Church Terrell as president
1896–1898		
		Du Bois works in Philadelphia's Seventh Ward
1899		
		Du Bois publishes *The Philadelphia Negro*
	April	Sam Hose lynching
	May	Du Bois's son Burghardt dies
	May	Washington offers Du Bois a job at Tuskegee
	Fall	Washington and Du Bois cooperate to challenge Georgia law that would take away black voting rights
1900–1904		
		Washington and Du Bois cooperate on challenge to segregation on Pullman sleeping cars
1900		
		Washington organizes National Negro Business League
		Du Bois attends First Pan-African Congress in London
1901		
	July	Washington publishes his autobiography, *Up from Slavery*; Du Bois reviews it in *The Dial*
	October 16	Washington dines with President Theodore Roosevelt at White House
	November	William Monroe Trotter and George Forbes found *Boston Guardian*
1902		
		Militants such as Ida B. Wells lose their officer positions in Afro-American Council as Washington gains control
1903		
	January	Philanthropist William H. Baldwin pressures Du Bois to accept employment at Tuskegee
	April	Du Bois publishes *The Souls of Black Folk*

July	Du Bois teaches at Tuskegee and dines with Washington
July 30	Boston Riot; Du Bois sides with the Anti-Bookerites

1904

Carnegie Conference forms Committee of Twelve; Du Bois resigns within six months

1905

January	Du Bois charges Washington with bribing the press
July	Du Bois launches Niagara Movement

1905–1909

Washington pursues full campaign of persecution against Du Bois and his allies

1906

September 22–26	Atlanta Riot
October	Brownsville Affair

1909

National Association for the Advancement of Colored People founded

1910

Du Bois becomes editor of *The Crisis* and moves north

National Urban League established

1911

Washington is beaten in street in New York City

1912

Washington loses president's patronage when Woodrow Wilson wins election

1913

Federal government offices segregated

1915

Washington and Du Bois protest racist film, *The Birth of a Nation*

Great Migration begins to pick up steam

November 14	Booker T. Washington dies

1919

Race riots erupt across United States

1920s

Du Bois comes into conflict with Marcus Garvey

1934

Du Bois resigns from NAACP although he briefly rejoins from 1944 to 1948

1950s

Du Bois comes under suspicion for "subversive activities"

1961

Du Bois emigrates to Ghana

1963

August 27	W.E.B. Du Bois dies
August 28	Martin Luther King Jr. gives his "I Have a Dream" speech at March on Washington in nation's capital before 250,000 civil rights protestors

1 | Jim Crow and the Rise of Segregation

Booker T. Washington and W.E.B. Du Bois rose to fame in a period of American history known as the Era of Jim Crow. The objective conditions for blacks during this era strongly shaped their beliefs, as did their personal experiences. But Washington's and Du Bois's philosophies had their basis in earlier ideas about how to improve the race. For an understanding of the two men and the larger debate over racial uplift, therefore, it is important to examine the context in which they lived and the influences they, and most African Americans, absorbed at the turn of the twentieth century.

In the 1830s a new type of entertainment appeared in America, the minstrel show. In these shows white (and sometimes black) musicians and comedians would appear in blackface—that is, they would darken their faces with burnt corks and apply red lipstick to make their lips appear larger, in a racist caricature of black faces. They would then perform song-and-dance routines and comic sketches that were supposed to reflect slave life on the plantation. The performers grinned and acted the buffoon, creating an image of slaves as happy-go-lucky, lazy, and ignorant. The best known of the early American minstrels was Thomas Dartmouth Rice. In 1828, he staged his first show in Louisville, Kentucky, featuring his caricature of an old and crippled slave who sang and danced to a song with the chorus "Eb'ry time I wheel about, I jump Jim Crow." As Rice toured the country with his act, "Jim Crow" became a national phenomenon. He may have chosen the name of a slave he knew or perhaps simply drew it from the saying "black as a crow," but Rice's character became synonymous with slaves and African Americans in general. The term evoked an extremely unflattering image of blacks, but by the end of the nineteenth century it was so common that the laws southern states passed to segregate blacks from whites in public places became known as "Jim Crow laws." In fact, the image of Jim Crow as a lazy and not particularly intelligent human being helped to provide justification for those laws in the first place.

The Era of Jim Crow for African Americans was also the Gilded Age and Progressive Era for most other Americans. It was during the Gilded Age that America became a major world industrial power, largely through the innovations of business entrepreneurs such as Andrew Carnegie in steel and John D. Rockefeller in oil. But these men could be as ruthless as they were innovative. Moreover, industrialization brought many new problems to America such as pollution, overcrowded cities, and unsafe working conditions. Mark Twain labeled the period the Gilded Age because, like the thin layer of gold paint with which we "gild" cheap metal to make it look more expensive, what appeared shiny and valuable in American society on the surface was simply a deception.

The Progressive Era that followed tried to compensate for the excesses of the Gilded Age through a variety of reforms aimed at making American politics, society, and economics more democratic. This democracy did not usually extend to African Americans, however. During the Era of Jim Crow, race relations between blacks and whites reached an all-time low with the rise of segregation and the increase in lynchings. It was not that racism against African Americans was new, as the existence of slavery and the popularity of minstrel shows demonstrated; but its nature changed to reflect a larger context that was also part of the Gilded Age and Progressive Era.

Several factors contributed to changing racial attitudes in the Progressive Era. The new movement to create an American empire like the European ones fueled racial stereotypes. American imperialists believed that the largely nonwhite, "primitive" societies they wanted to take over needed white supervision and, by extension, that all nonwhites were incapable of self-government. The large influx of southern and eastern European immigrants in the Northeast and Chinese and Japanese immigrants in the Far West also contributed to growing ethnic tensions. Unlike most earlier immigrants, these southern and eastern Europeans were not Protestant and in some cases were not even Christian. They were mostly poor, did not speak English, and tended to cluster together both in fields of employment and in housing patterns. They prayed differently, ate strange and spicy foods, had what people described as "swarthy" complexions, and seemed to be taking over urban America and threatening its ideals.

At the same time that immigration was on the rise, European and American social science began to absorb the influence of Charles Darwin's theory of the evolution of species. One resulting movement, known as Social Darwinism, contributed heavily to the rise of racism in the Western world. Social scientists, trying to identify different sub-species within humanity, began to classify the world in terms of its different ethnic groups and to rank these groups in order of superiority. Naturally, they began with the assumption that western Europeans were the ideal, and so the more any ethnic group differed from that ideal, the more inferior that group must be. Most believed that intervening to help the weaker groups was simply delaying their inevitable end and interfering with the natural order. Others went as far as to advocate "eugenics," or selective breeding of desirable ethnic groups. Social Darwinism caught on rapidly in the United States in the late nineteenth century.

When "scientific" studies of race and ethnicity, largely at white southern universities, began suggesting that racism was justified, progressives generally accepted the words of the "experts" without questioning their methods. To most whites, who had already absorbed negative stereotypes of blacks such as Jim Crow and Little Black Sambo, "scientific racism" made sense. Southern white scholars focused largely on physical differences to justify segregation. Studies in the 1890s collected statistics on the size of heads, the angle of foreheads (more slope implied less intelligence), the shape of noses, and other physical measurements—all, of course, concluding that whites were superior. Although flawed methodology led to inaccurate results, faced with such scientific "evidence," few progressives challenged them.

There were some reformers who believed it was possible to improve the so-called weaker races. These reformers probably first developed their ideas while working with Native Americans. Through superior force the United States had brought most Indians under government supervision on reservations, but it was clear the Indians did not want to settle there. Reformers decided that rather than trying to keep them separate, it would make more sense to practice a policy of assimilation: they would teach Native Americans to speak English, convert them to Christianity, and make them into little American farmers with the same values as whites. The Dawes Act of 1887 divided up reservations into individual plots of land to try to accomplish this goal, but eventually most of the land went to speculators rather than to the Indians themselves. In the 1870s and 1880s, missionaries with the same goal of assimilation established a series of schools both on the reservations and in the East. The policy was not very effective overall, but there were some successes. That same desire to eliminate cultural competition led to the ideal of America as a melting pot and efforts to assimilate the new European immigrants into American society through classes in English, nutrition, and citizenship education. Nonetheless, most Americans still reacted with hostility toward anyone ethnically different from themselves, and there was a movement to exclude new immigrants completely. Animosity was so strong toward the Chinese that Congress passed the Chinese Exclusion Act in 1882, banning all immigration from China for the next ten years. Renewed permanently in 1892, the act remained in effect until 1943.

Reformers made no attempts to help former slaves assimilate to Western culture, largely because they were already a part of it: blacks seemed to occupy a permanent place at the bottom of American society. Indeed, new immigrants soon learned that a quick way to prove one's "American-ness" was to make racist remarks about African Americans. Yet many blacks continued to hope that they too could assimilate to the larger society. They believed in the ideals of American democracy and expected that with slavery abolished, whites would recognize their worth and accept them as equals. In reality, few whites seriously challenged traditional stereotypes of blacks as lazy, dishonest, and lacking mental capacity for anything beyond manual labor.

It would be a mistake, however, to assume that African Americans were passive victims who simply reacted to their situation. Even though racism was the environment under which they operated, the ways in which blacks chose to act demonstrated a firm belief that they could control their own destiny and force change. From their earliest arrival in the American colonies, slaves had found ways to resist control by their masters through work slowdowns, "accidental" destruction of tools and crops, and food theft, among other tactics. Although these acts unfortunately contributed to the stereotypes that blacks were dishonest or too incompetent to be trusted with complicated tasks, such behavior was a sophisticated form of resistance that allowed the slaves to have some control over their lives.

Free blacks found more direct ways to achieve control. Some chose economic advancement as the means of gaining independence. Many believed that racial discrimination was the result of socioeconomic position: in other words, whites looked down on them because they were poor and lacked education and refinement. They believed the key to assimilation therefore was to improve their economic status. Families such as the Fortens of Philadelphia, the Ruffins of Boston, and the Cooks of Washington, DC, earned fortunes in business and real estate transactions, gaining the respect of blacks *and* whites in their respective cities. They also used this money to fund activities to help abolish slavery. James Forten, for example, almost completely funded the first year of *The Liberator*, a radical journal edited by white abolitionist William Lloyd Garrison. Garrison later gained financial support from other white abolitionists, but Forten made a key contribution at a time when abolitionism was not a popular movement.

Other leading blacks benefited from their blood relationships to prominent white families. Robert Harlan maintained close ties with his white relatives, a wealthy Kentucky family, and even as a slave he gained an education and could travel freely throughout the country. In 1849 he earned a fortune in the California gold rush and later moved to Cincinnati, where he became a part of black high society. Norris Wright Cuney of Texas and Blanche K. Bruce of Mississippi began their lives as favored sons of white masters and slave mothers. Both received an education and became prominent in state and national politics after the Civil War.

Having achieved a measure of social status themselves and thus recognition in the white community, many of those blacks who succeeded chose to distance themselves from the poorer classes of blacks, believing that Jim Crow stereotypes did not apply to them. Some even shared white views that the less fortunate blacks simply had not worked hard enough to get ahead and so must be lazy or stupid. Yet whites did not generally distinguish between rich and poor blacks, and even the richest and most prominent experienced some form of racism. Nonetheless, their success convinced many blacks that economic advancement and good manners were the keys to assimilation. Booker T. Washington's ideas came partly from this larger tradition, although he conceived of more widespread economic advancement.

Other free blacks, while still maintaining faith that whites would ultimately accept them as equals, began to think that they would have to practice a more cooperative form of self-help if they wanted to progress. Individual efforts to succeed were admirable, but in times of racial hostility, blacks could not depend on their ties with whites for help, nor could they expect to gain their respect. By the 1850s, many black leaders had begun to advocate racial solidarity as the key to success. African Americans should help each other by patronizing black businesses and supporting independent black institutions. Black fraternal organizations such as the Prince Hall Masons, the Knights of Pythias, and the Good Samaritans functioned largely as mutual benefit associations. Members paid dues and in turn were entitled to burial benefits or help for the family in times of illness. These organizations also provided opportunities not found in the larger society for blacks to practice leadership skills, as well as places where they could meet socially in a friendly environment.

Black churches, offering spiritual as well as social freedom, were probably the most important of these independent institutions. As a result of discrimination in white churches, blacks had formed separate congregations, some of which united under separate denominations. The African Methodist Episcopal (AME) and AME Zion denominations spread widely throughout the North and, after the Civil War, made strong inroads in the South. Black Baptists separated from southern Baptist congregations that supported slavery, and, after the Civil War, affiliated with northern Baptist groups, then created their own National Baptist Convention. As spiritual centers of the black community and often the social and political centers as well, the black churches would continue to play important roles in the late nineteenth century. Increasingly, however, they faced competition from other independent institutions such as settlement houses, the Young Men's Christian Association (YMCA), the National Urban League, and Du Bois's National Association for the Advancement of Colored People (NAACP).

Beginning in 1830, some of the most prominent blacks in the country called a series of national and state meetings to debate race matters. This black convention movement helped to put in focus what their leaders thought were necessary conditions for advancement and the ultimate goals for African Americans. Although they never organized any permanent association to coordinate their efforts, they did succeed in outlining the problems and suggesting solutions. In general, they regarded education as the key to success, specifically education for skilled manual labor or agriculture. White abolitionists proposed establishing schools for this purpose as early as the 1830s. Black leaders realized that the majority of the black population needed a basic education and skills that would enable them to live independently. However, they also called for the admission of exceptional black students to white colleges for the purpose of breaking down stereotypes of blacks as incapable of higher thought and sentiments. In the mid-1860s, with the Civil War almost over, black conventions met to push for full political and civil rights and in 1864 created the National Equal Rights League to protest discrimination and fight prejudice. The organization did not meet beyond its second year, however, in part because Radical Republicans were fighting on behalf of blacks and in the mid- to late 1860s achieved passage of the Thirteenth, Fourteenth, and Fifteenth Amendments, which abolished slavery and instituted citizenship and voting rights.

The debate over the abolition of slavery raised other possibilities for black progress and established some basic differences over approaches to racial advancement, which would continue even into the twenty-first century. White abolitionists were divided on the best way to end slavery. Some favored immediate abolition; others preferred a sort of grandfather clause that would free slaves one generation at a time. Although most blacks wanted immediate abolition, the gradualism versus immediacy question would prove a divisive one between Washington and Du Bois in the early twentieth century. It would also feature prominently in disagreements between moderate and militant civil rights activists in the 1960s.

The possibility of abolition also raised another issue: What should become of the slaves after emancipation? Some people advocated integration with whites and assimilation to white culture; others argued that blacks should try to set up a separate society and practice self-government. This separatism, or nationalism, took a variety of forms. Some favored simply avoiding contact with whites; others recommended temporary separation. Radical nationalists advocated an actual physical break from whites, the establishment of a separate black territory out West or even migration back to Africa to found an independent country somewhere on that continent. Despite the enthusiasm for moving "back to Africa" from the 1820s to the 1850s, many blacks discovered that they felt at home in America and became disillusioned with the idea of colonization. The movement for emigration would resurge in the late 1870s, the 1890s, and again in the 1920s, however. Du Bois himself emigrated to Ghana in 1961.

The majority of African Americans, although seeing some practical benefits of nationalism such as financial independence, continued to believe that they could integrate into mainstream American society, a belief that strengthened as support for abolition grew. Despite continued stereotypes, it was clear to many leading blacks in the North, such as James Forten or former slave Frederick Douglass, that some whites were willing to work with them to find solutions to race issues. In the 1850s and 1860s, white Republicans sought political support in the black community. Such political activities, largely centering on abolitionist circles in Boston, Philadelphia, and New York, helped to create a group of black leaders who, during Reconstruction, became major power brokers.

After the Thirteenth Amendment abolished slavery at the end of the Civil War in 1865, these black political brokers firmly believed that African Americans would achieve full equality in time. Frederick Douglass, who first gained notice for his published slave narrative and then became an active abolitionist, was a key figure. He moved to Washington, DC, during Reconstruction, consulted with leading Republicans on race issues, and reaped rewards for his political service with appointments as marshal of the District of Columbia, as recorder of deeds for the District, and, in the 1880s, as U.S. minister to Haiti. Other black political leaders included Blanche K. Bruce and P.B.S. Pinchback. Bruce was the first African American to serve a complete term in the United States Senate (and the last until 1966). Pinchback served in a variety of political offices in his native Louisiana and for a brief period was acting lieutenant governor of the state. Both Bruce and Pinchback moved to Washington and worked actively with the Republican Party at election times. Other black politicians were influential in their home states.

During Reconstruction, the efforts of the Radical Republicans as well as the federal government's creation of the Freedmen's Bureau, which lasted from 1865 to 1872, showed blacks the possibilities of racial cooperation. The passage of the Fourteenth and Fifteenth Amendments were attempts to provide a constitutional guarantee of black rights, particularly the right to vote. Supporters believed that the vote would allow freedmen to protect themselves, even if the government could no longer protect them. African Americans had every reason to believe that the federal government had their best interests at heart and that they would eventually gain political equality.

Radical Republican sentiment had reached its peak between 1866 and 1868 when Congress united in opposition to President Andrew Johnson, a southern Democrat. In 1872, Congress approved the Amnesty Act, which allowed all former Confederates to vote except for the highest officials and military generals. As a result, white southerners elected Democrats to office and retook control of the South. As southern states regained admission to the Union, the Republicans had little choice but to withdraw troops from those states once they had restored order. Left to themselves, the new southern state governments quickly adopted laws requiring voters to pay a tax or prove they were literate before they could vote. Such laws effectively prevented many blacks from voting because they had little spare money to pay a poll tax, and, as it had been illegal for them to learn to read while they were slaves, few freedmen were literate. By the election of 1876, the Radical Republicans no longer controlled Congress.

Reconstruction came to an abrupt end with the Compromise of 1877, which decided the outcome of the election. Meeting in Washington, DC, at a hotel owned by prominent black businessman James A. Wormley, Republican and Democratic Party leaders reached an agreement to end Reconstruction programs and all military occupation of the South in exchange for a promise that the South would respect the rights of the freedmen. Neither Republicans nor Democrats expected the South to keep this promise, and African Americans were horrified by the compromise but could do little to stop it.

Political cooperation between blacks and whites did not end completely, but conditions were deteriorating for the majority of African Americans, who did not have the same economic options as the black political brokers. Left to its own devices after the Compromise of 1877, the South soon initiated a social system that separated blacks and whites by custom and attempted to give blacks a permanently subordinate status. Most of the freedmen, with no money, skills, or education, ended up farming rented land on the plantations where they had worked as slaves. Since most could not afford to pay cash rent, however, they quickly became sharecroppers, paying their rent with a portion of their crop. Many of these sharecroppers could not afford to purchase tools and seeds, or even food and clothing for their families, until harvest time, so they entered into agreements for credit with "furnishing merchants," using their future crop as collateral. The merchants would then have a lien on the crop, meaning that before the farmer took any money for himself, he had to pay back the merchant. This crop-lien system generally put the farmers further in debt; not only did the merchants charge higher prices for goods on credit, but dishonest ones miscalculated the amount the sharecroppers owed them at the end of the year. At "reckoning time," after paying rent and the furnishing merchant, the sharecropper usually had nothing left for himself and often still owed the merchant more money. As a result, he was bound to continue farming the following year to pay off his debt. In essence, black sharecroppers were not much better off than slaves.

In the increasingly hostile environment, nationalist sentiment resurged among southern blacks. Although a movement to establish a Negro Territory never achieved its goal, during the 1870s a number of black entrepreneurs did help to establish all-black towns in Oklahoma, Texas, Kansas, and other western states and even a few in the Deep South. In some cases, large groups migrated west together in search of the Promised Land. In 1879 a group of 6,000 known as the Exodusters (after the biblical Exodus of the Hebrew slaves), under the leadership of Benjamin "Pap" Singleton and Henry Adams, moved to Kansas, where Singleton and his business partners purchased more than 1,000 acres of land on which to start a colony for former slaves. Not many of the Exodusters could afford to buy more land, however, and although some became farmers and ranchers and even cowboys, many ended up moving to cities such as Topeka, so that the towns they had established all but disappeared.

In the 1880s and 1890s the Farmers' Alliance offered one last hope for biracial political cooperation. The poor farmers who joined the alliance, including the purported million-member Colored Alliance, united in opposition to the sharecropping system in 1890 and decided to form the People's Party, or Populist Party. When white farmers, the majority support for the Democrats in the South, threatened to leave their party for the Populists, the Democratic leaders saw the need for drastic action to retain power. They took two approaches to recapturing the farmer vote, the first of which was adopting watered-down versions of the reforms that farmers were asking for. The second was to attack the concept of biracial cooperation among the Populists and call for white racial solidarity against the "evil race mixers" and those who would allow blacks to mingle socially with whites. The Democratic call for white solidarity was so effective that by the late 1890s, even Populist leaders who had earlier called for biracial cooperation were themselves preaching white supremacy.

In the late 1880s and early 1890s, all the southern states made a concerted effort to disfranchise blacks, to eliminate black voters from the electoral rolls. They passed a series of laws that prevented blacks from voting including more literacy tests and poll taxes, adding escape clauses for poor or illiterate whites. Ironically, many white southerners depicted these laws as reform of the political process: they argued that blacks were not intelligent enough to vote and so corrupt politicians could easily buy their ballots. Eliminating black voters was simply eliminating the opportunity for corruption, they said.

There were always a few exceptions for "reasonable" black men whom they counted on to vote in line with whites. Lewis Adams, a tinsmith in Tuskegee, Alabama, for example, worked his way up to owning a general store and becoming one of the wealthiest men in town. He worked actively with the Republicans during Reconstruction but, at a key time in 1880, switched his support to the Democratic candidate for state senate, who approached him to sway the black vote. The Democrat won the election with substantial support from the black community, and, in return, Adams asked for a grant from the state legislature to set up a school for blacks. This political deal initiated a long history of political cooperation and was the origin of Tuskegee Institute, whose principal, teachers, and students voted in every election.

For the most part, however, the South was gradually segregating blacks in all areas of life. As the states established public school systems in the 1870s and 1880s, they created provisions for separate schools for blacks and whites. In 1883 the Supreme Court declared unconstitutional one of the last Reconstruction measures, the Civil Rights Act of 1875, and the southern states began to pass laws excluding blacks from public places such as parks, hotels, and restaurants; banning intermarriage between blacks and whites; and, by the end of the 1880s, segregating trains and other forms of public transportation. In 1896 the Supreme Court heard the case of *Plessy v. Ferguson*, in which a black man who had been arrested for refusing to leave a whites-only car on a Louisiana train sued, claiming violation of his civil rights. The Supreme Court concluded in this case that it was not in the government's power to force social equality; it was therefore within the states' rights to pass laws segregating blacks and whites, as long as they provided equal accommodations. The decision created the "separate but equal doctrine" and, in effect, gave the Supreme Court's blessing to segregation. Interestingly, Justice John M. Harlan, who wrote the sole dissenting opinion, was the half-brother of former slave Robert Harlan, who had made his fortune in the California gold rush. In the wake of the decision, southern states passed a whole series of Jim Crow laws. The state of Oklahoma segregated telephone booths. Atlanta segregated Bibles for blacks and whites to swear on in courtrooms. Blacks suffered segregation from birth to death in hospitals, schools, housing, job opportunities, retirement homes, and cemeteries.[1] They could not serve on juries or testify against whites in most southern states.

Jim Crow facilities generally meant inferior facilities—separate, but hardly equal. The Jim Crow car on a train was usually overcrowded and dirty. There was no first-class seating for blacks, even those who could afford it. Jim Crow waiting rooms at train stations often had no benches or bathrooms. Appropriations for the black schools were usually around one-third of those for white schools, and overcrowding and lack of equipment or decent buildings often made even the best schools a nightmare for the students. In Washington, DC, overcrowding forced the black elementary schools to hold two half-day sessions. In Washington's M Street High School, one of the best black secondary schools in the country, teachers frequently held two different classes in the same classroom simultaneously. M Street teachers often purchased equipment themselves to make up for shortcomings. Other schools in the District lacked proper plumbing or running water. In many cases there was not even a pretense of creating equal facilities for blacks. There might be a white public swimming pool, for example, but no pool for blacks.

Not coincidentally, at the same time as the rise of Jim Crow laws, black disfranchisement, and scientific racism, lynchings of African Americans reached their peak. About 150 lynchings took place each year in the 1880s and 1890s. In 1892 there were 235; in the first two years of the twentieth century, 214.[2] Protests in the black community fell on deaf ears. Black journalist Ida B. Wells started a campaign to expose the true nature and causes of lynching but received little coverage in mainstream newspapers. Increasingly, protest seemed only to aggravate white hostility. Historian Rayford Logan called the turn of the century the nadir of race relations, the lowest point, and he was certainly right. But what that image overlooks is the creative efforts that African Americans were making to change their situation within their community. Once again, blacks would turn to racial solidarity and self-help as the best temporary solutions.

It was in this context, then, that Booker T. Washington and W.E.B. Du Bois rose to prominence and came into conflict. They faced formidable obstacles to what was essentially still a common goal: equality for African Americans. The ways in which they approached the problem were not new, just more crystallized and organized, but each man added new elements to the debate that reflected his own personal philosophy. The environments in which they grew up helped to shape their positions, as did the experiences of each man. For that reason, an examination of their early lives is necessary to understand the personal contexts for their disagreement.

Notes

1. C. Vann Woodward, *The Strange Career of Jim Crow*, 3d rev. ed. (New York: Oxford University Press, 1974), 97–102.
2. August Meier, *Negro Thought in America, 1880–1915* (Ann Arbor: The University of Michigan Press, 1963), 20; John Hope Franklin and Alfred A. Moss, Jr., *From Slavery to Freedom: A History of African Americans*, 8th ed. (Boston: McGraw Hill, 2000), 291.

2 | Booker T. Washington and Tuskegee Institute

Booker Taliaferro Washington was born a slave in 1856 in Franklin County, Virginia, near Hale's Ford. Like many slaves, he was uncertain of his exact birthdate and, indeed, had only one name on the census: Booker. He belonged to a man named James Burroughs and was likely the son of one of the white men in the neighborhood. His mother gave him the name Taliaferro because she liked the sound of it, but although the Taliaferros were one of the leading families in the county, there is no evidence to suggest that there was any blood tie. There was a family story that Jane, Washington's mother, briefly ran away from the Burroughs family because she was angry with the way they treated her. During that time, she stayed with Benjamin Hatcher, a white man who was part owner of the largest tobacco factory in town and who regularly employed slaves. When Jane returned to the Burroughs plantation, she was pregnant. Whoever Booker's father was, he never claimed him as a son; and legally, because his mother belonged to Burroughs, her children did too. Booker had one older brother, John, and a younger sister, Amanda; all three had different fathers. Not long after Booker was born, Jane married a slave named Washington from the Ferguson plantation across the road. When a teacher first asked Booker for his full name, he gave his stepfather's, and from then on he was Booker Washington.

Washington spent his first nine years in slavery and experienced many of the same hardships as other slaves. His basic physical needs often went unmet. He did not own a pair of shoes until he was eight, and his only item of clothing was a shirt made of homespun flax, very rough and scratchy when new. In his autobiography *Up from Slavery* he said that one of the most self-sacrificing deeds he ever witnessed was his brother's volunteering to wear a new shirt for him until it was broken in. Booker had very little to eat overall and an erratic diet of whatever was available. One night, he remembered, his mother woke him up to feed him some chicken she had somehow obtained. The family never sat down to eat on the plantation but took scraps from

As an adult, Booker T. Washington loved working on the farm at Tuskegee. Here he feeds the chickens, but his favorite animal was the pig. *Courtesy of the Library of Congress*

the owner's kitchen where Jane worked and ate from their hands. Their home was a one-room slave cabin with a dirt floor on which they slept, next to the storage hole for the master's sweet potatoes. In the winter the cabin was cold and subject to drafts coming through chinks in the log walls. In the summer it was hot, and the family opened all the windows and the door to let in a breeze, along with mosquitoes.

We know about Booker's experiences in slavery only from his autobiographical writings, but they were unusual in some respects. He was too young to do the heavy work on the plantation, but he did help his brother, John. He delivered messages and collected packages from the post office; and he also worked in the Burroughses' dining room, operating ceiling fans attached to pulleys and ropes. Booker did see harsh treatment of other slaves, including his uncle, whom a member of the master's family tied to a tree and whipped for misbehaving in some fashion. But he also frequently saw slaves run away and outwit their masters.

His stepfather had sometimes gone away with work parties to the salt mines in Malden, West Virginia, for months at a time, and returned with stories of his life away from home that fascinated Booker. His last years in slavery were during the Civil War, and almost all of the Burroughs sons enlisted in the Confederate Army. James Burroughs himself died in 1861 before his boys went to war. Two sons died, including the popular "Mars Billy," who as a boy had played alongside many of the slave children. Two other sons suffered wounds. Washington later wrote that the slaves showed great affection for their master when he died as well as for his sons, but it is likely this affection was simply a front the slaves put on to please their owners. During the war, with the plantations in uproar and regular life not possible, slaves generally found ways to take advantage of the chaos to lighten their loads, particularly when there was no white male supervision.

Overall, Washington recalled his childhood years almost with pleasure when he wrote about them, and it is likely that his personal experiences allowed him a kinder view of slavery. Moreover, he almost certainly downplayed the negative aspects because he was writing for a white audience that wanted to forget the bad old days. He was also trying to convince whites that he did not resent them for their past treatment of blacks—an easier feat if he could argue that he had received fair treatment even during slavery.

In 1865 the Washington family moved to Malden, where Booker's stepfather again found work in the mines. When they arrived, they were disappointed to find that their cabin was not much better than the one they had left and that all the cabins around them housed the poorest and most uneducated whites and blacks. Booker thought that poor whites were all drunkards who gambled and fought. Malden had once been prosperous, and there were still several rich families left who ran the town. But the salt mines were drying up; the demand for salt was lessening; and a flood had destroyed many boats and the docks from which they shipped the salt. Malden was entering an economic depression.

Booker's stepfather worked as a salt packer, a job that involved heavy physical labor. The mine paid him by the barrel, and he soon brought his stepsons to the mines to help him. Although Booker and John received wages for their work, their stepfather kept it all for the family. Such behavior was common practice for the time, but the boys never really understood it and never thought of Washington as a real father.

It was while Booker was working in the salt mines that he began to long for an education. As a slave he had often delivered things to the Burroughs children at the local schoolhouse and wondered what went on inside. In the salt mines he learned his first numbers from the marks the workers put on the barrels they packed to identify them. He soon realized he wanted more, and when the first school for blacks opened in town, he begged his parents to let him attend. Family finances did not permit him to leave work for day school, but he persuaded his mother to buy him a spelling book and learned the alphabet on his own. Knowing the letters made him more eager to learn to read, and through persistent effort he gained permission to attend classes first at night and then for an hour or so before work. He also enrolled in Sunday School. He was never a brilliant student, but he was diligent and made good progress.

About two years after the family moved to Malden, Booker found a new job working as houseboy for one of the rich ladies in town, Viola Ruffner. Her husband, former slaveowner Lewis Ruffner, was from a wealthy family who had owned and operated mines in the area since the eighteenth century. He had served as a general in the Union militia and had a reputation as a firm but fair man. Viola, his second wife, was twenty years younger than he and came from New England; originally, she had served as governess to Ruffner's children. With all the characteristics of a Yankee schoolmarm, she had great difficulty in finding servants who could meet her high standards of cleanliness. Booker jumped at the opportunity to get away from the mines, and although he sporadically ran off from his job to try other things, for the next few years he worked for her for $5.00 per month.

The relationship that developed between Mrs. Ruffner and Booker was typical of many aristocratic associations with servants. Ruffner was strict, demanding near perfection, expecting punctuality, politeness, and courtesy from Booker at all times, and insisting that he always appear presentable. Yet she was also interested in helping him to improve himself. She encouraged him in his schoolwork and lent him books from her library. She allowed him to take an hour from his work each day to attend classes. She also trusted him to sell fruit and vegetables from her garden to the neighborhood. Washington later said that she had taught him the lessons that helped him most in life: the value of hard work and of cleanliness.

On one of Booker's periodic disappearances from the Ruffner home, he worked in a coal mine. There he discovered that he had finally learned the value of cleanliness. Objecting to the endless dirt that coal miners endured, he knew that whatever he did in life, he would have to be where he could maintain clean living standards. It was also in the mine that he first heard about Hampton Normal and Agricultural Institute near Norfolk, Virginia, a school for blacks that emphasized industrial education. Founded by a white, Samuel Chapman Armstrong, a former Union army general, the school offered blacks a chance to get a basic education and also learn a trade that would enable them to support themselves. Washington decided that he had to attend Hampton and began saving for the travel and tuition. His brother and other blacks in his church and in the surrounding community donated money toward his goal, and finally, in 1872, he set off on the 500-mile trip to Hampton.

The journey itself has become part of the legend of Booker T. Washington because he wrote and spoke of it so often later in life. Since the train did not go all the way, he rode the stagecoach to the end of its line and then hitchhiked and walked the rest of the distance. At one hotel where the stagecoach stopped, the owner refused him a room because of his race and so he had to walk around for most of the night. When he reached Richmond, he had no money left for food or lodging, so he worked briefly on the docks loading ships. To save money he slept under the wooden sidewalk, a story he loved to tell in later years whenever he visited the city as an honored guest. He finally saved up enough to complete his journey but arrived at Hampton in early October with almost nothing to pay his way. He was so thrilled to see the great school he had heard so much about, however, that he was determined to stay.

Because he had arrived after the beginning of the school year looking shabby from sleeping under the Richmond sidewalks, the teachers at Hampton were uncertain whether to admit him. General Armstrong had created a program whereby students could work off their room and board by cooking and cleaning for the school, and Washington pleaded to be admitted on that basis. The teacher admitted him after giving him the practical test of cleaning a classroom, in which he proved he had absorbed Ruffner standards. He worked as a janitor for the school for the three years he was there to pay part of his expenses and later received a scholarship for his tuition from a northern white philanthropist.

Hampton Institute was an industrial education school—sometimes called a manual training school—and part of a larger movement toward educational reform. Until the last quarter of the nineteenth century, most Americans did not believe in universal education, the idea that everyone should have basic schooling. Even then, many intellectuals still thought some people were incapable of abstract learning. One of the reasons was the very nature of traditional education itself. The curriculum of most colleges was that of a classical education, emphasizing the *trivium* (the basic curriculum of universities since the Middle Ages, consisting of grammar, rhetoric, and logic) and the *quadrivium* (arithmetic, music, geometry, and astronomy). In order to take all these subjects students had to learn Greek and Latin. College preparatory courses in high schools focused on the seven subjects and the two classical languages. Most of the people who went to college were studying for the ministry, and since high school was largely preparation for college, few others got an education beyond elementary school.

Among the factors that began to change the nature of education was the rise of industry and business. For a start, basic literacy and arithmetic skills were essential to running a commercial enterprise of any sort, and America was a country of small business enterprises before the Civil War. But business owners did not advocate education for workers for purely selfless reasons. In the early 1800s, industrialization brought workers into factories for the first time. Those used to working on their own now had to account for their time to employers. They had to be on the job every morning and take only authorized breaks, if any. The factory whistle set the pace of life. Business owners, who noticed a tendency among former agricultural workers to slack off and take "sick" days when they felt like it, proposed that children receive training in the sorts of things necessary to factory discipline. To them it was less important that schools teach working-class children to read and write than that they enforced good behavior, such as getting to class on time and paying attention to the teacher. Businessmen thus advocated a curriculum that would emphasize sober habits and obedience.

It was from these sorts of demands that reformers proposed the idea of industrial education, which would prepare students not necessarily for the university but for a practical role in life and would also instill good habits and enforce proper discipline. Such an education would create happy and productive workers for the business owners but also teach the students skills they could use in life: practical trades such as carpentry rather than Latin or Greek. Such a curriculum focused on the needs of the student rather than some prescribed body of knowledge. It was also a way for poor people to improve their lives through gaining a basic education and skills to which they would not otherwise have had exposure. In the 1830s, reformers thought that such a practical curriculum would also help to democratize the schools, since opponents of universal education had fewer objections to industrial training.

But it was possible to abuse the philosophy to serve other agendas. A good industrial education was progressive, training people for skilled work or in new technologies. A curriculum that focused only on training people for manual labor or domestic service, however, also created a permanent working class. Students who went through such schools would have only a minimal academic education and little chance to advance into more professional occupations. When those who were to be educated were not just poor but from a different ethnic background, the abuse became more acute. For example, because most whites thought that Indians and African Americans were incapable of more than basic thought processes and simple work, it was easy to justify limiting their access to classical schooling. Industrial education seemed ideally suited to teaching "backward" races and civilizing "savages," because no one expected them to be able to do more than manual labor. There was no reason to train blacks to be lawyers or Indians to be doctors, because that would challenge the idea that they were socially inferior.

Industrial education was very much in vogue after the Civil War, thanks to the rapid pace of industrialization, and when the question arose of how best to educate the freedmen, it seemed to most whites the ideal solution. Certainly, Samuel Armstrong thought he had the best interests of the freedmen at heart when he established Hampton Institute in 1868. Armstrong was born in Hawaii, the son of Presbyterian missionaries who ran a school for Polynesians that offered an industrial curriculum, particularly teaching skills such as basket weaving. Armstrong attended college in the United States and then enlisted in the Union army. His bravery in battle led to quick promotion, and the army made him lieutenant colonel in charge of the Ninth U.S. Colored Troops. Armstrong had a missionary perspective of blacks, viewing them, and the Polynesians, as simple "children of the tropics." He was sympathetic to their plight and wanted to help, but he thought that it would take them perhaps several hundred years to reach the same level as whites. After the Civil War, he served with distinction in Mexico and gained promotion to brigadier general at age twenty-six. He knew that army life was not for him, however; instead, he wanted to help people in need. In 1866 he volunteered his services to the Freedmen's Bureau and worked as the general agent for eastern Virginia and the superintendent of education for the region.

Armstrong worked for the bureau for two years from his office in Hampton Roads, Virginia. In 1868, with the aid of the American Missionary Association—an organization active in setting up schools for the freedmen—he embarked on what would become his life work. Armstrong established Hampton Institute with an industrial curriculum designed to train blacks and, later, Indians to be useful in American society. He allowed students to work off some of their tuition not because he expected the school to sustain itself but because he thought it was good discipline for them to learn the value of working toward a goal. In creating a school intended to lift blacks from poverty and ignorance and placing it in the South, Armstrong could have encountered opposition. His advocating industrial education, however, placated conservative whites by assuring them that he did not intend to upset the social hierarchy. At the same time, he had a genuine opportunity to improve the quality of life for his students.

Certainly, Hampton had some noted graduates, including Booker T. Washington and Robert S. Abbott, the founder and editor of the *Chicago Defender*, a leading black newspaper. But most students never went much beyond fourth grade in their studies. The main part of the Hampton experience was less in its academic classes than in its regimen. Because the school was coeducational and Armstrong did not want any scandal, he made sure that the students kept busy for every waking hour from five in the morning until nine-thirty at night. They took lessons, practiced military-style drills, and learned such basic trade skills as laundry work and domestic service for the girls and proper farming techniques for the boys.

Armstrong imported many Yankee schoolteachers of impeccable moral character to serve as role models, and he himself showed the students that he was willing to sacrifice as much as they did for the good of the school. The students worshiped him. When a dormitory shortage arose and he asked for volunteers to sleep in tents until there were new accommodations, Washington and others volunteered gladly. Armstrong made a point of visiting them regularly in the mornings, particularly after very cold or stormy nights, with words of encouragement and appreciation. He maintained the style of a commanding officer but one whom his boys and girls loved.

For his part, Washington thought of Armstrong as the father he had never had; he modeled himself after the man, and Tuskegee after Hampton. He absorbed most of Armstrong's conservative racial views and remained his lifelong friend. Armstrong was proud of his most famous graduate but never truly saw blacks as equals. In a letter of recommendation he later wrote for Washington, he said that he was "no ordinary darkey." But Armstrong always lent money to Tuskegee when it was in financial difficulty and became one of its founder's biggest supporters.

Washington's three years as a student at Hampton were thus formative ones. When he arrived, he had only rudimentary literacy and a desire for something more in life. Because of his years with the Ruffners he was probably not quite the country bumpkin he later portrayed himself to have been, but Hampton certainly transformed him. Armstrong placed great emphasis on appearances, and each student had to have clean clothes with no missing buttons, as well as proper manners. Washington internalized these values and would give long lectures about the civilizing effects of the toothbrush. He came to believe that whites would more readily listen to blacks who were polite, well spoken, and neatly dressed. In a sense he was right, although he perhaps overestimated white generosity, even to polite and tidy blacks. Most southern blacks and many poor whites did not understand basic sanitation; as sharecroppers and farmhands, they lived in appalling conditions in shacks where keeping clean was extraordinarily difficult. Improved sanitation, however, meant improved health, and taking care of appearances brought them some sense of self-pride.

Washington explored the possibility of a variety of professions while he was a student. Wanting to do something to help other blacks achieve what he had and to improve their overall conditions, he ultimately decided, undoubtedly following Armstrong's advice, that teaching was the best way for him to uplift his race. Consequently, he worked to perfect those skills he would most need, including taking active part in debating societies. He soon discovered a flair for public speaking and developed the style that would make him so persuasive throughout his life. He liked to use simple language and folksy stories to illustrate his points, and as a result, his arguments came across as plain common sense.

In 1875, Washington graduated from Hampton and participated in an exhibition debate at the commencement exercises. The topic was whether or not the United States should annex Cuba. Washington took the position that it was better to solve the problem of the freedmen at home before adding the problems that Cuba would bring. He argued that large numbers of Roman Catholic immigrants, whom he viewed as already degrading the working classes, would add to the nation's social problems. Washington was certainly no egalitarian and perhaps internalized Armstrong's ideas a little too much. But his views were very much those of white, especially southern, Americans. Such beliefs would enable him to maintain friendly relations with even the most conservative white southerners, which allowed him to accomplish a great deal without arousing too much white opposition.

Washington worked as a waiter in a resort hotel in the Northeast following graduation, but he was so inept at first that the headwaiter demoted him to busboy. Vowing to improve, by the end of the summer he was once again a waiter. On his return home to Malden in the fall the townspeople appointed him teacher in the local school, where he tried to teach his students the lessons he had learned at Hampton— including the use of the toothbrush. Perhaps remembering his own early inability to attend school because of his work schedule, he established night classes. Eventually, he had nearly ninety students in both the day and night schools and was hard pressed to keep up. In addition, he taught Sunday School and established a local debating society. He also set up a public library and wrote letters to the local newspapers and the official Hampton journal, the *Southern Workman*. His mother had died in 1874, and the family had drifted apart. Washington nonetheless worked to put his brother, John, through Hampton (his sister, Amanda, chose an education elsewhere).

One of the lessons Washington had learned at Hampton was that it would be foolish for blacks to try to advance the race through political activity. In 1875 the tide was already turning against Radical Reconstruction, and Armstrong warned his students not to force themselves where whites did not want them. He advised using segregated facilities when they were available and not pushing for the vote until they were educated enough to use it wisely. Although Washington discouraged African Americans from political activity, he did get involved in one political cause in Malden that had nothing to do with race: the question of where to situate the state capital. White businessmen solicited his debating skill to gain support for Charleston among black voters. When West Virginia voters overwhelmingly chose Charleston, Washington got a taste of the political influence that he would enjoy later in his life on a much larger scale.

Following a few years of uncertainty about his future career, Washington accepted an invitation to speak at Hampton's 1878 commencement. His address must have been impressive, because Armstrong invited him to come and teach the night school. Washington relished the opportunity and took great pride in his students, most of whom worked all day on the campus before coming to his classes. He designated them the "Plucky Class," and gave them certificates. His experiences with these students convinced Washington even more that there was tremendous value in industrial education and that truly dedicated students could overcome almost any obstacle if they wanted to improve themselves.

Because he had done so well with the night school, Armstrong asked Washington to become the head resident in the Indian dormitory. Armstrong, who saw Native Americans as savages who just needed taming in order to progress, had begun a program to train Indians from the reservations to fit into mainstream American life. Most of those who came to Hampton were Kiowa, Sioux, and Comanche, recently defeated Plains Indians with a long and bitter history of hostility to whites. Such groups were not ideal candidates for cultural assimilation, but Armstrong believed that they might accept a black role model. Washington was not especially popular with the Indians and, in general, the black and Indian students at Hampton did not get on well together. Nonetheless, Armstrong was more than satisfied with his performance. In May 1881 the Alabama state education commissioners asked Armstrong to recommend a suitable white man to be principal of a new normal school for blacks in Tuskegee. He replied that he knew of no one better qualified than Washington, as long as they did not object to his race. The commissioners agreed and asked Armstrong to send him immediately. Black Tuskegee businessman and former Republican Lewis Adams had reaped the rewards of shifting his political support, and Washington had found his life's work.

Arriving in Tuskegee, Washington was stunned to find that there was no established school, no state appropriation until October, and no designated campus. He was determined to open the school on July 4 nonetheless and so went to work diligently seeking both students and a location. He toured Tuskegee and the surrounding area, speaking in churches and to individuals, to discover the needs of the community and the sort of pupils he could expect. Since Tuskegee was supposed to be a normal, or teacher-training, school, he refused all applicants under sixteen, and most of his early students were already teaching in local schools. The demand for black schools in the South after Emancipation was so great that many teachers were pressed into service who had had only a few years of education themselves. Washington hoped to attract these teachers so that they could improve their training. He also wanted to recruit bright students who would make good teachers in the future.

He held his first classes at the local AME Zion church but began to look for suitable property for a permanent location. He found a farm with several buildings and an orchard and, with General Armstrong's advice, borrowed the money from him to purchase the farm, promising to pay back the loan when the state funds arrived. Because that money was not due until October 1, and Tuskegee had no budget, Washington and the board of three commissioners, which included Lewis Adams, knew that they would need to charge tuition. But since Washington had seen the impoverished conditions in which most blacks in the area lived, he realized that tuition was not an option. Instead, he proposed setting up a manual training system on the Hampton model: students were to work off their tuition by helping to clean up the farm, repair the buildings, and plant crops that the school could both sell and consume.

Many of the teachers who came to Tuskegee turned up their noses at the idea of manual labor, particularly growing cotton. The black community had strong faith that education was the key to success and believed it would allow them to escape the cotton fields and sharecropping. Only with a great deal of persuasion and by setting the example of clearing the fields himself did Washington manage to persuade most of the students that there was dignity in common labor. The few who never accepted the idea ultimately left the school.

Washington's next task was to find qualified teachers. Not surprisingly, he turned to Hampton for suitable graduates and chose several, including Olivia A. Davidson, whom he hired to be Tuskegee's Lady Principal. Davidson would become a key factor in Tuskegee's survival and eventually Washington's second wife. Born in Virginia in 1854, she had moved with her family to rural Albany, Ohio, at a young age and attended Albany Enterprise Academy, a private black school. She taught in Mississippi and in Memphis, Tennessee, during Reconstruction and then enrolled in Hampton in 1878. She graduated in just one year and caught the attention of a wealthy white woman from Boston, who became her patron and paid for Davidson to attend a normal school near Boston. There she made many friends among her fellow students, most of whom were white. Like Washington, she was the product of a white father and black mother and was so fair-skinned that she could have passed for white, but she took great pride in being African American and wanted to devote her life to teaching and serving her race.

Davidson came to Tuskegee and immediately helped with school organization and finances. Realizing that he would have to depend on donations to keep the school afloat, Washington had begun organizing benefits to raise money. Davidson refined this process to an art with literary evenings, potluck suppers for which people bought tickets, and door-to-door fund-raising. Washington often said how impressed he was with the willingness of the local black community to help out with a few pennies here and there. To Tuskegee's black residents the normal school represented their future, for it would train the teachers who would train their children. Washington told the story of one poor black woman who brought him some eggs as a donation because she had nothing else to give; he said he treasured those eggs because of the sacrifice they represented. But Washington also noted how willing local whites were to help. Not all white Alabamians were completely convinced of the value of an education for African Americans, but because the school had an industrial curriculum, it was less threatening to the social hierarchy. And because Washington insisted that his students be on their best behavior and dressed neatly at all times, the school gained a reputation for turning out polite blacks who respected their superiors, as whites thought of themselves.

Herein lay Washington's genius. Following Armstrong's lead he forged a compromise between African Americans and conservative white leaders which allowed both to maintain their goals. Whites did not object to Tuskegee when they thought it was educating blacks for menial positions such as maids and manual laborers. Blacks flocked to Tuskegee to gain an education and improve their chances in life by learning a skill. And under the guise of maintaining the social hierarchy, Washington was able to create a strong, independent, black-run institution that went far beyond Hampton's manual training programs and drills, even though he continued to emphasize proper appearance and the toothbrush. Washington's leadership combined with Davidson's fund-raising abilities put Tuskegee on the road to success.

Success did not come instantly, however. Students in Tuskegee's early years often had insufficient food or clothing and frequently not enough school supplies. Realizing Washington's program to make Tuskegee self-sufficient took time. Mostly, students learned skills when the school needed them. For example, when there were not enough benches for the classrooms, the boys learned carpentry and made them. When the students needed more clothes, the girls learned to sew them. It was students who excavated a room from the dirt below the kitchen to serve as extra dining space. They did not complain but shared hard times in the spirit of sacrifice. Nonetheless, it was clear that the school needed more permanent buildings, and the state appropriation, when it came, was only a small portion of the operating costs. Washington began expanding his fund-raising trips to cover the whole state and beyond. At first, he relied heavily on Armstrong and Hampton's officials and teachers for loans, but Armstrong found other ways to help his former student. He took the Hampton Singers on tour to benefit Tuskegee, and he introduced Washington to some of Hampton's donors.

It was Olivia Davidson, however, who once again saved the day with her connections to wealthy philanthropists in the Northeast. She spent her summers there in relentless fund-raising activities, often sending checks back to the school just in time to avoid bill collectors. Through her friendships in Boston she gained introductions to philanthropists throughout New England. Never particularly robust, she found that these tours exhausted her physically and severely damaged her health but was determined to continue. Washington, who soon began his own fund-raising tours in the North, admired her dedication and persistence in such difficult and sometimes disheartening work.

Gradually, as Tuskegee's reputation grew, so did the size of the donations it received. By 1882 Tuskegee had paid off the mortgage on the farm, and it was becoming increasingly clear that the school needed more space. Washington proposed the first major new construction, Porter Hall, a large building with both classrooms and dormitories as well as a room for a library. Davidson and Washington printed a fundraising pamphlet describing the building and their plan to build it at minimum cost by using student labor wherever possible, and went North to get support. Work started on the hall when a local white merchant advanced some of the materials, and by the end of the year it was completed. Funding arrived to pay the bills just in time, and the students were extremely proud of what they had built with their own sweat. A few years later, Washington decided that the school needed more permanent brick buildings, and he proposed that the school establish a brickyard to make the bricks and sell the surplus to the surrounding community. After several complete failures to produce bricks, the students finally succeeded and from then on learned the art of bricklaying as part of the process of constructing new buildings. Students who attended Tuskegee during these years took great pride in the work they had done, and younger students who attempted to deface the buildings with graffiti received stern lectures from the older students about respect for property.

Washington soon found himself occupying an increasingly public position. After 1885 he employed agents to raise money for him, and he also established the Tuskegee Singers, modeled on similar groups from Fisk University and Hampton, to tour the country on behalf of Tuskegee Institute. Washington was making important contacts in the black community. At every commencement he took the opportunity to invite prominent people to give speeches and tour the campus. He brought Frederick Douglass, Blanche K. Bruce, and P.B.S. Pinchback to the institute and pursued friendships with them. He also made friends in the North as he traveled throughout the country. One of his closest friends was T. Thomas Fortune, editor of the *New York Age*, a black newspaper with a national circulation. Fortune became one of Washington's strongest champions in the debate with Du Bois. In 1887, Fortune founded the Afro-American Council, which advocated court challenges to civil rights violations and black disfranchisement. Although Washington was supportive of the organization, he stayed true to his conservative outlook on political action and did not attend national conventions.

By the 1890s, Tuskegee was becoming a leading employer of black college graduates, another factor that led to Washington's increasing importance in the black community. In 1894, W.E.B. Du Bois, fresh from his studies in Germany, applied for a position at Tuskegee as part of his job search but accepted an offer from another school before he got a response.

Washington was also becoming known to important people in the white philanthropic community. The two major philanthropic resources for southern schools were the Peabody Education Fund and the John F. Slater Fund. The Peabody Fund, named for philanthropist George Peabody, set aside $2.5 million for the education of poor people in the South. Peabody, an English industrialist, was instrumental in building low-income housing in London and wanted to make some similar contribution in the United States. The John F. Slater Fund, named for a wealthy industrialist who donated $1 million specifically for the Christian education of freedmen, contributed mostly to private schools and teacher-training institutes. Both funds had begun by making small grants to a variety of schools, but in the 1880s they made their first large donations to Tuskegee. The Slater Fund in particular began to focus its efforts on industrial schools on the Hampton/Tuskegee model. Once these major philanthropic organizations gave the seal of approval to Tuskegee, other donors followed. Indeed, Washington's work inspired major donors to create funds for black education. In 1902, Anna T. Jeanes, for years a friend of Tuskegee, established a fund of $2 million for rural black schools in the South, especially for teachers' salaries. Caroline Phelps Stokes and her sister Olivia began donating money to Tuskegee in the early 1890s and almost entirely financed the construction of Phelps Hall on the Tuskegee campus. In 1910, Caroline established a special fund to improve existing facilities for African American schools in the South as well as to build new ones.

As Washington gained the attention of important people, he began publishing articles in both the black and the mainstream press. He continued to espouse a conservative racial position, stressing that he did not advocate universal voting rights or social intermingling. Mostly talking about the virtues of an industrial education as the best approach for blacks to improve themselves, he earned a reputation as an accommodationist, a man whom whites could rely on to keep an even temperament and propose conservative solutions. But he was still only one of several black leaders espousing similar views. Hollis Frissell, for instance, who succeeded Armstrong as head of Hampton in the early 1890s, was also well known in educational circles as a conservative leader.

Tuskegee became a model for industrial schools for blacks. Students took classes in academic subjects in the morning and trained as skilled workers in the afternoon. *Courtesy of the Library of Congress*

Nevertheless, many whites did not consider consulting even conservative blacks on racial matters. In 1890, a group of white philanthropists, including former U.S. president Rutherford B. Hayes, then president of the Slater Fund, met to discuss the "Negro Question" at Lake Mohonk, New York. They did not invite a single African American. This group represented the "best" white people with the most concern for the problems that African Americans faced, and the decisions they made at this conference and another held the following year set the agenda for white philanthropy for the next generation. Excited by the possibilities of industrial education, these people concluded that industrial schools on the Hampton and Tuskegee models were the best way for blacks to improve. Armstrong was a leading figure at these proceedings, and his ideas reached a receptive audience. Having decided for African Americans their best course of action, white philanthropists became convinced that it was the only wise course and gave little attention or money to alternative projects or to schools such as Atlanta University, which emphasized a more classical curriculum.

In 1895, Washington became the most noted of the black conservatives as a result of one speech, his address at the opening ceremonies of the Atlanta Cotton States and International Exposition. The favorable impression he had made in speaking before a white conference in Atlanta in 1893 led to an invitation from some white men in the city to be part of a delegation to Congress to ask for a grant to support the planned exposition. Washington, stressing conservative themes about how blacks could use the exposition to showcase their accomplishments rather than push for political rights, impressed the commissioners so much that they asked him to take charge of the "Negro Exhibit." Pleading that his other duties at Tuskegee prevented him from committing the necessary time to the project, Washington turned down the offer. When the white commissioners decided that a black man could speak at the opening ceremonies and invited Washington to be that speaker, he accepted.

Since the commissioners had originally proposed a separate ceremony to open the Negro Exhibit as a way to avoid having a black speaker on the same platform with whites, the assignment was a difficult one. Washington knew it would take all his skills as a speaker and a diplomat to give a speech that both blacks and whites would accept. He also recognized that he had an unprecedented opportunity to address an audience of influential white southerners, as well as people from around the world, and that what he said could significantly influence white opinion on race issues. True to his beliefs, he said nothing that he and other conservative blacks such as Frissell had not said before. But the forum in which he spoke gave Washington great publicity, and its timing made white America more willing to listen. In 1895, just a few years after the Lake Mohonk conferences and one year before *Plessy v. Ferguson*, whites were turning away from helping blacks and were content to hear that blacks wanted to help themselves. Convinced that industrial education would solve all problems, they were pleased when Washington made fun of blacks who tried to become politicians even though they had neither the income nor the skills to support themselves. He was an instant hit.

What Washington actually proposed in his Atlanta address was a compromise: blacks would agree not to push for social and political equality if whites would agree not to exclude them from economic progress. He began by praising the commissioners for their generosity in allowing him to speak and for supporting the Negro Exhibit. He apologized that blacks had not progressed further; that was so, he stated, because they had tried to start at the top of life as politicians and lawyers instead of starting with hard work at the bottom. Advising blacks to recognize that there was "as much dignity in tilling a field as in writing a poem,"[1] he said they should settle down in the occupations and jobs they were already familiar with and not try to jump ahead too fast. In return, he asked whites to look to blacks rather than to the new immigrants when they wanted to hire workers. Invoking a rather romantic view of the Old South, Washington emphasized that blacks had always been faithful in the past, and so whites should trust them to help in the future. The most quoted sentence of the speech—"In all things that are purely social we can be as separate as the fingers, yet one as the hand in all things essential to mutual progress"—was actually advising whites to work together with blacks in restoring the South. He warned that unless whites helped, black poverty and ignorance would be a continual drain on southern resources and would drag the region down further in the long run. But he did reemphasize that blacks could not force change and should not expect instant success or full rights: "It is important and right that all privileges of the law be ours, but it is vastly more important that we be prepared for the exercise of these privileges." Pushing for immediate social equality would be the "extremest folly."[2]

He captured the mood of his audience perfectly, and his speech ended to thunderous applause. Georgia's former governor, Rufus Brown Bullock, rushed across the stage to shake Washington's hand, and ladies in the audience fluttered their handkerchiefs. Blacks who attended were thrilled. Black and white newspapers around the country reprinted at least excerpts of the address if not the complete text, and telegrams and letters of congratulation poured in. Du Bois himself was enthusiastic and congratulated Washington, telling him his speech was "a word fitly spoken."[3] Washington began receiving requests from around the country to speak; Tuskegee began taking in more donations; and politicians began approaching him to consult on racial issues. A star was born.

Washington's rise to power was helped by the fact that many of the older black political leaders from Reconstruction were fading from the scene in the late 1890s. Douglass died in 1895, Bruce in 1898, and in the inevitable efforts of the black press to identify comparable leaders, Washington came out on top. He was able to maintain such a high-profile position in part because of the public relations machine that developed at Tuskegee. With the help of his personal assistant, Emmett J. Scott, the institute became a central clearinghouse for information on race issues. Tuskegee published its own magazine, issued regular press releases, and, using ghostwriters, sent regular articles under Washington's name to such prestigious journals as the *Atlantic Monthly*. Washington became an extraordinarily busy man. He brought in his brother, John, to help run the day-to-day affairs of Tuskegee Institute and devoted himself almost full time to speaking and fundraising. Having initially gone door to door soliciting funds in northern towns, he now had access to some of the wealthiest people in America. John D. Rockefeller donated substantial sums once Washington had cultivated his support; Andrew Carnegie became one of his greatest allies. Carnegie, who had risen from rags to riches, believed that it was his duty to give back to society as much as he had earned. As a businessman, he was especially interested in practical programs with concrete results and was therefore attracted to industrial education; besides, it had the potential to train workers for his steel factories. To Carnegie, Washington was a kindred spirit, a practical man of action. Through Washington and Tuskegee, Carnegie ultimately funneled several million dollars to the cause of black education.

Washington solidified his position as the preeminent leader of black America in 1900 and 1901. In 1900, he established the National Negro Business League (NNBL), an organization dedicated to promoting black businesses. With chapters in almost every major town and city, the NNBL gave him a mechanism for maintaining contact with leading black businessmen. It accomplished little in the way of practical programs but did offer meeting places where those businessmen could share their experiences. Local chapters became centers of loyalty to Tuskegee, and when the debate with Du Bois arose, Washington used the NNBL as one of his weapons.

In 1901, Washington further enhanced his image with the publication of his autobiography, *Up from Slavery*, to widespread acclaim. He wrote the book to inspire other blacks to succeed as he had, but he also wanted to further his agenda for racial uplift. He tried to convince whites that blacks were capable of intelligent thought and action and to break down some of the more obnoxious stereotypes. He was firm in his insistence that whites give blacks a chance whenever possible but equally firm in his reassertion that blacks did not seek political or social equality. The reaction to his book was overwhelmingly positive. After reading it a second time, George Eastman of Kodak Eastman Company sent a check for $5,000, saying he could not think of a better use for the money than to further Washington's work.

Washington also began advising politicians on a much larger scale. Local leaders around Tuskegee had consulted with him even in the 1880s, and as Tuskegee expanded, so did his influence, especially in Alabama state politics. In the late 1890s and early 1900s he began to advise on the national level. His most important relationship was with Republican Theodore Roosevelt, the former governor of New York, whom he probably met through T. Thomas Fortune of the *New York Age*. As with Carnegie, Washington found a kindred spirit in Roosevelt as a man of action, although the New Yorker's racial views were more in tune with those of a less benevolent Armstrong. Roosevelt strongly believed in the natural superiority of the white race, but he was also a practical man who recognized the potential importance of the black vote, and a moral man who was outraged by the worst injustices that blacks faced from white zealots. Roosevelt turned to Washington for advice on racial matters, and continued to solicit his opinion when he became president in 1901, not just on appointments to positions traditionally reserved for blacks but in all appointments throughout the South. Washington advised Roosevelt to appoint conservative white Democrats rather than the rabid race-baiting politicians who arose in the 1890s. The president not only valued his advice on appointments but also consulted him on all racial issues.

On October 16, 1901, Roosevelt invited Washington to dine with him at the White House. The event showed both how far African Americans had come and how far they still had to go. Blacks praised Roosevelt for his invitation, as did reform-minded whites, but some white southerners poured forth abuse—not on Roosevelt for the invitation but on Washington for accepting it. They accused him of pushing for social equality by eating publicly with a white man. Washington rushed to reassure white southerners that he had no such intentions. In fact, although he had dined frequently with whites in the North, he maintained segregated practices in the South; even at Tuskegee he separated the students from white visitors at mealtimes. Nonetheless, despite Washington's reassurances and generally conservative outlook on race relations, a few whites still labeled him a troublemaker.

By 1901, Washington was easily the most powerful black man in America. He had the acclaim of both blacks and whites, the ear of the president, and friendships with the most influential people in the country. Tuskegee Institute had become more than just a well-funded and successful school; it was a local empire in Alabama. From Tuskegee, Washington unofficially controlled not only most of the funding for black schools in the South but also jobs and other patronage in the black community. African Americans seeking jobs, approval for a project, or financial support first had to go through Tuskegee. Through the NNBL, Washington had created a network of Tuskegee supporters around the country. His allies began privately referring to him as "the Wizard of Tuskegee." The question remained, however: Was the course he proposed the right one for black America?

Notes

1. See page 126, this volume.
2. See page 128, this volume.
3. W.E.B. Du Bois to Booker T. Washington, September 24, 1985.

3 | W.E.B. Du Bois and Atlanta University

William Edward Burghardt Du Bois, called Willie, was born on February 23, 1868, in Great Barrington, Massachusetts, to Alfred and Mary Du Bois. Unlike Washington, he was born free, but like Washington, Du Bois had no relationship with his biological father. Alfred Du Bois, the grandson of a French planter aristocrat and his slave, was born in Haiti. Sometime before the Civil War, he came to the United States probably to be with his father, Alexander Du Bois, a free black who had returned to New England shortly after Alfred's birth. Alfred served with the U.S. Colored Troops without distinction during the war and afterward moved around the Northeast doing various jobs. He became the black sheep of the otherwise fairly respectable Du Bois family. In 1867 he settled briefly in Great Barrington and married Willie's mother, but within a year he had moved to another town and begun another series of jobs. Willie remembered that his father wrote to ask them to join him, but whether he actually did write or not, Mary Du Bois and Willie never went. Willie had almost no contact with the Du Bois side of the family except for one brief visit to his grandfather, Alexander, when he was a teenager.

Mary was one of the Burghardts, also a free black family. Her great-great-grandfather had fought in the Revolutionary War and earned his freedom. Her grandmother, born Elizabeth Freeman but whom locals called "Mom Bett," successfully sued for her freedom in the courts when her mistress abused her. The Burghardts were never wealthy, but they occupied a position of relative respectability in the

A dapper Du Bois at the Paris Exposition in 1900. *Courtesy of the Special Collections and Archives, W.E.B. Du Bois Library, University of Massachusetts, Amherst*

community. Mary left her family briefly when she had her first child, Adelbert; there was some scandal about the father, who did not meet Burghardt standards of propriety. She probably then met Alfred Du Bois while she was in upstate New York and was attracted to his manners and seemingly high-class background. She returned with him to her hometown, and Adelbert went to live in Albany. When Alfred ran out of money, the Burghardt family took them in. Willie later blamed the Burghardts for his father's departure, believing that they made it too uncomfortable for him to stay. Mary had worked out of town as a maid and possibly salesgirl before her marriage, but after Alfred left, she chose to stay in Great Barrington and take care of her son. After her father died, she and Willie lived in a series of small rental houses, which they shared with other family members. When her mother died, they moved to one of the poorest sections of town in a house next to the railroad tracks, several saloons, a few gambling houses, and a brothel. Mary suffered a small stroke and became unable to work, so they lived on what other family members could give them, some money Adelbert sent, and what Willie earned from after-school jobs. The boy and his mother were very close, and he did what he could to make her life easier.

Willie did well in school and came to see an education as the road out of poverty and a way to make his mother proud. He attended high school, the first of the Burghardts to do so, and gained the attention of some prominent whites in the community who took an interest in him. One of these men rented a house to him and his mother and uncle in a more respectable neighborhood, even though the family could not always pay the rent. Willie had all the usual boyhood chores and jobs. He had a paper route, mowed lawns, and sold things door to door. He worked hard and his family was poor, but he knew early on that he was destined for greater things.

Great Barrington seemed in many ways an ideal place for a boy to grow up, and Du Bois remembered it as a typical little New England town on a golden river. But the town was not perfect. There were fewer than thirty black families in the area, most of whose members worked in service positions such as waiters and maids. White racial attitudes were fairly progressive, probably as a result of having so few blacks in the community. Nonetheless, adult whites and blacks did not mingle socially, although students attended integrated schools. When large numbers of Catholic immigrants began to arrive to work at the new mills, both white and black townspeople made a point of distancing themselves from the newcomers, showing their acceptance of many of the turn-of-the-century stereotypes surrounding ethnicity. Du Bois, like Washington, thought of these poor whites as lazy drunks.

Du Bois wrote that in his early years in school he never felt different because of his race; only when people came to visit from outside Great Barrington did he begin to think of himself as something unusual. Part of the Du Bois legend is a story he told about a small white girl who had newly arrived in Great Barrington. Du Bois and his classmates were exchanging calling cards, imitating adults' behavior when they visited one another's houses. The girl refused to accept Willie's card because he was black, and the boy suddenly realized that there would always be a barrier separating him from whites. This anecdote, which Du Bois told in *The Souls of Black Folk*, was typical of his romantic style of storytelling and may have been true, but it is likely that he was aware of racial prejudice long before that incident. It is also true, however, that his best childhood friends were white and that he competed with whites academically in school without any fear of reprisal.

Nonetheless, because of his poverty, his physical size (he was short and skinny), the taint of his father's absence, and his superior intellect, Du Bois had many reasons to feel like an outsider. He had only a few close friends and was shy in unfamiliar social situations. He was supremely confident in his academic ability, however, and decided early that he would make an important contribution to his race. He continued to attract the attention of leading townspeople who encouraged him to take the college preparatory course at the local high school. Even as a teenager he was an intellectual, borrowing as many books as he could and paying on installments to buy a five-volume deluxe edition of a classic history book. He also became a contributor to the *New York Globe*, T. Thomas Fortune's predecessor to the *Age*. Willie was the local distributor for the *Globe* and first sent regular reports of the social events in Great Barrington's small black community, especially those at the AME Zion church. He editorialized that blacks should create a literary society to improve themselves and later wrote stirring calls to arms against racial discrimination in local politics. Like Washington's early writings, Du Bois's articles for the *Globe* reflected what would be the basis of his own philosophy in years to come.

In 1883, Willie went for the first and only time to visit his grandfather, Alexander Du Bois, in New Bedford, Massachusetts. Alexander had retired a relatively wealthy man and had all the aristocratic bearing that the son of a French planter should have. For Willie, this first long trip away from home by himself involved a series of missed trains and a visit to the state legislature, but it was Alexander who impressed him the most. The Burghardts, though respectable, regarded fancy manners and clothes as affectations that people put on to impress others when there was nothing else to impress them. But Alexander Du Bois not only affected an aristocratic background; he truly had one, with the home and friends to prove it. For Willie it must have been a tremendous contrast to his previous image of the Du Bois family. Before, thinking only of Alfred, his father, he had perhaps been a little ashamed of the name. After the visit with his grandfather he gained a sense of himself as descended from important people both European and Caribbean. Perhaps the knowledge enabled him to overcome the humiliation of his father's desertion. He also gained a glimpse of what life could be like if he could succeed in the world. His own carefully cultivated aristocratic image may have had its origins with his image of his grandfather.

Willie entered his senior year of high school with great dreams for the future. Primary among them was his desire to go to Harvard University. He knew that Harvard was one of the best schools in the country and hoped for a scholarship from the townspeople who had supported him in the past. A scholarship eventually did come, but the townspeople raised money for him to go to Fisk University in Nashville, a black college, instead of Harvard. Du Bois was greatly disappointed when they told him he should go and study with his "own people" down south. To him, his "own people" were fellow intellectuals at schools like Harvard. He had had little exposure to all-black environments, having lived in a mostly integrated town. But going to Fisk, as he admitted later, changed the direction of his life for the better and helped shape his philosophy of racial uplift.

Fisk University, established in 1866 with the help of the American Missionary Association and the Freedmen's Bureau, was probably the most famous of all the black colleges. Fisk's Jubilee Singers were the first group of their kind to tour the country on behalf of a black school, and they gained a stellar reputation singing slave spirituals and folk songs. Fisk also had an excellent academic reputation and attracted some of the nation's leading black scholars, all of whom had an almost missionary zeal to provide the students with the best possible education and teach them to contribute to their race. Fisk students assumed that it was their duty to help other African Americans whenever and wherever they could and often spent their summers volunteering to teach in rural areas. The university offered a classical curriculum but did emphasize putting education to practical use. As Hampton was a model for Washington, Fisk became the model for Du Bois.

His years at Fisk were not only his first time living almost exclusively among other African Americans but also his first taste of the South. Nashville was rapidly becoming a segregated city, and his trip there was probably his first ride on a Jim Crow train car. In fact, he experienced more racism personally in his first year than ever before in his life. Most Fisk students came from the South and were used to an all-black environment, but Willie's only previous experiences in this regard were a few church revivals that he had attended. He later said these had given him both his first sense of what it meant to be black and a sense of fellowship with his race. At Fisk, Du Bois encountered the whole range of the black community, from sons and daughters of sharecroppers and maids on scholarship to the children of those few blacks who had become wealthy and prominent. He was at Fisk at the same time as Margaret Murray, an exceptional student who later became Lady Principal at Tuskegee and Booker T. Washington's third wife, after Olivia died. Du Bois made lifelong friends such as Thomas J. Calloway of Washington, DC, who would become a lawyer and ally in the debate with Washington and Tuskegee.

Under the influence of Fisk's missionary zeal, Du Bois went with a group of students to look for a summer teaching position in rural Tennessee. Fisk students saw themselves as the vanguard of the race, whose duty it was to go among their people and lead them out of bondage—not physical bondage, of course, but the bonds of poverty and ignorance that they believed were keeping the race from progressing. They shared a spirit of noblesse oblige, the idea that as persons of superior breeding and class they had an obligation and special responsibility to care for those less fortunate. The objects of such charity, although grateful, did not always view themselves as people of inferior status, nor did they always think that they needed help of the sort that was offered. Nonetheless, such impulses served as inspiration to many leading African Americans to do something to help the race and did bring some positive results.

Du Bois went to the Teacher's Institute in Lebanon, Tennessee, for a week of classes to qualify him for a first-grade teaching certificate and then set off on foot to find a school. In Alexandria, in rural Wilson County in the backcountry of Tennessee, he found the school where he would spend two summers working with poor black farmers and their families and learning how desperate their situation really was. By the end of his first summer, Du Bois had lost some of his aristocratic attitude and come to understand that southern whites did not react well to blacks "putting on airs." His school consisted of one room with precarious benches and a leaky roof. When it rained, one of the students had to stand at the front of the class and hold an umbrella over his head as he worked. Du Bois taught about thirty students when they all attended, but he soon found that the children frequently missed school to work on the farm or take care of other children. His students varied in intellect and dedication, but local blacks were happy to have a teacher available to them. He boarded with a succession of families and was shocked to see the conditions in which some lived. Undoubtedly he saw much the same conditions as those Booker T. Washington had found in rural Alabama when he first arrived at Tuskegee. Du Bois saw firsthand that hard work did not automatically bring success, for some of these people were the hardest workers he had ever seen. When he returned to Alexandria ten years later, he found that some of the laziest people seemed to be doing just as well as before, whereas some of the hard workers' lives had not improved at all. He concluded that there needed to be some overall change in the system if blacks were to prosper and overcome barriers. Economic progress was not possible if blacks could not control the furnishing merchants or protect their land rights.

In the middle to late 1880s, when Du Bois was at Fisk, blacks were still voting in the South in relatively large numbers, and legal segregation was only just beginning. Faculty and students at universities such as Fisk, Howard, and Atlanta kept faith with the ideals of abolitionism and Radical Reconstruction. They still looked to political solutions and expected that more enlightened whites would work with them. Even as disfranchisement began, many African Americans believed that it was aimed not at blacks but at poor and ignorant people in general. When the full extent of Jim Crow and disfranchisement became clear, it hit them extremely hard; they demanded that whites keep the promises they had made to respect blacks' civil rights. Du Bois had come from a childhood in which he had experienced little discrimination to a school that emphasized superior education for blacks along with the idea that graduates would lead the way for other blacks to follow. It was not surprising that he would be optimistic about the future of the race and his role in advancing it. But what he saw in Alexandria, and later in Philadelphia, shattered that faith in inevitable progress. He would later realize that only more decisive action would change things.

At Fisk, Du Bois continued his academic preparation for his career. He began as editor of students' submissions to the *Herald*, Fisk's magazine, and wrote two articles about his summer teaching experiences. By his senior year he had become editor in chief and was writing many editorials on race issues. Chosen to speak at commencement in 1888, he praised the German chancellor, Otto von Bismarck, champion of practical politics in diplomacy and someone who had united his country through strict discipline and order. He said that African Americans must have similar discipline if they were to advance but should not get so tied up in the practical aspects of progress that they forgot the ultimate goal of helping people.

In one of his autobiographies, Du Bois grandly titled the chapter on his experiences at Fisk "Going South," clearly thinking of himself as having been there on a mission from the North. He always assumed that he would return to Massachusetts and attend Harvard's graduate school. He also clearly still saw himself as superior to the poor farmers he met in rural Tennessee. Yet Fisk had given him a sense of pride in his race as well as in himself and had knocked off a few of his rough edges and social pretensions. It had taught him that he could be more at ease in the company of blacks than whites and had given him an appreciation for the real barriers that blacks faced in their struggle for equality. Although he always preferred the North to the South and generally remained aloof from people, he was capable of an insight into southern society that most northerners could not achieve.

In the summer of 1888, after he graduated from Fisk, Du Bois and some friends worked as waiters at a resort hotel in Minnesota. Like Booker T. Washington in upstate New York, he did a poor job waiting tables; he wrote that he did not get tips because he was not willing to ignore rude customers. Patrons expected him to turn a blind eye to their drunkenness and vulgarity, but Du Bois refused to do so. It is revealing that at the same point in their lives, Du Bois and Washington had similar experiences but gained different insights from them. Washington used his experience to illustrate that blacks could succeed if they just applied themselves and learned the necessary skills;

Du Bois, to show that blacks should not be willing to tolerate indignity, no matter what the source. This difference in attitude would intensify the debate between the two men in later years.

From 1888 to 1892, Du Bois did indeed attend Harvard, the school of his dreams, though all was not entirely as he expected. In order to enter the graduate program in philosophy he had to take his junior and senior years over again at Harvard, whose faculty did not think Fisk had high-enough academic standards. He never made close friends with white students at Harvard; in fact, he later wrote that he purposely held himself back from social interaction with whites because of his Fisk experiences. He did not want to force his company on anyone who might not want it, a possibility he had never really considered before going South. But Du Bois willingly complied with Harvard's academic standards and was thrilled to be in Cambridge.

The only other African American in his graduating class was Clement G. Morgan, who was ten years older, and the two men became friends. Morgan, originally from Virginia, had attended the prestigious M Street High School in Washington, DC, before moving west. He had been working as a barber in St. Louis when he gained the attention of, and married, one of the city's black schoolteachers, who encouraged him to pursue a higher education. They moved to Boston, and Morgan attended Harvard's preparatory school and then entered the university as a freshman. Having known many of his classmates for so long and because of his unassuming and friendly personality, he was quite popular. He was also an excellent public speaker, and he and Du Bois competed for the distinguished Boylston Prizes for oratory in their junior year. Both prizes came with $50, which Du Bois needed to supplement his small scholarship. Morgan won first prize, and Du Bois came in second, marking the first time that African Americans had taken both Boylston Prizes.

Du Bois's classmates broke all traditions in 1890 by nominating Morgan as their class orator, the first black man to earn such an honor. He gave an excellent speech, confounding all the people who had warned of the dire consequences of his nomination. Du Bois was one of six others the faculty selected to speak at commencement that year. Both men received a lot of attention in the black press as examples of what the race could accomplish, and black society matron Josephine St. Pierre Ruffin held a formal reception to introduce them to Boston's black elite. In the summer following their graduation, Morgan and

Du Bois became even closer friends as they embarked on a tour of speaking engagements to raise money for their further education. Morgan attended Harvard Law School and became a prominent attorney.

In his first graduate year, Du Bois also met incoming Harvard freshman William Monroe Trotter, who had grown up in a well-to-do black family in Hyde Park, a mostly white suburb of Boston. His father had served in the traditionally African American appointment of recorder of deeds in Washington, DC, under Grover Cleveland. Trotter was popular and outgoing, and the students at his predominantly white high school elected him class president. Like Du Bois, he was extremely intelligent and excelled at Harvard, graduating Phi Beta Kappa. Du Bois first met him when a group of friends from the Boston area went to see African Americans George Forbes and William H. Lewis graduate from Amherst College. Some of Boston's black elite had begun a series of visits to black students at other colleges in the region, and the friendships they formed often remained long after their college days were over. Lewis, who graduated from Harvard Law School with Clement Morgan, maintained his friendship with Du Bois and Trotter for many years, but in the end had to choose between that friendship and his career as a result of Du Bois's attack on Booker T. Washington. Du Bois admired Trotter's outspokenness and social grace.

With an inheritance of $20,000 from his father, Trotter was almost in a class of his own. He typified many of the strong-minded Boston black elite in his unwillingness to compromise and his firm belief in the possibilities of gaining full social equality. Boston had been a center of abolitionist activity, and leading blacks prided themselves on their connections with whites. They attended predominantly white schools and churches and refused to submit to any racial segregation. Somewhat socially exclusive, members of the city's black elite tended to look down on working-class blacks and to distance themselves from them as much as possible.

But black Boston Brahmins, as the city called its elite, were also political activists. Josephine St. Pierre Ruffin was a militant supporter of woman suffrage, publishing articles on the subject and participating in campaigns to get women the vote. Archibald Grimké, who also lived in Hyde Park, was the nephew of famous white abolitionist sisters Angelina and Sarah Grimké of South Carolina. With the help of his aunts, Archibald attended schools in the North, graduated from Harvard, and became a well-known attorney and leading spokesman on racial issues. He maintained fierce political independence, switching to support the Democrats in 1886 but never fully identifying himself as one. In the late 1890s, Grimké served as American consul in Santo Domingo (today the Dominican Republic). Upon his return, he and his daughter lived in Washington, DC, with his equally independent brother, Presbyterian minister Francis Grimké, and Francis's wife, abolitionist Charlotte Forten Grimké, who was the daughter of black businessman James Forten of Philadelphia.

The Boston black leadership provided the earliest and chief opposition to Booker T. Washington's conservatism, and undoubtedly Du Bois's personal relationships with many of the Boston radicals, particularly Trotter, influenced his own position. Still, it is clear that Du Bois had already formed many of the same attitudes as the Boston elite, and those personal relationships were as much a matter of shared political beliefs as pleasant company. Du Bois had finally found somewhere he seemed to fit in.

Du Bois also found himself at home academically. The faculty at Harvard was pleased with his scholarship on the whole, and several members treated him as a favored student. The professors in the philosophy department particularly impressed Du Bois, especially William James and George Santayana. But, as biographer David Levering Lewis points out, Du Bois was less impressed by their somewhat radical philosophies than by the men themselves as models for the intellectual that he felt himself to be. James and Santayana were both unconventional and seemed to be outsiders. They did not fit the professorial mold that Du Bois expected. It was James who advised Du Bois that he should not become a philosopher because philosophers were withdrawn from the world, and if he wanted to make a difference he should go into a field that dealt with real problems, such as the then new field of sociology.[1]

Since Harvard did not yet offer sociology, Du Bois took his master's degree in history in 1891, studying under the famous historian Albert Bushnell Hart, then just starting his Harvard career. Du Bois's thesis was on the Atlantic slave trade, and after he had successfully defended it before his Harvard professors, he presented it before the American Historical Association. He then tried to get permission to expand his master's thesis into a Ph.D dissertation, but by 1892 he had begun to look beyond Harvard to greater things. As good as Harvard's reputation was in the United States, and as good an education as he had received there, internationally an American degree was still slightly suspect. Du Bois had begun to plan his life's work. What he wanted to do was teach and research the truth about African Americans. He believed, perhaps naively, that one main reason for so much prejudice against blacks in America was that whites believed the stereotypes of Jim Crow. Moreover, he was frustrated with the trend among scholars to theorize on the basis of alleged racial characteristics without investigating the facts. If he could prove these stereotypes wrong, then whites would have to recognize the essential equality of the races. What Du Bois wanted to do required impeccable credentials and the most up-to-date training. For those, he had to go to one of the great universities of Europe.

In 1890, he had seen a newspaper clipping that showed him a possible route to his new goal. Rutherford B. Hayes, former U.S. president and then head of the Slater Fund, had made a crude remark about blacks being incapable of advanced study of literature or other academic subjects. He commented sarcastically that the Slater Fund would gladly finance a European education for any black student who showed such a capacity, if it ever could find one. It was just at this time that whites meeting at Lake Mohonk were deciding to support industrial education for blacks, and Hayes was echoing sentiments that many shared. Through Booker T. Washington's influence the Slater Fund had already begun to shift toward almost exclusive support of industrial schools. Du Bois, furious at the statement, decided to take advantage of Hayes's sarcastic comment. He applied to the Slater Fund to finance his studies in Europe toward his doctorate. Hayes first denied the statement, then qualified it, and then said he had withdrawn the offer. Du Bois, however, was so insistent that he keep his promise and so persistent in writing that Hayes finally agreed to have the board consider his application. In 1892 the Slater Fund offered him a $750 stipend, half in the form of a repayable loan, renewable for the following year. An elated Du Bois had won a small victory.

His original plan was to spend time in Germany, England, and France, studying at different universities. Britain and France, however, did not recognize American degrees, so he realized that he would do better to stay longer in one place. After he received the stipend in 1892, he gained admission to the University of Berlin and spent the next two years in Germany. The experience once again reshaped his thinking. The change began on the boat from Rotterdam in the Netherlands to Berlin, when he was amazed to discover that a white Dutch family treated him like anyone else on the river steamer and insisted that he accompany them on tours in the cities where they stopped. Du Bois was in awe of Europe and all its famous landmarks. He made several short trips from Berlin to see as much as he could and, later, before returning home, spent a few months touring with friends in England and Poland.

In Berlin, he first stayed in a small boardinghouse and carried on a romance with the landlady's daughter. He mixed easily with white students and attended many social events. He danced with German women at balls without seeing the slightest raised eyebrow. He was amazed at the difference in race relations. His relationship with the landlady's daughter ended, however, when a white American couple came to stay and objected violently to it. Du Bois, realizing that even in Europe he could not completely escape racial prejudice, moved to another boardinghouse. But for the most part, his stay in Berlin provided him with a glimpse of what a truly equal society might be. Most people judged him on his intellect and manners rather than on his skin color, and the experience made Du Bois more determined to fight discrimination at home. He also adopted many German mannerisms and styles, including the mustache he grew in imitation of Kaiser Wilhelm.

The other change for Du Bois was that in Germany he got the training he needed for sociology and discovered his true passion in life. He found no mentor like Santayana or James—in the European university the professors did not have close relationships with their students—but he studied economics and history with some of Europe's most noted scholars. After three semesters of work, his professors began to suggest that they might propose him for his doctorate in economics at the university. He had taken the necessary examinations and completed a dissertation; all that remained was approval by the universitywide faculty committee. But in most departments, students had to complete six semesters of study to earn a doctorate, and although professors might waive one or two semesters for exceptional students, waiving three semesters seemed excessive to the other departments. They refused to approve his degree until he had taken at least four semesters of work. Du Bois applied to the Slater Fund to renew his stipend one more semester, but Slater officials stated that they were no longer supporting graduate work abroad. Greatly disappointed, Du Bois took a few months to tour Europe before returning home to Harvard in 1894.

Resigned to finishing his doctorate at Harvard, Du Bois expanded his master's thesis on the slave trade. He argued that Americans had been active participants in the illegal importation of slaves after Congress outlawed the trade in 1808, and that these illegal imports accounted for the increase in the slave population in the fifty years before the Civil War. Although he overestimated the total number of slaves smuggled into the country, his thorough research made his work the standard on the subject for years to come. Albert Hart, his dissertation supervisor, approved the work in June 1895, and Du Bois became the first African American to earn a doctorate from Harvard. Hart also recommended publishing *The Suppression of the African Slave Trade* as the first in a series to be called Harvard Historical Studies. By the time Du Bois graduated in 1895, he was already gaining a reputation in academic circles for his sound research.

Almost immediately on his return from Europe, he had begun looking for a job to support himself while finishing his dissertation. At first, he applied to teach in the Tennessee rural schools near Alexandria, but the white school board felt that a Harvard- and University of Berlin-trained black scholar would not be the appropriate choice for a backcountry school in the South. He also sent out letters to universities and colleges catering to blacks, including Howard, Hampton, Fisk, Wilberforce, and Tuskegee. Most schools had no vacancies, but finally, in mid-August 1894, Wilberforce University in Ohio offered him the chair of the classics department for $800 per year. Du Bois gladly accepted and then promptly received two other offers, which he felt he had to turn down, since he had already accepted Wilberforce's. The first was for $250 more teaching classics and mathematics at Lincoln Institute in Missouri; the second was an offer from Booker T. Washington to teach mathematics at Tuskegee, terms unspecified.

Wilberforce, a product of the AME Church and abolitionist zeal, was established in 1856 near Xenia, Ohio. Its campus was a former resort hotel called Tanawa Springs, previously patronized by rich slaveowners. Named for famous British abolitionist Bishop William Wilberforce, the school for blacks came under the control of several different white denominations until the AME Church bought it in 1863. After 1887, Wilberforce also housed a state-funded Combined Industrial and Normal Department, ensuring its financial stability. Du Bois's two years at Wilberforce, however, were not happy ones. To begin with, he had only just returned to the United States from an environment in Europe that had allowed him great freedom. Back in what he called "nigger-hating America," he experienced tremendous disillusionment. He had been soaring for the past six years and had great plans for how he was going to bring about change for African Americans. But now he felt thwarted in even the simplest of his goals. If he had taken offense at racist remarks and racial discrimination before he left for Germany, he was even more sensitive to them after he returned. Europe had shown him that things could be different, and he wanted to make white America realize that fact, too.

Adding to his general disillusionment and his disappointment at not being able to finish his Berlin degree was the political situation at Wilberforce. In November 1893, AME head Bishop Daniel Payne had died, and the university administration had changed. Payne had been a driving force behind higher education for blacks and proper training for ministers, and often it was only his tireless fund-raising that had kept the school open. His successor, who had served as Payne's subordinate and longed for the power himself, had begun the process of replacing Payne's men with his own supporters at Wilberforce, even adding his own sons to the faculty. He chose as president a man who, Du Bois said, was more concerned with pleasing the trustees and enhancing his own reputation than with meeting the needs of the students. When Du Bois arrived in late August 1894, he found that he was replacing one of Wilberforce's most talented and popular scholars, who had fallen victim to the new administration—an unenviable position at best. Moreover, Du Bois's grand ideas for raising Wilberforce's standards to match those of Harvard or Berlin and his rather superior attitude rubbed administrators the wrong way. He did make some improvements in the teaching of Greek and Latin and added German to the curriculum but did not get much support for his efforts. He particularly wanted to add sociology classes and even offered to teach them on his own time, but the administration did not agree.

Finally, Du Bois and some other faculty members objected when the bishop tried to appoint one of his unqualified sons to teach literature. Although they won their fight, they also laid themselves open for revenge. For Du Bois it came when he tried to stage *A Midsummer Night's Dream* in a wooded area on campus, and school officials refused him permission. They gave no clear reason for their decision and waited until after the students had already begun rehearsing to announce it. Realizing that he would never be able to make any substantial changes at Wilberforce, Du Bois began to think about moving elsewhere. It was at this time, in September 1895, that Washington addressed the Atlanta Exposition, and Du Bois found time to send him a brief message of congratulation.

Two good things resulted from his few years in Ohio. First, he met and married his first wife, Nina Gomer, the daughter of a respected black hotel chef and his German wife. Second, he met the Reverend Alexander Crummell for the first time. Crummell, the leading U.S. black intellectual before Du Bois became prominent, had been a member of Trinity Parish, an Episcopal church in New Haven, Connecticut, where Alexander Du Bois had lived. In 1842, Crummell had led blacks to form St. Luke's, an independent Episcopal church, after the white members at Trinity became less hospitable to them; Grandfather Alexander had actively supported that endeavor. Crummell later studied at Cambridge University in England and became an advocate of black emigration to Africa. In the early 1850s he had gone to Liberia as an Episcopal missionary and returned in the early 1870s to found one of the most prestigious black congregations in the country—also called St. Luke's Episcopal Church—in Washington, DC. He published many books on racial issues, including two on Africa and the role of African Americans in "civilizing" it.

Crummell spoke at the commencement exercises at Wilberforce in 1896 and instantly impressed Du Bois, not only with his intellect but also with his noble bearing. Like Du Bois, Crummell had a fairly elitist attitude. He had little faith in the ability of poor people to help themselves, as he had had little faith that Africans could improve without the help of educated African Americans. But he also believed that it was the moral duty of the more fortunate blacks to help raise the rest of the race, and he emphasized the good that Wilberforce's graduates could do by setting a moral example for less fortunate people to follow. Du Bois would remain friends with him until Crummell's death in 1898, and one of the essays in The Souls of Black Folk was a tribute to the man. He also helped Crummell with one of his last projects: organizing the American Negro Academy, a group of black scholars who would publish information and research to counteract negative stereotypes.

Crummell first discussed the idea of a black scholarly association in 1894. He and William H. Crogman, an African American professor and future Clark University president, proposed bringing together fifty of the nation's best black scholars to study the literature, folklore, and ethnography of Africans and people of African descent. By 1897 the idea had evolved into the American Negro Academy. With Crummell as its first president and headquarters in Washington, DC, the ANA tried to devote itself to study and publication of works on race and black culture. The organization never gained full membership but did include such notable scholars and thinkers as sociologists Kelly Miller and Alain Locke of Howard University, Archibald H. Grimké, and of course Du Bois, who became its second president after Crummell's death. Du Bois remained president until 1903, although after 1900 he largely directed his energies elsewhere. Archibald Grimké succeeded Du Bois and tried to make the organization more active, but the ANA never really became the central clearinghouse of information for the race that Crummell had envisioned. Du Bois would largely duplicate its efforts at Atlanta University, as did Booker T. Washington at Tuskegee.

In 1896, however, Du Bois's path lay east, not south. Knowing he had to leave Wilberforce, he accepted an offer to assist a sociology professor, Samuel McCune Lindsay, of the Wharton School at the University of Pennsylvania, in collecting data for a study of African Americans in Philadelphia. Once a center of Quaker abolitionism and home to black abolitionist James Forten, in the course of the nineteenth century, Philadelphia had gradually become more hostile to its black citizens. Political corruption also flourished; during the Gilded Age it was clear that the city's politics ran on money and influence. But what reformers saw as corruption was not always bad for poorer residents. Studies have shown that immigrant neighborhoods pooled their votes in exchange for municipal services, such as better sanitation and street lights, which they might not otherwise have received. In addition, the ward bosses who represented the political machine in these exchanges often took the time to get to know the residents and did not treat them as objects for improvement.

In Philadelphia, there was a strong municipal reform movement centered on the Philadelphia Settlement. The majority of settlement house workers were white middle-class women, most of whom had a college education. They were expanding the idea of appropriate work for women by saying that settlement work was simply housekeeping on a municipal scale. The new progressive emphasis on scientific research added to the movement by focusing on the collection of statistical data for the purpose of bringing about change. Jane Addams, the most famous American settlement house reformer, had perfected the technique of research and reform at Hull House in Chicago, and in 1895 she published a statistical summary of its neighborhood.

The Philadelphia Settlement catered primarily to the Fifth and Seventh Wards, the poorest in the city. These were racially mixed wards and only 30 percent of the population of the Seventh Ward was black. However, about half of the city's black residents lived there. Most worked as domestic servants or in manual labor. Some had no permanent jobs and supported themselves through occasional work or petty criminality. With few job opportunities many blacks were glad to give their votes to the Republican machine in exchange for promises of municipal appointments and jobs on the city payroll. Philadelphia reformers, concerned about political corruption, tried to get their own candidates elected to office to end these sorts of deals. But black voters, fearing that they would no longer have access to city jobs and resenting the reformers' condescending attitude, tended to oppose the reform candidates. Indeed, when poor whites began to move out of the Seventh Ward in the late 1890s and more blacks migrated to the district from the South, the administrators of the Philadelphia Settlement moved to a predominantly white residential district.

The Philadelphia Settlement was in part a product of the College Settlement Association, which encouraged women from the nation's leading colleges to become involved in settlement work. It also received funding from Susan Wharton, a prominent white Philadelphian whose family had established the Wharton School in 1881. Wharton, the first business college in the country, was part of the post-Civil War emphasis on teaching practical knowledge at universities. In its first decade it expanded its program from economics to social science in general and incorporated sociology. The school supported the settlement movement, and particularly its emphasis on research. Professor Lindsay was not only a teacher at the school but a graduate of its program. When the women of the Philadelphia Settlement proposed a study of the black community similar to what Addams had done at Hull House, the Wharton School fully supported the idea and persuaded the University of Pennsylvania to agree to publish the findings.

When Du Bois arrived in Philadelphia in late 1896, he feared he was trapped in another political situation. He believed that whites expected him to confirm that black voters were corrupt as a result of some inherent racial characteristic. White southerners claimed that they were eliminating the potential for voter fraud by disfranchising blacks; some Philadelphia reformers thought they were facing a similar situation. In the Era of Jim Crow, there was not much difference between the North and the South when it came to white stereotypes of

African Americans. Du Bois's suspicions became more acute when the university did not list him in the college catalogue as a member of the faculty. As a result of his recent experiences, he was perhaps a little oversensitive to academic politics. But Lindsay, apparently an honest scholar who respected Du Bois's ability, requested that the catalogue list him for the second school year since his official appointment lasted from January 1897 to January 1898.

Anxious to leave Ohio, Du Bois had accepted the offer despite the fact that he was newly married and could not be certain he would find employment once the year was up. He and Nina moved into the Seventh Ward and the Philadelphia Settlement to collect data. It was a rough neighborhood, and Nina could hardly have enjoyed her life there, but her husband's work came first. When the birth of their first child was due, however, she moved to Great Barrington to get proper care from Du Bois's family. Their son, Burghardt Gomer Du Bois, was born October 2, 1897. Willie, like Booker, was a doting father but also spent more time with his work than his family.

Throughout 1897, Du Bois went door to door making surveys of conditions in the neighborhoods of Philadelphia's Seventh Ward. He personally interviewed about 5,000 residents and sent canvassers out to speak with others. Without asking advice from anyone, he created the methodology, standardized questions, and information for the canvassers; sorted through the results; and created an immense database on black Philadelphia and its history. The finished product, which he completed in early 1898 and published in 1899, was *The Philadelphia Negro*, an unprecedented work of sociological research into urban black America. Du Bois painted a rich history of black life in Philadelphia and carefully enumerated the many institutions that blacks had established in the community to help one another. He told both success stories and failures. He did not always sympathize with the working-class blacks he studied and thus tended to accuse them of low moral standards and high levels of promiscuity and drunkenness. Still, his overall argument was that the main cause for the poor condition of blacks in Philadelphia was unemployment. In part, their inability to get jobs was a result of their lacking skills, but only in part: Du Bois recounted story after story of educated and skilled blacks who could not find employment in the field for which they had trained. The real problem, he implied, was not lack of ability but lack of opportunity—in short, racism. Furthermore, many blacks who had begun with high hopes during Reconstruction had so often faced defeat because of discrimination that they had given up trying; many had turned to crime.

The reviews of *The Philadelphia Negro* praised Du Bois for his meticulous research and objective restraint. He had not pointed any finger at whites in assigning the blame and was quick to identify what he saw as faults within the black community. As a result of this work, he was soon receiving offers of similar research positions from around the country. He conducted and published a study for the Bureau of Labor Statistics on the economic conditions and progress of blacks in Farmville, Virginia. He chose the small southern agricultural town as typical of ones that were starting to lose their black populations as they migrated North. It was his practice to collect hard statistical data before drawing conclusions in order to determine the actual facts about African American activities, rather than theorizing on the basis of alleged racial characteristics. He was still convinced that knowing the truth would break down stereotypes and racial prejudice.

In August 1897 the *Atlantic Monthly* published an extraordinary essay, "Strivings of Our Negro People," which would appear again in *The Souls of Black Folk* in 1903. In this essay Du Bois outlined what it meant to be both American and black, two souls striving for oneness and not finding it. He described the veil that hung between blacks and the white world, excluding blacks from complete participation in it but also hiding their true feelings and characters from whites. Blacks should neither reject the white world nor embrace it, he argued. Instead, they needed to find a way to make being black and being American compatible: in other words, a way to eliminate racial tension. Moreover, he wrote, although blacks needed vocational training, they also needed civil rights and higher education because they could not be assured of defending themselves without the vote, nor could the race expect to rise without making use of its most gifted people. Du Bois's article no doubt shocked many white Americans with its forthright tone and demands. Unlike Washington, he did not reassure readers that there was no fundamental racial problem. Instead, he challenged them to think about what it meant to be an American, and how racism had become tied up in that definition.

Meanwhile, Du Bois had found permanent employment. Atlanta University, headed by President Horace Bumstead, was desperately trying to maintain its classical curriculum and high academic reputation at a time when industrial education for blacks had become the standard. One of the university's trustees had proposed in 1895 that the school conduct a series of studies on the conditions of blacks in urban areas, something Tuskegee and Hampton were starting to do for rural blacks. The board of trustees approved, but the project was delayed by the death of the economics professor who was to have conducted the studies. Du Bois's old history professor at Harvard, Albert Hart, recommended him as a replacement, and Bumstead visited him in Philadelphia. Impressed with Du Bois's commitment to his research and his willingness to live in the Seventh Ward, Bumstead decided to offer him the position. In 1898, Du Bois started his illustrious career as a professor at Atlanta University.

At this point he was not yet ready to break completely with Tuskegee, nor was Washington ready to break with him. In 1899, Washington would quote Du Bois when stressing that industrial training was simply a means to achieving equality. The goal was not to make men into carpenters but to make carpenters into men, Du Bois had said.[2] But the seeds for the break were already there. Du Bois had begun to oppose Washington philosophically on the best sort of education for blacks. He had started to argue that the best way for the race to progress was by relying on its leaders to show the way. He believed that political rights were essential to reaching its goals, and he resented any kind of discrimination against blacks based on racial stereotypes and prejudice. As Jim Crow laws began to segregate the South, Du Bois became impatient with Washington's seeming support of social separation. As lynchings increased, he became outraged by the injustices of racism.

Meanwhile, at Atlanta University, Du Bois began training a whole generation of black sociologists in proper statistical methodology and instilling in them a sense of duty to publish the truth about the race. He also emphasized to his students and in his writings that conditions could change and that the social structure need not be a fixed one. In 1898 he began work on the series called the Atlanta University Studies, moving beyond urban areas to investigate conditions for blacks in all of America. Applying the same rigorous standards he had used in Philadelphia and Farmville, he envisioned a long-term cycle of data collection that would repeat every ten years. He proposed the study of different aspects of black life each year, including the church, education, crime, health, literature and art, and the general distribution of the black population. Du Bois hoped that by collecting hard data over a long period, he could document black progress and prove his ideas about changing conditions while undermining stereotypes about blacks. His first publication in the series in 1898, *Some Efforts of Ne-groes for Social Betterment*, catalogued black achievements since Reconstruction. Du Bois also became responsible for organizing the annual conferences held at Atlanta University to discuss black problems. These conferences mirrored the annual Tuskegee conferences and allowed Du Bois to make connections with leading sociologists and social workers, both black and white.

Although he never realized his long-term goal, under his direction the Atlanta University Studies program collected a tremendous amount of valuable information on black life in America and established Du Bois's reputation as one of the nation's leading scholars. The longer he lived in the South and the more research he did, however, the more he understood that simply showing whites the truth was not going to bring about the necessary change in race relations. If anything, conditions seemed to be getting worse.

In 1899, two events in particular helped to radicalize Du Bois's thinking. In April an especially gruesome lynching took place in Palmetto, Georgia, about twenty-five miles southwest of Atlanta. A mob of 2,000 whites had gathered to watch the lynching of Sam Hose, a black farmer who had killed a white man in an argument. The leaders of the mob burned Hose alive, strung him up from a tree, and then cut his body into small pieces as souvenirs for the crowd. Enterprising whites sold these pieces to souvenir hunters who had not attended the lynching. Crushed pieces of bone went for a quarter, and Hose's knuckles ended up on display in a store window in Atlanta. Du Bois passed the window on his way to give the editor of the *Atlanta Constitution* an objective and statistical editorial on lynching. Sickened by the display, he turned around and went back home, realizing that he could not fight such horrors with objectivity and social science. He became committed to doing something more active in the fight against racism.

The second event that pushed Du Bois into activism came a month after the Hose lynching and involved a death closer to home: his son, Burghardt, died of diphtheria on May 24. Atlanta had few black doctors, and many white doctors refused to treat black patients. Since Du Bois had tried without success to find a doctor the night before Burghardt died, he blamed his son's death on the evils of segregation and racism, a conviction that grew stronger when whites hurled racial slurs at the funeral procession. The death devastated him, and Nina never quite recovered from the tragedy. Du Bois would publish an extraordinarily sentimental essay on Burghardt's death in *The Souls of Black Folk*. Racism had touched him on a personal level in a way he had not thought possible. He became committed to fighting against it in the trenches, not just from his ivory tower.

Notes

1. David Levering Lewis, *W.E.B. Du Bois: Biography of a Race* (New York: Henry Holt and Company, 1993), 86–89, 91–92.
2. Booker T. Washington, "The Case of the Negro," *Atlantic Monthly* (November 1899).

4 | The Conflict

Between 1899 and 1903, Washington and Du Bois had gained national reputations for their work, and each eyed the other with some suspicion. There was no open break between the men, however, and the differences remained largely philosophical. In fact, they cooperated on a number of projects, and Du Bois even taught a summer seminar at Tuskegee as late as 1903. Of the two, Washington had the upper hand. He had more money and influence behind him than Du Bois and a powerful patronage machine in Tuskegee. Yet Washington was growing wary of opposition. He knew that there were some grumblings against his accommodationist stance, and he worried that public disagreements would lessen his ability to make deals with whites. In order to obtain concessions, he needed at least the appearance of unanimous support from the black community and therefore the assurance that he was speaking for the race. He could handle a few outspoken comments from young upstarts such as William Monroe Trotter or *Washington Bee* editor Calvin Chase, but Du Bois was becoming the most respected black scholar in academic circles, and his opposition would draw attention. So for several years Washington cultivated him as an ally, and Du Bois kept his peace.

The differences between the men were not as great as they appeared. On the issue of education, Du Bois acknowledged that industrial education was appropriate for some blacks, and he believed that Tuskegee and Hampton were doing valuable work. Washington, for his part, acknowledged that some blacks should get a higher education. In fact he sent his own daughter to Wellesley College and later to Berlin to study music, and Tuskegee was one of the largest employers of black college graduates. The difference was in the emphasis each man placed on his preferred method. Washington argued that industrial education should come first so that southern blacks could gain basic schooling and useful skills with which to make something of themselves. Du Bois argued that without higher education for blacks, there would be no black teachers for the industrial schools and therefore no chance for blacks to improve.

Even the methods of racial improvement the two men advocated were not irreconcilable. Washington envisioned blacks rising up from the bottom of society through individual effort and hard work. Du Bois's vision was that blacks would rise with the help of educated leaders, the top 10 percent of the black population, who would use their training and skills to help others and to fight for rights for the race. This Talented Tenth would lead the race out of poverty and ignorance while battling discrimination. But Du Bois was also an advocate of individual self-help, and Washington's vision was not incompatible with his own. There was no reason why individuals could not make efforts to improve on their own while the Talented Tenth guided them. Similarly, Washington recognized the value of sound leadership and recruited members of the Talented Tenth to help carry out his programs around the country.

More important, although publicly Washington proposed accommodation to segregation and advised blacks to stay out of politics, privately he was largely in agreement with Du Bois's call for full civil rights, and he himself was very involved in politics at all levels, local to national. He advised presidents on appointments and lobbied for and against specific bills. He strongly opposed black disfranchisement and privately financed test cases in many southern states to challenge the constitutionality of the new voting laws. He did not advocate that all blacks be allowed to vote, but he objected to exclusion from voting purely on the basis of race. At times he supported literacy tests but insisted that southern states should apply them equally to illiterate whites. He signed petitions to state legislatures to oppose bills that would disfranchise blacks unfairly. In short, he and Du Bois often worked toward the same goal. The difference was that Du Bois made his opposition known, and Washington did not. When their dispute became public, it was more rhetorical than real, more personal conflict than theoretical debate.

One of the main reasons Washington worked behind the scenes was his fear of losing white backing if he started to protest racial conditions. He had made a bargain with southern whites for economic support in exchange for blacks' not pushing for full rights. He had made a similar bargain with northern whites: money for black education in the South in exchange for his promise to maintain an industrial curriculum. Washington was worried that if he did not keep his part of the bargain, he would lose everything for which he had worked so hard. As the voice of reason, he was able to obtain concessions that no one else could. If he lost that reputation, he worried there would be no one left who could effectively persuade whites to help. Even his acceptance of an invitation to dine at the White House had outraged some southerners; open protest would provoke a much harsher reaction.

For the most part, however, whites were the ones not honoring their part of the bargain. Since Washington's Atlanta address, overall conditions for blacks had become worse rather than better. Jim Crow laws and disfranchisement spread across the South; lynchings were on the rise; and scientific racists were convincing northern whites that segregation and discrimination were justified. Washington envisioned a progressive form of industrial education, but whites heard only that he wanted to educate blacks for menial positions. Washington advised that blacks not force themselves where they were not welcome; whites heard only that blacks did not mind segregation. Washington realized that blacks were getting the short end of the stick, and he would have liked to speak out more forcefully by the late 1890s, but he was trapped by his own carefully cultivated image. Consequently, critics who did not face such obstacles increasingly began to speak out against him. In reaction, Washington started using questionable methods to ensure public control.

His first effort to co-opt Du Bois came in 1899. That year, the topic for study for Atlanta University's annual conference was "The Negro in Business," and Du Bois proposed the organization of local black business leagues with the ultimate goal of forming state and national associations. Later that year, as director of a black business bureau for the Afro-American Council, he collected a list of black businessmen from around the country for the purpose of establishing such an organization. As a result of various political disputes with T. Thomas Fortune, who wanted to control the group, Du Bois was never able to get an organization started. When Washington later borrowed the list to form the National Negro Business League, his critics accused him of stealing the idea in order to control the group himself. Du Bois also felt slighted, but he was more angry with Fortune than with Washington.

The Afro-American Council provided one of the first public arenas for criticism of Washington. The council was a reincarnation of

New York Age editor T. Thomas Fortune's Afro-American League, which had advocated active protest for civil rights. Defunct for several years, the organization re-formed in 1898, partly in response to rising racism. Following the Hose lynching in 1899 the council issued an appeal to southern officials to protect blacks from physical harm. Washington had published a letter in which he also asked for an end to lynching but concluded with a warning to blacks to control "the beast" that allegedly led them to crime and inspired the lynch mobs. He had withdrawn a much harsher editorial because Fortune had warned him that such language would only antagonize whites and lose him support for his other efforts. At the Afro-American Council's annual conference in Chicago in 1899, Washington stayed in the background. He had conversations with many of the participants but did not attend any official sessions. A few radical members tried to pass a resolution condemning Washington for his unwillingness to take a public stand; however, a vocal group of his supporters managed to stop the council from passing the resolution or expelling him from the organization. That group included, ironically, W.E.B. Du Bois.

That year Washington also began actively courting Du Bois, hoping to bring him to Tuskegee. Du Bois was unhappy in Atlanta following his son's death and was looking for another position. In May, Washington made him a job offer, but Du Bois told him he was obligated to Atlanta for at least the next school year. In October, Washington repeated the offer with more specific terms: Du Bois would come to Tuskegee and conduct sociological studies of the sort he had been doing, and Tuskegee would publish his findings. He could teach one course if he wanted to; and he would be paid a salary of $1,400 and given a house to live in. Toward the end of 1899, Du Bois also received an offer to teach at Howard, which, like Atlanta University, favored a classical curriculum and was becoming a center of opposition to Tuskegee.

Du Bois and Washington worked together that fall to oppose a proposed state law in Georgia. The bill before the legislature created an "understanding" qualification whereby prospective voters would have to prove that they could read, write, and *interpret* any paragraph of the state constitution before they could register to vote. The bill left the question of whether or not an individual actually understood the paragraph to the discretion of the registrar. Although the measure did not mention race anywhere (the Fifteenth Amendment forbade it), it was clear that the legislature intended it as a way to disqualify black voters. The law also created a loophole for illiterate whites in the form of a grandfather clause that exempted all persons who had been eligible to vote before 1867 and their descendants from the "understanding" requirement. Washington and Du Bois took a two-track approach to oppose the bill. Du Bois and other less conservative leaders signed a petition to the Georgia legislature agreeing that the state needed election reform but opposing any sort of literacy clause that would be left to the discretion of the registrar. They also objected to the grandfather clause that created separate standards for blacks and whites. For his part, Washington issued press releases and gave interviews to influential southern papers criticizing the specific types of qualifications in the proposed law but not the concept of voter qualifications nor the Georgia law by name. He also enlisted the help of influential friends in the state to oppose the bill. The bill did not pass and, in fact, the Georgia legislature did not enact a law disfranchising blacks for another nine years.

By February 1900, however, Du Bois was becoming more suspicious of Washington's motives for job offers at Tuskegee. In addition, he learned of a third job opening that appealed to him more than either Howard or Tuskegee. The Washington, DC, school district was looking for a new black superintendent of colored schools to replace George F. T. Cook, who had filled the position for the previous twenty-five years. The black public schools in the District were among the best in the country, particularly M Street High School, and the nation's capital would have been an ideal location for Du Bois. It was home to Howard University and some of the nation's leading black scholars, including sociologist Kelly Miller. Its lively black elite community included Archibald Grimké, whom Du Bois had met in Boston; his brother Francis; P.B.S. Pinchback; Harvard graduate Robert Terrell and his wife Mary Church Terrell, daughter of a black Memphis millionaire; and many others like those people he had known in Boston. It was also the headquarters of the American Negro Academy, of which Du Bois was then president. And although it was still technically a southern city, because of its unique status as the national capital it had resisted some of the worst forms of segregation, and it had a far more cosmopolitan air than Atlanta. Du Bois asked Washington for a letter of recommendation for the superintendency without completely rejecting the Tuskegee offer. Washington gave him the letter but later asked Du Bois not to push his application. Du Bois, meanwhile, tabled the Howard offer so as not to offend Washington.

The District's school board decided that it could better control the black schools by reorganizing the system, and a series of minor problems in the white schools gave them an excuse to do it. Under the new organization, black and white schools each had an assistant superintendent who answered to a white superintendent of schools. M Street, moreover, now came under the control of a white director of high schools. With more control over the black schools the white superintendent appointed a Washington resident and Tuskegee ally, William S. Montgomery, to the assistant superintendency and left Du Bois with only one offer remaining: the position at Tuskegee. In Du Bois's mind, going to Tuskegee would be little improvement over Atlanta because it was still in the South; in fact, conditions might be worse, since it was in a rural area. In addition, he began to hear rumors that Washington's allies in the District had actively campaigned against him and he believed that Tuskegee was behind the campaign. In April, Du Bois definitively turned down the Tuskegee offer and resigned himself to staying at Atlanta University.

Meanwhile, he had started a new fight. In February 1900 he had boarded an overnight train from Atlanta to Savannah, and the Pullman sleeping car porters had refused to give him a berth. Du Bois had to spend the night sitting up in the dirty Jim Crow car. Georgia had recently segregated Pullman cars but provided none for blacks. Since the train had originated in Cincinnati and was en route to Jacksonville, Florida, however, Du Bois complained that the company had no right to segregate interstate transportation. The head of the company explained that the porters were only following orders, because he had started and ended his journey in Georgia. Du Bois decided to pursue the matter before the Interstate Commerce Commission, and, needing a lawyer, he requested Booker T. Washington's financial support in the case.

Washington had already been working behind the scenes to challenge Pullman car segregation in the South. One of Tuskegee's most loyal trustees was William H. Baldwin, the white president of the Southern Railway, and Washington had asked him to try to persuade the head of the Pullman Sleeping Car Company to change his policy. But his efforts were not successful; in fact, shortly after Du Bois requested financial support for a legal case, Baldwin advised Washington not to push any specific lawsuit. The railroad owners did not fully support the state segregation laws, Baldwin said, but it was best to lie low and let them sort the matter out themselves. Washington continued to put behind-the-scenes pressure on the railroads and promised to support Du Bois's case privately as long as no one mentioned his name in connection with it. The case dragged on for four years, until Washington hit a brick wall in his negotiations and advised Du Bois that a lawsuit would not succeed.

For most of the rest of 1900, Washington worked behind the scenes to consolidate his control, setting up the NNBL, and courting political allies. Du Bois was not his main target; even though he had turned down the Tuskegee appointment, the two men were still on friendly terms because of the Pullman fight. Du Bois concentrated his energies on setting up a "Negro Exhibit" for the Universal Exposition in Paris. He amassed statistical data showing black progress since Reconstruction, based on his Atlanta University Studies, along with photographs, charts, and other material from Fisk, Howard, Tuskegee, and Hampton, among other black schools. The other major event in Du Bois's life that summer was his participation in the first Pan-African Congress in July 1900, in London. Those who attended were mostly persons of African descent from England, the United States, and the West Indies, who sought to shape a kinder European imperialism in Africa as well as address international race issues.

The congress was in part a result of Washington's efforts to establish ties between Tuskegee and Africa. Like Alexander Crummell before him and like Du Bois, he thought of Africa in much the same way Europeans did: as a savage continent in need of civilizing. Washington believed that his program of industrial education would be ideally suited to Africans and sent several students to Togoland to train natives in proper methods of growing cotton. Though the experiment was something of a failure, a few African students did eventually come to Tuskegee to study. Through those efforts, however, Washington met a group of West Indians who had formed the African Association in 1897 to promote unity among persons of African descent. He agreed to sponsor the Pan-African Congress in London and encouraged others to attend, although he himself did not. Du Bois played a minor role in the proceedings, but it was here that he first gave the address in which he pronounced that "the problem of the twentieth century is the problem of the colour line."* Du Bois would not become more active in the Pan-African movement until after World War I, but he had been a part of its founding, as had Washington.

*Lewis, *W.E.B. Du Bois*, 248–51.

After Washington established the NNBL in the summer of 1900, he increasingly faced public criticism. Journalist Ida Wells was among those who accused him of stealing Du Bois's idea for the sole purpose of dominating the new organization. William Monroe Trotter and George Forbes of Boston were also outspoken in their criticism. The anti-Bookerites, as they became known, argued that blacks needed an association to fight for political rights rather than one for business-men.

In 1901, Trotter was one of the founders of the Boston Literary and Historical Association, modeled on the prestigious Bethel Literary and Historical Association in Washington, DC, and dedicated to the de-bate of political issues for the race. The group rapidly became a forum for the Boston militants who were challenging segregation and criti-cizing Tuskegee. As Washington made efforts to downplay the opposi-tion and discredit the call for protest, the anti-Bookerites began to take the issue personally. In November 1901, Trotter and Forbes founded the *Boston Guardian* in order to air their views more publicly. They intended the paper to act as an antidote to T. Thomas Fortune's pro-Tuskegee *New York Age*, which Washington was increasingly using to berate his enemies. Trotter wrote scathing editorials about Washing-ton and Fortune. Many of these attacks were simply petty insults, but others represented serious criticism of Washington for painting too optimistic a picture of race relations. Trotter also assailed Washington's relationship with Theodore Roosevelt, who he believed did not have the best interests of the race at heart. Further, after establishing the Massachusetts Racial Protective Association to investigate discrimi-nation, he used the organization to create a network of anti-Bookerites around the state. The *Guardian* was the first large-circulation paper to criticize Tuskegee, and Washington made efforts to challenge Trotter.

Most blacks dismissed Trotter as a hothead and a fanatic, but it was increasingly clear that race relations were getting worse, not bet-ter. Washington became obsessed with the need to maintain unity in the fight for racial equality under his leadership alone. He truly be-lieved that he was the only one capable of negotiating with both the white North and the white South and that outspoken protest would simply make matters worse. He could not afford to have public oppo-sition that would lessen his claims to speak for the race. He therefore began a concerted campaign to silence that opposition, which eventu-ally he began to take personally. This campaign was the true origin of the debate between Washington and Du Bois.

Over the next few years, Washington would fund the creation of several newspapers in Boston to compete with the *Guardian*, although these efforts failed. He published editorials in other newspapers, attacking Trotter and promoting his own accommodationist stance. He also began to use his patronage powers to reduce his opponents' funding. Since Trotter was independently wealthy, thanks to his inheritance and his insurance business, Washington could not silence him, but George Forbes was another matter. Forbes worked at the Boston Public Library, and Washington had a connection to the head librarian. Tuskegee ally Roscoe Conkling Bruce, son of Blanche K. Bruce and a Harvard student, suggested that Washington ask for Forbes's dismissal unless he toned down the *Guardian*. The head librarian explained that he could not fire Forbes outright because of civil service rules but would gladly put pressure on him to toe the line. Washington later became quite proficient in using this tactic against other enemies.

In 1902 the anti-Bookerites moved to take control of the Afro-American Council. Washington's allies held most of the key offices in the organization, and since the 1899 meeting it had become clear that Washington was controlling things from behind the scenes. Hence, the militants faced tremendous opposition and in the end suffered a devastating defeat. The last of the militant officers lost their positions, including recently married Ida Wells-Barnett and Bishop Alexander Walters, the prominent black Democrat who had been president. Washington thus retained control of the organization but paid a price: he drove Walters, among others, into the anti-Bookerite camp. Even people who still agreed with Tuskegee's philosophy began to resent Washington personally.

Du Bois's role in the split was unusual. He was still a Washington ally but disagreed with his philosophy. Despite his friendship with Trotter, he thought the *Guardian* too radical and disliked Trotter's making personal attacks in print. Reasoned criticism of the Tuskegee philosophy was one thing, but he objected to attacking a man's character. In 1901, Du Bois reviewed *Up from Slavery* in *The Dial* and made this point quite clear. He praised Washington for his efforts but said that his accommodationist stand was only one of many approaches the black community advocated and that he did not have universal support. Nonetheless, Du Bois remained polite, if not friendly.

By 1902, however, Washington's manipulations had begun to affect Du Bois beyond just hurting his acquaintances. Washington's control of philanthropic donations to black schools gave him a way to pressure nonindustrial schools to ally with Tuskegee. Washington, knowing of Du Bois's philosophical beliefs as well as his long friendship with Trotter, assumed that Du Bois was one of the anti-Bookerites. He therefore saw Atlanta University as a fair target, and the amount of money that the school received in donations gradually began to drop off. Within ten years the university would announce that it could no longer afford to support the Atlanta University Studies, but even in 1901, Du Bois realized he was being pressured to take sides.

Booker T. Washington in his office at Tuskegee, the center of the Wizard's empire. *Courtesy of the Library of Congress*

Philanthropists followed Washington's advice and lead. A few prominent whites such as Francis J. Garrison, the son of abolitionist William Lloyd Garrison, argued that higher education was as important as industrial education and deserved equal support, but most preferred to believe in Washington's ideals for black education. Robert C. Ogden, a white philanthropist who made his fortune in department stores, had devoted his life to the promotion of black education. Tuskegee so impressed him that he had become one of its most active trustees and promoters. He became involved with all the major educational funds for the South, and began to bring northern philanthropists south on a private train each year to visit black schools in person and see the work they were doing. The "Ogden Express" was basically a finely coordinated way to funnel northern money into southern schools. In 1901, the Ogden Express stopped in Atlanta, but if it had not been for the fact that George Peabody was to give a speech on campus, the delegation would have entirely skipped Atlanta University. As donations fell off, President Horace Bumstead began to feel pressure from his trustees to change the curriculum and to get subtle messages that his university would attract more money if it got rid of Du Bois.

Between 1901 and 1903, tensions rose between Washington and Du Bois. Du Bois attended the Tuskegee Conference in 1901 and then asked Washington to speak at the 1902 Atlanta University Conference. But his letter of invitation almost accused Washington outright of not supporting Atlanta's work despite the support Du Bois had given Tuskegee's annual conferences. When a publisher approached Du Bois about printing a collection of his essays, Du Bois saw an opportunity to make his position clear. The essays for *The Souls of Black Folk*, which would come out in April 1903, were largely revised versions of earlier publications. They included a tribute to Alexander Crummell, the story of Du Bois's son's death, and two chapters outlining the plight of the southern sharecropper and his experiences in rural Tennessee. He began with his discussion of the double nature of African American identity and the two souls within: African and American. He explained his philosophy of a Talented Tenth to lead the race. He particularly warned of the dangers of blacks paying too much attention to material goals and not enough to the ultimate goal of equality. He outlined the importance of institutions of higher education for blacks, such as Atlanta University, and discussed the cultural foundations of African American society in the black church and in slave spirituals.

The third chapter of the book, however, read like a declaration of war, although Du Bois said he did not intend it to be. "Of Mr. Booker T. Washington and Others" was a devastating critique of Washington's philosophy and leadership. Du Bois argued that Washington was the leader of the black community only because whites had appointed him as such. African Americans needed to learn to choose their own leaders if they were to improve themselves. Moreover, Du Bois said, Washington's ideas were holding back racial uplift. Washington argued that only by giving up claims to political power and civil rights in exchange for material prosperity and focusing on industrial instead of higher education, could blacks survive. Du Bois argued that the only results of these sacrifices had been the disfranchisement of blacks, the rise of segregation, and the withdrawal of money from black universities offering a classical curriculum.

Du Bois went on to outline what he called the triple paradox of Washington's career. First, his goal was to make blacks productive workers and property owners, yet without the right to vote, black workers could not protect their property rights. Second, Washington called for thrift and self-respect, but he advised submission to whites and accepted an inferior social status that would rob blacks of that very self-respect. Third, he advocated the priority of industrial education over higher education, yet without people trained in institutions of higher learning, there would be no one to teach in the industrial schools. Wiser men, said Du Bois, recognized that the right to vote, civic equality, and the education of students according to their ability were essential to racial progress. Some conciliatory moves toward the South were necessary to achieve their goals, but Washington was flattering southerners without regard to their actions. Blacks needed to praise honest efforts but also to criticize any attempt to rob them of their manhood.

Washington's "propaganda," as Du Bois referred to it, had left three dangerous impressions: first, that southerners were justified in their prejudices and actions because blacks were in such a degraded state; second, that blacks had not made faster progress since slavery because they had pursued the wrong type of education; and third, that it was primarily the responsibility of blacks to improve themselves with minimum help. The truth, Du Bois said, was quite different. First, he argued that southern prejudices and actions had led to the degraded state of blacks, not the other way around. Second, educational progress for blacks had been slow not because blacks had chosen the wrong education but because it was impossible to create industrial schools until the universities had trained teachers for them. Third, although it was true that blacks had to make efforts to help themselves, without the support and encouragement of the white community and the elimination of discriminatory barriers, progress was not possible.

Du Bois summarized his criticism in one point: that Washington had given whites an excuse to step aside and do nothing to help blacks, whereas a solution to the so-called Negro Problem required everyone's participation. White southerners needed to take responsibility for the effects of slavery and begin to make up for past wrongs. White northerners had to become active partners in this process rather than just throw money at the problem. Finally, blacks had a duty to support Washington in his constructive efforts for the masses but also to stand up to injustice and oppose him when he condoned political and social inferiority.

Du Bois's argument was persuasive, his criticism well formed, his logic clear. Yet the Era of Jim Crow was not a logical time when it came to race relations. Even before Washington's Atlanta address, whites were already moving toward segregation and toward limiting black education to an industrial curriculum. It would be difficult, then, to prove a direct connection between his statements and the rise of discrimination. Nor was it realistic to expect whites from the North or South to be willing to help blacks any more than they already did. The fact that Washington was able to funnel millions of dollars into black education at a time in which there were such racial hostilities was itself surprising. In addition, Du Bois chose to overlook the behind-the-scenes efforts that Washington was making on behalf of civil rights, including supporting his own lawsuit against the Pullman Sleeping Car Company. So, in some sense, his logical arguments defied the actual context in which Washington operated.

Nonetheless, it is clear that Washington made it easier for whites to turn their backs on "the race problem." They could use his public speeches to show that blacks themselves did not want political rights or social equality. Furthermore, Washington overestimated the generosity of whites when he made his bargain with them. They would give money to support his schools, but only to train servants and manual laborers. Washington thought he was training blacks to gain the respect of whites through hard work as he had. But most whites never truly believed that blacks deserved respect. Blacks could not expect to improve their situation through hard work alone as long as whites were not willing to admit their part in creating that situation.

Du Bois regarded his *Souls of Black Folk* essay not as a personal attack on Washington but merely as a political criticism. After all, he later argued, he could have outlined Washington's increasingly underhanded tactics and objected to the Tuskegee machine's control of patronage, but he had stuck to purely philosophical disagreements. Perhaps naively he did not expect that Washington would be offended. He was wrong. It did not matter that Du Bois had not made a personal attack; he had made public the division in the black community and threatened Washington's claim to leadership by calling on people to oppose him. In so doing, he set the terms of the debate for years to come. In many ways, however, he misrepresented both their positions. The two men's views were not as wholly incompatible as he made them sound.

In 1903 the gloves would come off between Tuskegee and the anti-Bookerites. Washington began the year with the hope of keeping Du Bois on his side. He invited him to a local conference in New York in January to discuss racial issues, after which Tuskegee trustee William H. Baldwin invited Du Bois back to his magnificent estate. There, Baldwin made every effort to persuade Du Bois to go to Tuskegee to teach, saying that he could make improvements to the school that Washington was not capable of. Such flattery was hard to resist, but Du Bois saw it for what it was: an attempt to coerce and co-opt him. Shortly thereafter, he did visit Tuskegee and agreed to give a series of summer lectures but did not give in to Washington. Then in April, when *The Souls of Black Folk* came out, Washington was furious. In order to show that he was above such matters, he kept his agreement to pay Du Bois's expenses while he was teaching at Tuskegee that summer, and even invited him to dinner in July. The fact that Du Bois saw no difficulty in lecturing at Tuskegee is consistent with his belief that he had not made a personal attack. But Washington now assumed that Du Bois was behind *all* attacks on him and labeled him an enemy.

In late July an event occurred that finally pushed Du Bois into the opposing camp. The Boston chapter of the NNBL invited Washington and T. Thomas Fortune to speak on the evening of July 30 at the Columbus Avenue AME Zion Church. Hearing of the invitation, Trotter prepared to ambush Washington with a series of embarrassing questions such as, "Is the rope and the torch all the race is to get under your leadership?" He had attempted to humiliate Washington from the floor of the annual convention of the Afro-American Council, but the pro-Tuskegee delegates and President Fortune had silenced him. On his home turf, Trotter expected to have the advantage. About 2,000 people filled the church, and several policemen, anticipating trouble, were standing by. After the preliminary speeches, Fortune addressed the crowd and goaded Trotter with comments about his behavior at the council convention. In the middle of his speech an anti-Bookerite created a disturbance, and someone sprinkled cayenne pepper on the podium and emptied the water pitcher. Fortune, despite a violent coughing fit, eventually completed his speech.

When it was Washington's turn, the anti-Bookerites in the crowd began to shout out objections to his appearance, and a series of small fights broke out. Amid the chaos, Trotter stood on a chair to read out his questions, and policemen moved in with clubs. They ultimately arrested four people: the man who had made the first disturbance during Fortune's speech, a man who was stabbed in one of the small fights, Trotter, and his sister Maude, who allegedly had stabbed a policeman with a hat pin. The police dropped the charges against Maude and released her, but they charged Trotter with disturbing the peace. The so-called Boston Riot made all the major newspapers the next day, and many people realized for the first time that Washington had a sizable opposition. Tuskegee allies pressed charges against Trotter, and he received the maximum thirty-day jail sentence.

Washington was concerned about this very public opposition and determined to silence his critics. He made a blacklist of his enemies and began to issue editorials under various aliases attacking these enemies by name. His allies, eager to punish the perpetrators of the riot, urged him on and took it upon themselves to report to him on a regular basis about the activities of the anti-Bookerites. At the time of the riot, Du Bois was en route from teaching in Tuskegee to the Trotters' house, where he was staying for the rest of the summer. The event and its aftermath deeply upset him, and he became more alarmed as Washington's behind-the-scenes manipulations increased. Although he did not agree with Trotter's tactics, he was outraged by the way Tuskegee had treated his friend, and moved to make a public break with Washington. He published a sympathetic letter he wrote to Trotter shortly after his arrest.

Washington took this letter as proof of Du Bois's involvement in the riot and wanted revenge. He stepped up his financial pressure on Atlanta University, writing to all his white philanthropist friends that it was an unworthy school. He falsely told Robert C. Ogden that he had proof that Du Bois was behind both the riot and all the opposition to him in the preceding few months. One by one, anti-Bookerites began losing political appointments and jobs. Washington also secretly funded a libel suit against the *Guardian* when it made offensive comments about someone he had supported in the past. George Forbes, co-owner of the *Guardian*, was so alarmed by the suit and the possibility of losing his job at the library that he printed an apology while Trotter was still in jail. Washington claimed a small victory. Through spies, he learned of many of Trotter's activities in advance and was able to prevent another Boston Riot from occurring, but it was clear that both sides had declared war.

Still hoping to salvage his claims to leadership, Washington tried to reconcile the two factions in late 1903 by calling for a conference in New York to discuss race issues. For most of the rest of the year, he and Du Bois negotiated over whom to invite as delegates. Washington, despite his offer of peace, wanted to ensure that he controlled the agenda of the meeting and that most delegates would be loyal to him. Du Bois, well aware of that fact, several times managed to get non-Tuskegee delegates invited only by threatening not to attend otherwise. The conference took place at Carnegie Hall in January 1904. Andrew Carnegie, who briefly addressed the delegates at the opening of the meeting, funded the event. Washington did not control everyone present, but the majority of attendees were Bookerites. The group decided to form a new organization, the Committee of Twelve for the Advancement of the Interests of the Negro Race, whose purpose was to collect information and serve as a unifying force for all the various race organizations. The Committee of Twelve was so packed with Tuskegee men, however, that Du Bois resigned within six months and urged Archibald Grimké and Kelly Miller to do the same. Grimké stayed with the committee for another year and tried to steer it in the right direction but would eventually abandon Tuskegee for the NAACP. The committee ceased most political activities after the first year, though it did continue to publish pamphlets on the race issue.

Throughout 1904, Du Bois became increasingly vocal in his criticism of Washington. In both articles and speeches he was more outspoken on the issue of Washington's character and methods, areas he had not been willing to attack in *The Souls of Black Folk* just one year earlier. He also began to forge alliances with the anti-Bookerites who could present a serious challenge to the Tuskegee machine. Meanwhile, sales of *The Souls of Black Folk* continued to soar; the book was already in its third printing by the end of 1903. Its author was gaining an audience, but he did not yet have the confidence of either the black or the white community.

In 1905, Du Bois published an article in a new journal, the *Voice of the Negro*, in which he offhandedly remarked that Tuskegee had spent at least $3,000 in bribes to the black press the previous year to silence Washington's enemies. Since such an accusation implied that he had even less actual support than he appeared to have, Washington was quick to reassure his white friends that the accusation was a complete lie. Most whites believed Du Bois was making up the story, and so the charges backfired. Oswald Garrison Villard, editor of the *New York Evening Post* and grandson of abolitionist William Lloyd Garrison, was willing to give Du Bois a chance to prove his charges and asked him to forward the evidence. When Du Bois could not find more than hearsay to support his arguments, some of which came from Trotter and his friends, Villard chastised him for his dependence on unreliable people. Villard and his associates did not doubt that overzealous Tuskegee allies had bribed the press for support, but they assumed that Washington himself was not directly connected to any wrongdoing.

Washington had, in fact, spent at least the amount in question on subsidizing the black press, had done so for a number of years in exchange for favorable coverage of Tuskegee, and would continue to do so as a way to silence opposition. In 1904, as Fortune began to succumb to alcoholism and became an increasing embarrassment to Washington, he proposed secretly buying the *New York Age* but keeping Fortune on as an employee; he followed through on this plan in 1907. But in the meantime, Washington used all his influence, if not his money, to silence Du Bois in the black press. Shortly after the bribery charges appeared in the *Voice of the Negro*, Washington asked the *Colored American Magazine* to downplay its coverage of them but not to seem so pro-Tuskegee as to raise suspicion. In supreme irony, Washington wrote his assistant that he had already told Fortune to stop covering the matter and that Emmett Scott should advise the rest of the black papers to do the same. In the same letter he enclosed an unsigned editorial attacking Du Bois for making unsubstantiated charges.

For Du Bois the press subsidy issue was the last straw. He secretly called a meeting of anti-Bookerites to meet and form a new organization in Buffalo, New York, in July 1905. Fifty-five men signed the call to the meeting. Not all could attend, but when those who could arrived in Buffalo, they faced segregated accommodations and so moved their meeting to the Canadian side of Niagara Falls. Twenty-nine men came from across the country to attend the meeting, including *Voice of the Negro* editor J. Max Barber, Trotter, former Harvard classmate Clement Morgan, lawyers and government workers William H. Hart and Lafayette M. Hershaw, and F.H.M. Murray of the Murray Brothers Printing House in Washington, DC. The result was the formation of the Niagara Movement, with Du Bois as general secretary. The organization was to have chapters in each state, and the chairmen of the state chapters would serve on a national executive committee. The group issued a list of demands including the right to vote, an end to segregation, equal employment opportunities, and equal access to education with a common curriculum for both races. One demand aimed at Tuskegee especially condemned any attempts to limit freedom of speech. The focus of the Niagara Movement was to encourage action and open protest to challenge racism and discrimination.

Washington had heard about the meeting at Niagara Falls from his loyal lieutenants and sent a spy there to find out what happened. Because he arrived after the group had moved to the Canadian side, however, the spy mistakenly reported that there had been no meeting. When the *Boston Transcript* carried a report of the proceedings, Washington's spy visited the Associated Press offices in Buffalo to make sure that other white papers around the country did not find out about it. Washington also used his influence over the black press, which almost completely excluded all mention of the Niagara Movement and its activities.

Under J. Max Barber, the *Voice of the Negro* became the unofficial organ of the Niagara Movement. Originally, Washington had sponsored the *Voice* and made Emmett Scott its assistant editor. But Barber and Scott quarreled, and Scott resigned. Barber grew closer to Du Bois and became a charter member at Niagara. Thereafter, he began to publish sharp criticism of Tuskegee, and he paid a high price for it. Forced to suspend publication of the journal in 1906 because of racial unrest in Atlanta, he moved to Chicago, where his attempts to reissue the *Voice* failed, and he faced constant pressure to sell to Washington. He tried to become an editor for several other papers, but Washington chased him out of journalism. He moved to Philadelphia to work at a manual training school, but Washington told the school principal that Barber taught black children to hate white people, and so Barber lost that job, too. Eventually, he had to withdraw from race politics and trained as a dentist, a profession in which Washington could not harass him. Barber endured Washington's most concerted efforts at revenge, but he would not be the only Niagara member to lose his job or his journal. When Du Bois sponsored a new periodical, *The Moon*, to report the group's activities and provide a more radical voice in the black press, it faced great financial pressures, too, and went bankrupt, taking with it a sizable amount of Du Bois's own money.

One of Washington's underhanded tactics uncovered an interesting fact. In March 1906 he asked one of his Georgia lieutenants to find out whether certain anti-Bookerites had voted in the previous election and who had paid their poll taxes so as to be eligible to vote. One of the names he checked on was Du Bois, who, the lieutenant discovered, had never voted in Georgia. For a man who made so much of the need to vote, he did not seem to be matching his actions to his words. Washington gleefully exposed Du Bois, who responded that he did not pay the poll tax on principle. Given his deep moral convictions and sensitivity to racial insults, that was likely an accurate explanation; Du Bois certainly voted in later elections after he left Atlanta. The irony here is that Washington, a man who claimed to scorn politics, did vote in every election, often returning home to do so. He also encouraged all the Tuskegee faculty and students who were old enough to cast their ballot.

Despite Washington's attempts to stifle all mention of the Niagara Movement, by the end of 1905 it claimed 150 members and seventeen state branches. Aside from cooperating with a few suffrage associations, however, the organization managed little in the way of concrete action, prompting criticism at its anniversary meeting at Harpers Ferry. But in the fall of 1906, two events began to invigorate the movement as well as to help discredit Washington's program and leadership: the Atlanta Riot and the Brownsville Affair. In August 1906, visiting Atlanta for the annual convention of the NNBL, Washington found that the white newspapers were stirring up racial hostilities in an attempt to compete for circulation. He also found that the press was misquoting his speeches and fixating on a brief mention of black crime. Although he tried to calm fears, there was little he could do, and he returned home discouraged. Du Bois had been in Lowndes County, Alabama, collecting data for the Census Bureau since late August and thus did not take part in the events that followed. On September 22 an armed white mob, enraged by accusations in the papers that black men were raping white women, began moving through the black business district, attacking blacks on the streets and in local businesses and pulling them off streetcars. This was the first of five violent nights in which white mobs attacked blacks and in some cases blacks defended themselves. As a result of the riot, ten blacks and one white person died, and many more suffered injuries and property damage.

Washington arrived back in Atlanta a day after the riot ended. He sent ahead the advice that blacks should practice restraint and that the city's prominent blacks and whites needed to come together to calm the disturbance. Du Bois hurried home to Atlanta as well. Although Tuskegee allies accused him of hiding out in fear while the riot raged, he in fact returned as quickly as he could. On the train he composed the very moving "Litany of Atlanta," a poem that the black press distributed widely. Washington proposed the creation of a biracial league to cooperate in achieving better relations between the races. He cautioned both blacks and whites not to let emotions get in the way of a true solution. Behind the scenes he asked Villard to hire a private detective to find out the cause of the riot. Du Bois proposed political action to challenge the discrimination that had created the racial tensions.

The Atlanta Riot made many blacks question Washington's approach for the first time. The violence of the riot and the reaction of white northerners to it (they largely blamed black crime) made them realize that the North and the South increasingly shared the same views of blacks and that no political compromise would change these attitudes. Du Bois's call to protest now made more sense than Washington's call for compromise.

In October a second event shook black faith in the federal government and Washington's most famous friend, Theodore Roosevelt. Three companies of the black Twenty-fifth Infantry, stationed in Brownsville, Texas, were involved in a small riot in that border town, during which one white man died and another suffered injuries. The fight was probably a mutual disagreement, but whites claimed that the black soldiers had come into town shooting. The soldiers refused to give the names of those involved in the fighting, and so Roosevelt, impatient with the affair, dishonorably discharged the entire regiment. His action infuriated African Americans. The Niagara Movement issued statements of outrage; various prominent citizens, including Mary Church Terrell, pleaded with Secretary of War William Howard Taft and President Roosevelt to change their minds; and even Washington tried to persuade the president to rescind the order. But Roosevelt stuck to his decision and thus earned the distrust of many formerly loyal black supporters. Unable to sway the president but continuing to support him nonetheless, Washington also lost some respect in the black community.

Black groups around the country held meetings to denounce the president, and when Taft's name came up as a possible successor to Roosevelt in the White House, they aimed their displeasure at him too. Washington tried with small success to silence the opposition. Roosevelt and Taft took the attacks seriously and began to distance themselves from championing any civil rights causes. Taft's administration would be the first in which the number of blacks in federal employment decreased. He even named southern whites to fill traditionally black appointments such as registrar of the treasury, a position that Blanche K. Bruce had held before his death. In these actions the Niagarites found new motivation for their efforts but did not yet have the power to remove Washington's control completely.

Following the failure of *The Moon*, Du Bois tried to found a new journal to speak for the Niagara Movement. Published from 1907 to 1910, *The Horizon* fared slightly better but still did not attract a large readership and suffered a shortage of funds. Du Bois's *Horizon* coeditor, Lafayette Hershaw, and the journal's printer, F.H.M. Murray, suffered similar pressures as had J. Max Barber. One of Washington's most trusted and influential lieutenants, the New York collector of customs, Charles W. Anderson, made it his purpose in life to hound the Niagarites out of their government jobs. He visited Teddy Roosevelt in May 1907 and told him that it was time to take action against those people who were stirring up opposition against him. When he named Lafayette Hershaw, an employee of the Interior Department, as the ringleader, Roosevelt gave Anderson a letter of introduction to the secretary of the interior, to whom Anderson explained the situation. He suggested that the secretary reduce Hershaw in rank or, if that was not possible, transfer him to a disagreeable job. On the same day, he visited Secretary of War Taft and informed him that his employee F.H.M. Murray was another administration critic and should perhaps suffer a fate similar to Hershaw's. It was, as Anderson said, a successful day.

Meanwhile, despite increasing signs that conditions were getting worse, Washington did not change his public conservative stance, still believing that protest would simply stir up more trouble. Moreover, he was starting to lose control and desperately wanted to hold on to the power he had left. In 1906 and 1907 he embarked on a concerted campaign to marshal all his influence to reward his friends and punish his enemies. He found political appointments for friends: former M Street principal Robert H. Terrell became the District's first black municipal judge, and William Lewis of Boston became special assistant district attorney in the U.S. attorney general's office. He found funds for newspapers that were willing to print pro-Tuskegee editorials. The *Washington Bee*, long a critic of Tuskegee and one of the few papers to criticize the Atlanta Exposition address, was falling on hard times in 1906, and its editor, W. Calvin Chase, was anxious to secure funding. In exchange for generous subsidies the *Bee* became a pro-Tuskegee paper, at least as long as Chase received prompt payment.

In centers of opposition like Boston and Chicago, Washington used the NNBL and black fraternal orders such as the Odd Fellows to rally his supporters, and he relied on his influence with whites to remove his enemies from various positions. In Washington, DC, formerly a center of strength for Tuskegee, cracks were gradually appearing. The Wizard of Tuskegee therefore not only unleashed the dogs on prominent Niagarites such as Hershaw and Murray, who worked for the federal government, but also used his influence to have Roscoe Conkling Bruce, a Tuskegee ally, appointed to an assistant superintendency in the District schools, a position that enabled him to punish more anti-Bookerites. Finally, in an attempt to show that he supported higher education and to silence his critics once and for all, he secured for himself a position on the board of trustees of Howard University. There was great panic among the Howard faculty that Washington would turn the school into a center for industrial education, but in fact he did a good job and managed to bring in a Carnegie Library, among other donations.

Increasingly, however, Tuskegee held its power more through fear than through genuine agreement with its principles. Increased violence against blacks concerned even some liberal whites, and many blacks longed to do something more active to change their lives. The Niagara Movement would not provide that possibility. The organization funded a few court cases challenging segregated transportation but ended up in debt. Not all its state branches were equally active, and most could not pay dues. By 1906 a division in the leadership had developed between Trotter and Clement Morgan. Du Bois sided with Morgan, and in 1908, Trotter split to form a rival organization, the National Equal Rights League, which fared little better than the Niagara Movement. In 1908, Du Bois advised blacks through *The Horizon* to vote Democratic in the presidential election, since Taft did not promise to treat blacks with much respect. Most blacks still voted Republican, however; Du Bois seemed too radical for them. Du Bois began to complain that Niagara Movement affairs were keeping him from the Atlanta University Studies, and the movement held its last annual meeting in 1909.

Mary White Ovington was one of the founders of the NAACP and a close friend to Du Bois. *Courtesy of the Library of Congress*

The organization that finally overthrew Tuskegee was a biracial one, born in the ashes of another race riot. Three whites—John Milholland, Oswald Garrison Villard, and Mary White Ovington—were key players in the founding of the National Association for the Advancement of Colored People in 1909. Milholland had earlier founded a biracial group, the Constitution League, to attack disfranchisement and other forms of discrimination through protest and legal cases. The Constitution League had cooperated on some cases with both Washington and the Niagara Movement, but when Washington remained loyal to Roosevelt even after the Brownsville Affair, Milholland sided with the Niagarites. Villard, editor of the *New York Evening Post*, had also gradually come to realize that Washington's program was not achieving results. Ovington, a former settlement house worker and a reporter for the *Evening Post*, had connections with social workers around the country and brought with her people such as Jane Addams of Hull House and anthropologist Franz Boas, whose work would later discredit scientific racism once and for all. It was largely at her urging that Villard called for the conference that initiated the NAACP, and it was her close relationship to Du Bois that brought him into the group. Ovington had known Du Bois since at least 1903 and had contributed to the Atlanta University Studies with both research and funding. She was in awe of his intellect and became a passionate supporter; he treated her as a confidante, and she was the only white person to whom he ever truly explained his feelings on racial issues. Ovington heard Washington speak once but believed he painted too rosy a picture of race relations, since as a result of her settlement work she had seen herself how bad conditions were for urban blacks.

In 1908, there was a race riot in Springfield, Illinois, the home of Abraham Lincoln, and the irony prompted reformers to call for a meeting on the race question. They approached Villard to issue the call for Lincoln's birthday the following year. Villard invited Washington, who declined the invitation, but Du Bois, Ida Wells-Barnett, and J. Max Barber were there to speak. The formal organization of the NAACP came out of a second conference in 1910, and it grew much faster than the organizations that had preceded it. One reason was that it was better funded and had a regular journal, *The Crisis*. Another was that the participation of such prominent whites provided protection from Tuskegee's attacks. Finally, the increasing discrimination against blacks had convinced many that it was time to speak out against injustice. Du Bois became the editor of *The Crisis*, and moved to New York to work from NAACP headquarters in Harlem.

Washington used the same tactics against the NAACP as he had against the Niagara Movement, but he was less successful in limiting its publicity in the newspapers. In addition, many people such as Kelly Miller, Mary Church Terrell, and Archibald Grimké, who had cooperated with Tuskegee in the past, became active in the new organization. Washington and Du Bois continued to trade barbs in the press. Both men visited Europe in 1910, and Du Bois published a group statement saying that Washington was misrepresenting the true nature of race relations in the United States. Under pressure from Villard and the NAACP executive committee, Du Bois had to follow up with a statement that he was not circulating the official position of the NAACP. But Washington did not differentiate.

The NAACP largely appealed to Du Bois's Talented Tenth at first, and many blacks thought of the organization in its early years as an elite social group. But increasingly, as it began to campaign against lynching and initiated lawsuits challenging disfranchisement and segregation, most blacks came to see it as accomplishing something worthwhile. *The Crisis* became the best-known black journal, and many African Americans thrilled at Du Bois's plain-speaking attacks on discrimination. He made a point of reporting events from around the country, including lynching, riots, and other violence against blacks. Du Bois insisted on editorial control of *The Crisis*, and built up a little empire of his own within the NAACP. Although he increased circulation rapidly and the journal almost paid for itself within a few years, Villard and other association officials often clashed with him for control.

Tensions with Washington began to decline after 1911. In that year a white New Yorker brutally beat Washington in the street, claiming, rather unbelievably, that Washington had been peeping through a keyhole before trying to rob his apartment. The police initially arrested both men, but when they found out it was Booker T. Washington, they released him with apologies. Washington pursued a civil suit against the man who had beaten him, but the judges acquitted the man because Washington could not explain how he came to be in the neighborhood. He received outpourings of sympathy from across the country, however, and in the wake of the incident he tried to make peace with the NAACP. He proposed to Villard that the NAACP send official delegates to the NNBL and vice versa, and Villard asked the NAACP to issue a public statement of sympathy for Washington. A mild resolution eventually passed, although radicals such as Trotter did not want to approve even that. The NAACP also eventually dropped the matter of delegates to the NNBL; nonetheless its relations with Tuskegee were far more cordial after 1911.

The election of 1912 was a turning point in race relations. The three candidates for president were the Republican incumbent, Taft; Teddy Roosevelt, who was running as a Progressive because he felt Taft had betrayed him; and Democrat Woodrow Wilson. Du Bois did not trust either Taft or Roosevelt, given the Brownsville incident and Taft's record since then, and so approached Wilson for assurances that he would support civil rights for blacks. Wilson gave them, and in his *Crisis* editorial, Du Bois once again urged blacks to vote Democratic. This time more blacks listened to him and did switch their support to Wilson.

The new president did not keep his word, however. A southerner from Virginia, Wilson had little sympathy with blacks on race issues, although he was more moderate than some whites. Once in office he appointed southerners to his cabinet who were less moderate than he on racial issues, and blacks soon found themselves pushed out of government appointments and federal employment. Most symbolically, it was Wilson who ordered the segregation of the government departments themselves. Department heads placed blacks in small windowless rooms or erected screens separating them from white workers. Segregated bathrooms often meant that black employees had to walk up several flights of stairs to reach the "colored" facilities. For black government employees, many of whom were NAACP members, such treatment was unbearable, and for African Americans as a whole it was a sign that the federal government had completely turned its back on them. It was one thing for southern states to practice legal segregation but it was simply unacceptable when the federal government itself did so. The District of Columbia chapter of the NAACP staged one of its first large protests surrounding segregation in government, although it did not succeed in changing the situation. Wilson's actions persuaded many blacks to adopt a more radical stand on protest. Here was the very moderate southerner Washington had been promoting as the salvation of the race, and he only made conditions worse.

Another reason that Wilson's presidency was a turning point was that Tuskegee lost its power to reward friends and punish enemies. Wilson, the first Democratic president since 1896, was eager to replace all officials with members of his own party; he could not ask Booker T. Washington, a regular Republican, for advice on appointments. Despite Du Bois's early support of Wilson, the president did not consult him either. When he consulted blacks at all, he turned to prominent Democrats such as Bishop Alexander Walters, and Du Bois soon regretted his support of the man. Even most of Washington's allies in government lost their positions to Democrats.

The Wizard of Tuskegee still had influence with white philanthropists in educational matters, but his overall power was much diminished. He continued to work behind the scenes to challenge segregation and disfranchisement and supported many of the same goals as the NAACP, but he rarely associated his name with these efforts. In his last year he did publicly join the protest against D. W. Griffith's racist film *Birth of a Nation*. The premise of the film was that during Reconstruction the South had fallen prey to evil Republicans who manipulated blacks and mulattos into doing their will and taking control of politics; only through the noble efforts of the Ku Klux Klan had the South rid itself of corrupt influences and black rule. The film inspired whites to attack black neighborhoods. The NAACP took the leading role in denouncing *Birth of a Nation*, organizing boycotts and issuing critical pamphlets, one of which actually quoted Booker T. Washington's condemnation of the film.

Throughout the summer of 1915, Washington struggled with ill health, largely as a result of stress and overwork. He tried to rest and recover, but his condition gradually got worse. In November, while on a visit to New York, he collapsed and was taken to the hospital. Against doctors' advice he insisted on returning to Tuskegee and took the train to Alabama with his wife on November 12. He made it to his home the next night but died early in the morning on November 14, 1915. Du Bois wrote his obituary in *The Crisis*, calling him the most distinguished man the South had produced since the Civil War and the greatest black leader since Frederick Douglass. Even so, he said, Washington bore a great part of the responsibility for disfranchisement and segregation, as well as the decline of black institutions of higher learning. Thus, Du Bois had the last word, and it was not very complimentary. With Washington's death the great debate was over, and for the moment it seemed that Du Bois had won. But it was not so much a personal victory for him as a reflection of changing objective conditions that had made a radical position more acceptable than a conservative one.

What historians have long viewed as a philosophical debate between Washington and Du Bois was far more complex. In many ways the debate was more of a personal conflict than a true disagreement. Their public arguments were often not true depictions of their views, and their actual views were not completely incompatible. Their public stands, however, did contribute to the debate over methods of racial uplift that had begun in the early nineteenth century. Washington was a gradualist, and Du Bois favored immediacy. Washington advocated economic advancement and self-help; Du Bois favored political advancement. Washington believed in working up from the bottom, as he had done; Du Bois favored the leadership of a Talented Tenth who would pull up the rest of the race. Washington was probably the most powerful black man in his time; Du Bois was the most respected black intellectual. The attention they commanded between them and the public nature of their dispute made it inevitable that their words and deeds would shape the debate for the twentieth century. Yet theirs were not the only voices in the struggle for racial uplift, and in many ways the alternative methods others proposed helped change the objective conditions that shaped their debate.

5 | Alternatives to Washington and Du Bois

The debate between Booker T. Washington and W.E.B. Du Bois came to involve people at all levels of the black community. It shaped the way that black leaders discussed how to improve the race, and it opened new opportunities for poor blacks in both the North and the South. Nonetheless, not everyone took sides. Some leading blacks found ways of combining the two views, emphasizing the points at which they were compatible. Large numbers of poor blacks had little time to consider how to improve their long-term situation and attempted more immediate methods of change. Even those who were most involved in the debate recognized that there were more than two methods of racial uplift, and a number of groups and organizations actively pursued other tactics. As segregation deepened in the twentieth century and racial tensions increased, many blacks found that changing conditions made the debate between Washington and Du Bois less relevant. The question was no longer "How can we improve our situation?" but "How can we stop it from getting any worse?" Blacks used segregation as a reason to build up black-controlled institutions and businesses, which made them less dependent on whites or the Tuskegee machine and created new opportunities. By the time of Booker T. Washington's death in 1915, the combined efforts of Washington, Du Bois, and the rest of the black community had already made parts of the debate obsolete.

Some people clearly sided with either Washington or Du Bois, and their fates often reflected these choices. Other blacks attempted either to reconcile the two sides or to tread the line between them. As we have seen, their differences involved personalities more than philosophies after 1905, for the beliefs of the two men were not necessarily mutually exclusive. Probably the most prominent intellectual to take the middle road was Howard University's Professor Kelly Miller. Just as Washington's and Du Bois's experiences had shaped their beliefs, Miller's background may have contributed to his position. Born in 1863, the son of a tenant farmer in South Carolina, he earned a basic education and then graduated from Howard University in 1886 with a bachelor's degree. After studying advanced mathematics at Johns Hopkins University, he returned to teach at Howard in 1890 and became one of the founding members of the American Negro Academy in 1897. Until 1907 he was professor of mathematics; then he became dean of arts and sciences. In 1918 he stepped down as dean and taught sociology until 1934, when he retired. Having had both a southern, rural childhood and an academic intellectual career, Miller's life blended the experiences of both Washington and Du Bois. Perhaps that is what enabled him to support aspects of both philosophies.

Miller believed in the need for industrial training schools and was a strong advocate of Tuskegee's educational work, but he thought it was "mischievous and silly" to prescribe only one kind of education for all blacks. He supported schools with a classical curriculum to train black leaders as well as industrial schools to train poor blacks. In this way, blacks could advance at both ends of the spectrum. He believed in taking a gradual approach to achieving civil rights, but he also advocated that blacks make full use of the rights they had. For example, he suggested that they should be active politically but use such political rights as the vote to support moderate white southerners. Most of all, Miller worried that internal disputes such as that between Washington and Du Bois held the race back, and so he tried, unsuccessfully, to heal the rift.

Miller was actively involved in most of the major race conferences of the early twentieth century. At first he was closer to Washington, but after the Boston Riot and Washington's reaction to it, he turned away from Tuskegee and took the middle road. He was an important figure at the Carnegie Hall conference in 1904, when Washington made a last attempt to bring the anti-Bookerites and Du Bois under his control. Washington thought Miller was an unreliable ally and complained privately that people were getting tired of his straddling the fence. Du Bois made a special effort to win Miller to his side, consulting him on strategy for the conference and outlining his plans to confront Washington. Nevertheless, Miller did not take sides at the conference. He wrote the official account of the meeting and became an active member of the Committee of Twelve. When it became clear that the committee was only another tool for Tuskegee, Du Bois asked him to resign, but Miller continued to work with it. Still, Du Bois invited him to become a founding member of the Niagara Movement in 1905. Although he did not join Du Bois at Niagara Falls, Miller did become an active member of the NAACP and spoke at its founding conference in 1910. Yet he also served on the board of the National Urban League, which had a much more conservative approach to racial uplift.

He remained somewhat conservative for most of his life—Miller was an opponent of labor unions and women's voting rights—but became more willing to speak out for black civil rights as segregation increased. In 1906 he advised Washington to oppose Theodore Roosevelt for dismissing the black soldiers during the Brownsville Affair. He warned Washington that unless he took a stronger stand, he would lose his credibility in the black community. Unfortunately, Washington did not listen. In 1909, when Du Bois was leaving Atlanta University to edit *The Crisis*, Miller led a campaign to hire him at Howard. With Washington by then on the board of trustees, however, such a campaign was futile. As Miller became more committed to protest, he took more action himself. He was part of a delegation to Congress in 1916 which testified against a proposed bill to segregate streetcars in Washington, DC, and he was active in other local NAACP protests. Historian August Meier has written that Kelly Miller's ideas typified the thinking of many intellectuals of his period, and the evolution of his thought toward more support for protest reflected the changing times in which he lived. In the process, Miller showed that the debate between Washington and Du Bois did not have to split the black community and that both approaches had merit.[1]

Another person who played both sides of the debate skillfully was clubwoman Mary Church Terrell. Her concern was less to reconcile the two views than to navigate the political situation to advance her own causes. She was the daughter of Robert Church of Memphis, one of the first black millionaires in the country, who made his money in real estate by buying up property during a yellow fever epidemic and then waiting out the slump. Church was a symbol of individual economic advancement, and his daughter reaped the benefits of his good fortune with a fine upbringing, a good education, and a sense of pride in her family background. In 1885, Mary Church graduated from

Mary Church Terrell walked the line between Washington and Du Bois and worked to improve the lives of black women. *Courtesy of the Library of Congress*

Oberlin College, an Ohio school with strong abolitionist ties. She first taught Latin at Wilberforce University, where Du Bois would later teach. In 1890 she moved to Washington, DC, to teach at the prestigious M Street High School. There she met and married Robert H. Terrell, head of the Latin department and, in 1900, school principal. Terrell came from a prominent Virginia family; his father had taken care of Ulysses S. Grant in his last years. Robert Terrell was a Harvard graduate like Du Bois and had a law degree from Howard University. He also invested in several business enterprises in the black community, including a savings bank that ultimately failed. Terrell was a great admirer of Booker T. Washington, and it was as a reward for his support that Terrell received his appointment in 1906 as the first black municipal judge in the District of Columbia.

Mary Church Terrell, for her part, knew where her husband's loyalties lay and generally sided with Tuskegee. She had her own agenda for racial uplift, however, and did not let her husband's obligations stop her from maintaining ties with the Niagara Movement or joining the NAACP. Washington's spies frequently commented that Mrs. Terrell was a loose cannon. When they reported that she had been attending meetings of the Niagara Movement, for example, Washington actually asked Robert Terrell to keep her in line. Mary hurried to explain that she was merely attending meetings to keep an eye on the enemy and that she could best serve Tuskegee by keeping them informed of anti-Bookerite activities.

Terrell learned her political skills through her work in many women's organizations as well as her service on the District of Columbia's board of education. In her clubwork she learned that it was important to create coalitions with other groups to accomplish similar goals. She came to believe that open protest was the best way to achieve her goals for black women. However, in her two terms on the board of education, Terrell learned that one could not push too hard for change without provoking backlash from whites in positions of authority. She also learned the importance of patronage in politics and recognized Tuskegee's hold on it. She became skilled at working for her goals without antagonizing too many people, skills that served her well in escaping the worst fallout from the debate between Du Bois and Washington. A good example of Terrell's tactics was to give public speeches that emphasized blacks' achievements rather than their harsh treatment. Behind the scenes, however, she was more forceful. She made personal visits to William Howard Taft to protest his part in the Brownsville Affair, and she regularly wrote editorials on the evils of lynching and the convict lease system in which local sheriffs would lease out convicts to work on plantations. Terrell came from an aristocratic background, and she expected both blacks and whites to treat her with respect. In one rather startling incident for the times, she actually slapped a white man on a streetcar who had called her a "nigger"and refused to move out of her way.

Whereas elite blacks such as Kelly Miller and Mary Church Terrell tried either to shape or to avoid the debate between Washington and Du Bois, many blacks were too involved with day-to-day existence to care. Conditions in the South were getting worse every day for sharecroppers, particularly in the 1890s. Plantation owners had overcultivated the soil during the cotton boom of the mid-nineteenth century, and so crops were less productive. Cotton prices dropped drastically following the Civil War, but few furnishing merchants would give a lien on any crop other than cotton. The depression of the 1890s made prices fall even lower, with the result that farmers under the crop-lien system could not make enough to pay off what they owed each year and gradually slipped further into debt.

If the situation was difficult for white sharecroppers, it was twice as hard for black sharecroppers, who faced racial hostility in addition to the troubles that beset all poor farmers. Increased numbers of lynchings added an especially frightening element for poor blacks in the South. Du Bois and Washington had observed the problem firsthand but could offer little in the way of immediate relief. In 1899, in response to the Sam Hose lynching, Du Bois resolved to begin active protest against discrimination, but few black sharecroppers had the luxury to do the same: a poor black man who protested would most likely become the next victim. A few blacks stood up to white violence and drove nightriders off their property with shotguns, but the majority were too afraid of the consequences to confront whites. And Washington's advice to avoid behavior that might provoke a lynching seemed pointless, because the black farmers knew that there was very little rationale behind the violence. Neither Washington nor Du Bois really spoke to their condition.

As their situation grew increasingly desperate, many poor blacks lost faith in the possibility of integration that both Washington and Du Bois held out as the ultimate goal. In the 1890s a new wave of black nationalism held strong appeal. Black nationalists of the period came in many shapes and sizes, but they stressed several common themes. First, blacks needed to control their own destiny. Nationalists had little faith that whites would ever grant them equality, so they wanted to make their lives as free from white control as possible. Second, nationalists believed that people of African descent had a special destiny. They supported this idea with a revised biblical text that referred to "princes" coming out of Ethiopia, which would soon "stretch forth her hands unto God." As the "Ethiopian," or black, empire rose, the white man's empire would fall. Third, nationalists frequently compared Moses leading the slaves out of Egypt with African Americans gaining their freedom by leaving for the Promised Land.

The idea of the Promised Land had several variations. The North was the most obvious place for it, but many blacks wanted to move as far away from whites as they could. To some, the West seemed to be the place to go. In 1889 they proposed making a separate all-black state in the Oklahoma Territory, just opened to settlement. Led by black Kansan Edwin McCabe, who wanted to be the first governor of such a state, they began a massive propaganda campaign to attract blacks. McCabe established several all-black towns, including Langston City, which had its own newspaper that promoters distributed throughout the South to attract more settlers. In the first year, more than 7,000 blacks migrated to the Oklahoma Territory. Although the plan to create an all-black state never succeeded, there was tremendous enthusiasm for the idea among poor blacks. Similar movements led to the establishment of all-black towns in western Arkansas and increased black migration to that state overall.

Conditions in these western towns were far from ideal. Southern white sharecroppers also moved into Arkansas looking to own land and brought with them the same racial attitudes that existed in the rest of the South. Consequently, Arkansas blacks soon found themselves victims of violence and intimidation. As more blacks began to enter the Oklahoma Territory, both whites and Native Americans grew hostile and tried to drive them off the land. Those who had already migrated once soon thought about going elsewhere, and there quickly arose a variety of schemes to leave the country completely, for either Canada, Mexico, or the black republic of Haiti. For many poor blacks in the 1890s, however, the ideal solution seemed to be to emigrate to Africa.

There had been several previous back-to-Africa movements in the nineteenth century, the strongest of which had led to the creation of the American Colonization Society. The ACS was a white-led organization whose express purpose was to provide passage and support for blacks to emigrate to Liberia. During slavery, many white abolitionists had supported colonization as the answer to the problem of what to do with the freed blacks. After the Thirteenth Amendment abolished slavery, the idea gained more support, and some emigrationists even advocated congressional appropriations to ship all African Americans to Liberia. In the black community, support for emigration decreased during Reconstruction, when it seemed that equal rights might become a reality. As conditions worsened, however, blacks of all classes embraced the idea.

Three black leaders in particular popularized the back-to-Africa movement in the 1880s and 1890s: Alexander Crummell, Bishop Henry McNeal Turner, and Edward Wilmot Blyden. Crummell had connections with both Du Bois and his grandfather: in 1842 he had led the movement for a separate black congregation in New Haven, Connecticut, which Alexander Du Bois supported. He was also the intellectual whose speech at Wilberforce University in 1896 had inspired W.E.B. Du Bois. Crummell had received his early education side by side with whites in New England, but when he decided on a career in the ministry, he faced discrimination from U.S. seminaries, so he took his degree in England at Cambridge University. From 1853 to 1873 he served as a missionary in Liberia, which was founded by the ACS and African American emigrants in 1822 and became a republic in 1847.

Not surprisingly, given his early education, Crummell shared many white assumptions about Africa, even after living there himself. He believed that all humanity was moving forward on a path toward some divinely ordained level of achievement. He thought, as did most Westerners, that all non-Christian societies were farther back in that line of progress and that African cultures in particular were savage and barbaric. Crummell argued that African Americans were ideally suited to "civilize" the Africans and recruited especially the "better" class of them to emigrate. He believed that African Americans had moved forward along the line because of their contact with Western society and Christianity, even though this contact had been a result of slavery. Crummell's ideas mirrored those of the ACS officials, who also hoped to attract "respectable" emigrants to help tame the wilds of Liberia.

When Crummell returned to the United States in the 1870s, he undertook a series of speaking tours and wrote several books about the importance of Africa to African Americans. These books did much to stimulate the Pan-African ideas that would become important to Du Bois. Although in later life he became less convinced of the need for emigration to Africa, Crummell influenced a generation of black leaders to consider it as a possible solution to racial problems in America.

One of the leaders he converted to supporting emigration was Henry McNeal Turner, who heard Crummell speak on the subject on a tour of the United States in 1862. Turner was a bishop in the AME Church. More than anyone, he deserves credit for starting a mass movement for emigration to Africa in the 1890s. Born free in South Carolina in 1834, Turner nonetheless worked side by side with slaves in the cotton fields. He escaped this apprenticeship, got a basic education in a law office, and then became a traveling evangelist at age twenty. He had always resented the prejudice he encountered, believing that whites should treat him as an equal, since he was as free as they were. When he first discovered the AME Church in 1858, he was thrilled to see African Americans controlling their own affairs. He trained to become a minister and rose quickly in the ranks. In 1868, as a result of his efforts in establishing the AME denomination in Georgia and as a reward for his political service in the black community, Turner received an appointment as the first black postmaster in the state, at Macon. White Georgia Democrats objected to the appointment, however, and hounded him out of office after two weeks, charging him with fraud and theft.

Turner's experiences convinced him that America was a racist country and that the only solution for blacks was to emigrate. In 1876 he became manager of the publishing arm of his denomination and in sales trips throughout the country he made personal connections with local pastors and converted many to his ideas about emigration. In 1880, these pastors nominated him for bishop over the objection of northern church officials who opposed emigration and charged that Turner was counseling blacks to run away from their problems. They believed that blacks had a duty to fight for equality in the United States and that whites would eventually have to accept them as equals. Washington himself opposed emigration, advising blacks to "cast down their bucket" where they were. Throughout the 1880s, Turner regularly wrote letters to the editor of the AME journal, keeping the subject of emigration at the forefront of discussion. Although the *Christian Recorder* did not have a large circulation, it did reach AME ministers all over the South, who then repeated many of its ideas in their own sermons.

It was through their churches that many poor and illiterate blacks first heard about the glorious continent of Africa.

In 1889 the third leader who promoted emigration, Liberian scholar Edward Wilmot Blyden, made an official visit to the United States at the request of the American Colonization Society, which was trying to attract qualified people for Liberia. Blyden lectured around the country about the special relationship between Africa and African Americans, who, he said, had a duty to help Christianize Africans. Blyden was suspicious of anyone but pure blacks, believing that mulattos, or people of mixed race, were more tempted to try to be like white people and take power for themselves. To pure blacks, he spoke of race pride and urged them to leave America and return to Africa, where they could control their own destiny. His message excited blacks across the country who came to hear him speak.

In 1890 and 1891 the fever for African emigration was reaching a peak. In 1890, threatened by a potential civil rights bill from President Benjamin Harrison, Congress renewed debate over appropriations to ship former slaves to Africa. In 1891 the AME Church finally allowed Turner to visit Africa in person, and he sent back glowing reports to his many followers. The black press reported these developments, and ministers across the South informed their congregations about them. Many poor blacks, after hearing both Blyden's and Turner's rosy accounts of conditions in Africa and fed up with worsening conditions at home, decided that the time was ripe for emigration.

Those who had already migrated to the West or North were the most likely recruits for emigration. Having uprooted themselves and moved to another town only to find the same conditions, many shared Turner's belief that the United States was a white man's country. With few roots in their new locations, blacks in Oklahoma and Arkansas embraced the back-to-Africa movement wholeheartedly. As whole towns experienced Africa fever, promoters were quick to take advantage of the situation. Unfortunately, so were con artists. The main problem was how to get the would-be migrants, most of whom had barely enough money to reach the nearest port, to Africa. The European nations, having carved up Africa into a series of colonies at the 1885 Berlin Conference, had barred trade with foreign countries. American shippers could therefore dock only in Liberia, and Liberia did not import or export enough products to make the journey profitable. Only one American shipping company continued service to Liberia, and it made only two or three trips per year. Otherwise, visitors to Africa had to sail first to England and then take another ship from there—a trip far too expensive for most black sharecroppers.

The only sure way for poor blacks to get to Africa was through the American Colonization Society, but it had been in a slump since the Civil War and did not have the funds to accommodate all the applicants. Moreover, the ship to Liberia had space for only about 100 passengers at a time. In 1892 the ACS faced a crisis when the group it had approved was unexpectedly joined by two other groups from Oklahoma and Arkansas, who appeared at the shipping offices in New York in February expecting to sail. The nearly 200 Oklahoma migrants had come because a swindler conned them into believing that the ACS had approved their application. He talked them into selling their land and possessions for bargain prices in order to pay their passage, and then left them en route to New York, claiming he was too ill to make the trip himself. The thirty-four Arkansas migrants had simply come regardless of warnings that the ACS could not accommodate them. These groups attracted tremendous newspaper publicity when it became clear that they had no money for food and no place to stay; some did not even have shoes for protection against the New York winter. The negative publicity surrounding the fiasco, combined with the death and retirement of two of its top officials, led to a reorganization of the ACS. After 1892 the society stopped arranging transportation for colonists to Liberia and concentrated instead on solidifying the Liberian economy and educating the public about that country.

Nonetheless, even though the shipping company canceled its African route, given the lack of profit and bad publicity, the mania for emigration did not subside. Bishop Turner encouraged blacks to form their own line to transport migrants, and a series of short-lived companies in the 1890s took public subscriptions toward buying a ship. The typical plan was for people to make an initial down payment for their passage and then pay the rest, up to $40, in monthly installments. Most of these companies failed, however. Although would-be emigrants enthusiastically made the initial down payment, they were not usually able to keep up the subsequent installments. Con artists also took advantage of the situation and promoted bogus companies, taking people's down payments and then disappearing.

Faced with a lack of funds in the black community, Turner turned to white businessmen to establish a shipping route, presenting the plan as a business proposition rather than a crusade. The result was the establishment of the International Migration Society in January 1894, which promised to charter steamships to transport emigrants to Africa. The cost of passage was $40 per passenger, payable in monthly installments. Within a few months nearly 800 migrants had made a down payment, but only fourteen were ever able to pay their full fare. The society could not afford to charter a ship, so it sent them individually via Liverpool, England. Eventually, after many struggles, the International Migration Society did send a group of 200 emigrants to Liberia in 1895 and another 321 in 1896.

That more blacks did not emigrate to Africa had less to do with desire than with their inability to pay for the trip and the simple logistical factors of transportation. Thousands of southern blacks wrote to the ACS or subscribed to emigration schemes, both real and fake. Although the emigration companies did not survive very long, they offered an alternative to staying in a racist society. Nationalists such as Turner and Crummell created a vision of a separate black nation, independent from whites, and promoted racial pride through their emphasis on the concept of an "Ethiopian" empire. Their rhetoric did much to convince African Americans that they needed to control their own destiny, even if they stayed in the United States. It also made many blacks less patient with Washington's gradualist approach and more willing to protest for equal treatment.

Although relatively few blacks could migrate to Africa, increasing numbers did leave the South. Around 1915, black movement to the North began to increase dramatically, earning the name the Great Migration. Historians estimate that nearly one million blacks left the South, encouraged by labor recruiters, relatives who had already gone on ahead, black newspaper editorials, and economic opportunities. African Americans went North looking for the Promised Land. Floods, a boll weevil infestation, and two brutal and highly publicized lynchings in Leland, Mississippi, and Waco, Texas, in 1914 and 1916 further convinced them that it was time to get out of the South.

The Great Migration substantially changed objective conditions for many African Americans and shifted the focus from poor rural blacks to poor urban blacks. Washington's program of industrial education to teach proper farming methods had little relevance to the new residents of Harlem, nor did Du Bois's emphasis on the Talented Tenth offer much in the way of an immediate solution. Many of the migrants were from the younger generation who had never known slavery and who did not understand their parents' deference to white southerners. They were less willing to tolerate Jim Crow, more determined to speak up for themselves. They were disappointed to find that there was equal discrimination in the North.

The movement of so many African Americans to northern cities had tremendous implications. Their numbers placed a great strain on both civic and charitable resources. Overcrowding was a serious problem, and discriminatory housing practices made it worse. The many migrants soon filled traditional black neighborhoods, but few whites would rent or sell to blacks outside these areas. White landlords who did lease to blacks often charged such high rents that it was necessary for the tenants to take in extra boarders just to make the rent. Moreover, the landlords had little incentive to make expensive building repairs, since they knew they had a captive clientele. Black neighborhoods were usually the last to receive public funds, which led to a lack of municipal services and poor sanitation. Overcrowding made the sanitation issue worse; epidemics of diseases such as tuberculosis were quite frequent, and the mortality rate among urban blacks was extremely high. The migrants received little welcome from northern whites, and even some northern blacks, many of whom had achieved a measure of economic stability, looked down on their "country bumpkin" cousins.

Nonetheless, northern cities that faced these new problems often discovered alternatives to Washington and Du Bois. The YMCA and the clubwomen's movement focused on redefining manhood and womanhood in the black community and in the process created new approaches to racial uplift. By focusing on individual character building, they created ways of thinking about race that addressed the realities of the twentieth-century urban environment. Despite a tendency toward elitism, these new approaches made positive contributions toward improving conditions for the race.

First introduced to America in Boston in 1852, the YMCA had as its goal to provide a clean and spiritual alternative for young single men in the newly industrial city. Away from home for the first time and away from family and church, many young men fell prey to the saloons or prostitutes, and there were few alternatives for wholesome entertainment. The YMCA set up prayer groups and meeting rooms and offered public lectures. In many ways, its work was quite similar in aim to that of manual training schools such as Hampton. Like Samuel Chapman Armstrong, YMCA workers believed that it was necessary to mold the morals and character of the less fortunate.

The YMCA's attitude toward African Americans was mixed. To avoid splits between northern and southern chapters, the organization's leaders never officially condemned slavery, and they removed abolitionist literature from the reading rooms. They did not discourage separate black YMCAs, but they did not provide them with financial support either. Black leaders were enthusiastic about the association's work nonetheless and established their first chapter in Washington, DC, in 1853. During the Civil War the "Y" worked with both white and black soldiers to improve the moral character of the troops. After the war it encouraged the formation of black associations to help freedmen but offered little financial support. Part of the problem was that all local chapters were largely self-sustaining at first and the central organization was too weak to provide additional funds.

When the YMCA became more centralized in the 1870s and 1880s, it began to appropriate money and personnel to create black associations. The executive committee believed that these chapters would promote racial harmony and encourage blacks to improve themselves. They also hoped to identify potential missionaries to send to Africa. The committee appointed a white secretary, Henry Edwards Brown, to supervise the process, and he began door-to-door recruitment of individuals to be executive officers, called secretaries. Faced with a lack of progress and opposition from many local churches, which saw the YMCA as competition, Brown tried calling regional conventions, but few people could afford to travel to them. After speaking at several black colleges, however, Brown realized that the natural source for "Y" workers was young male students, and he soon began establishing chapters on the campuses of black colleges in the South. The students were the future leaders in the black community, and the "Y" wanted to attract a respectable class of men as secretaries.

Black YMCA chapters arose all over the country in the 1870s and 1880s. The success of the movement in the black community was due to several factors. First, the YMCA stressed manhood and self-respect, two character traits that blacks traditionally had suppressed out of fear of white retaliation. Second, its emphasis on intellectual as well as spiritual improvement had very practical applications for freedmen. In South Carolina the state established public schools to teach black children, but adults also needed a basic education. When the

Freedmen's Bureau ceased to exist in 1870, the YMCA took over its educational programs and promoted literacy in the whole population. Moreover, although most black YMCA members objected to segregated associations, ultimately they came to support them as a way of maintaining independent control of their activities.

In 1891 the YMCA appointed its first African American international secretary, William A. Hunton, and placed him in charge of work in the black community. Hunton was a strong opponent of segregation and at first attacked the YMCA's segregation policy as unchristian. As segregation arose in all aspects of society in the late 1890s, however, he realized there was little he could do to change the policy. Instead, he concentrated on building up the black chapters and centralizing their administration. He published several newspapers to communicate ideas between local secretaries. Hunton also brought in Jesse Moorland to be his assistant. Moorland had joined the "Y" while still a student at Howard University and would become the leading figure in the black YMCA movement in later years. The Great Migration drastically increased the demand for YMCA services. Because of the combined efforts of Hunton and Moorland, by 1920 there were forty-four African American chapters in American cities, and 113 on college campuses. The Colored Work Department of the YMCA claimed nearly 26,000 members overall.

As the work spread, Hunton and Moorland concentrated on attracting qualified permanent secretaries for the local associations and constructing or purchasing permanent facilities. A good secretary had to be intelligent, morally upright, diplomatic, and able to keep track of financial matters. He also had to be willing to fix the plumbing and serve as janitor. Du Bois's Talented Tenth were ideal candidates for such positions, provided they had also a Tuskegee-like attitude toward the virtues of physical labor. With the aid of philanthropists such as John D. Rockefeller Jr. and Julius Rosenwald, the African American YMCAs began building campaigns. Both Rockefeller and Rosenwald donated money on a matching-funds basis, and often the citywide fundraising drives that followed united the black community around a common goal.

Although the money they could donate did not always match their enthusiasm for the project, most blacks saw the YMCA as providing a genuine service to the community, especially as more migrants arrived in the cities. They also saw the project as an opportunity for blacks to build something that they would control themselves. The African

YMCA chapters such as this one at Philander Smith College in Little Rock, Arkansas, emphasized building character and restoring manhood. *Courtesy of the Schomburg Center for Research in Black Culture, Jesse Alexander Photograph Collection, The New York Public Library*

American YMCAs often employed black architects, one of whom was William Sidney Pittman, Booker T. Washington's son-in-law. They also employed black labor wherever possible. Despite the initial dependence on white philanthropists for funds, ultimately the black YMCAs controlled what happened in their buildings, which not only housed gymnasiums, reading rooms, and parlors but also served as meeting places for a variety of black organizations.

The YMCA's strategy of improving men by instilling a sense of self-worth provided an alternative approach to racial uplift. Its emphasis on manhood was particularly significant to black men who had felt robbed of their masculinity. Both Booker T. Washington and W.E.B. Du Bois applauded the "Y" for its accomplishments. Ironically, out of a policy of segregation, blacks in the organization were able to create independent power bases, as well as spaces where they could just be men.

As middle-class black men looked to the YMCA to restore their sense of masculinity, middle-class black women used their clubwork to reclaim their femininity. Long before Washington and Du Bois fired their opening shots, African American women had seen themselves as uniquely suited to help improve the race. They argued that black women had a special insight into racial problems because they bore the dual burdens of racism and sexism. Clubwomen believed that by focusing on practical reform of conditions for women and children, they could elevate the image of the race and open doors for African Americans. They combined their activities with a strong feminist message: emphasizing their role as mothers, black women claimed common ground with white women and insisted on the same courtesies. They also argued that the race would improve only in proportion to the condition of its women. Educator, clubwoman, and feminist Anna Julia Cooper best expressed this idea in an 1892 speech: "When and where I enter in the quiet, undisputed dignity of my womanhood without violence and without suing or special patronage, then and there the whole Negro race enters with me."[2]

The most important goal of African American feminism was to reclaim "respectability." During slavery, black women had suffered tremendous discrimination and sexual harassment. White southern images of femininity centered on the plantation mistress, supposedly a fragile flower that needed protection at all times. Although most plantation mistresses were far from fragile, white men swore to uphold their virtue, and white southern culture often revolved around

ideals of chivalry. There was no room for this image in the slave quarters, however. Physical labor was unfeminine, yet slave women worked
side by side with men in the fields. Chastity was an important part of
the feminine ideal, but white men frequently used young black slave
women, often forcibly, to satisfy their sexual urges. They also encouraged black women to enter into sexual relationships with other slaves
in order to produce children and thus increase the slaveowners' black
"stock." To justify such behavior, whites claimed that sexual promiscuity was a racial characteristic of blacks and that black women willingly gave themselves to their masters or even seduced white men in
return for favors. The image of black women as Jezebels, or brazen
harlots, persisted long after slavery. Ironically, the only other image
black women had in the South was as the faithful Mammy who cared
for her white master's children as if they were her own. Faced with
the choice between slut and Mammy, it was not surprising that the
women chose to embrace the image of motherhood as a way to reclaim
respectability.

During Reconstruction, middle-class black women worked through
their churches to provide relief for the freedmen and women in the
South. Believing that education and moral training were the keys to
success, they formed a series of clubs to focus their efforts and often
prodded church leaders into taking further steps. Through their
clubwork, many of them realized their capabilities for the first time.
By holding a series of conventions they also began to create a national
network of women to share ideas. Southern black Baptist women, in
particular, began to see themselves as ambassadors to both white and
black northern women. As white women became involved in relief
efforts, they were impressed by the dedication and religious conviction of the black women organizers they encountered in the South. In
the 1880s they raised funds to bring some of the southern organizers
north to receive proper schooling in Baptist colleges. While pursuing
their education, black women helped to break down some whites' stereotypes about the intellect and moral character of African Americans.
In 1895, when black Baptists formed their separate National Baptist
Convention, black women were some of its most active supporters. In
1900 they organized an auxiliary Woman's Convention and centralized church-sponsored charitable activities.[3]

Much of the women's work centered on teaching black women
and men "proper" behavior, educational efforts that tended to take on
the same tone as Booker T. Washington's gospel of the toothbrush. In

1909 the Woman's Convention, under the leadership of clubwoman Nannie Helen Burroughs, established the National Training School for Women and Girls in Washington, DC. Emphasizing the importance of "Bible, bath, and broom," the school trained girls primarily for domestic service. But although the program prepared girls for menial labor, it also emphasized moral education. The belief was that such programs would help women win more respect in domestic service, where they often faced sexual harassment and discrimination. By training working-class black women to behave "respectably," the Baptist women hoped to disprove old stereotypes.

Clubwoman Nannie Helen Burroughs, founder of the National Training School for Women and Girls, meets with fellow Baptist Booker T. Washington. *Courtesy of the Library of Congress*

Despite their seemingly conservative approach to education, the members of the Woman's Convention did not support accommodation to the existing racial situation. Quite the contrary: once they had reclaimed their position of respectability as women, they believed they occupied a higher moral ground from which they had every right, and even a duty, to protest further discrimination. The Woman's Convention regularly petitioned local, state, and national governments to improve conditions for African Americans. In 1910 it petitioned the

Interstate Commerce Commission to require that railroads provide sanitary toilet facilities for women on the Jim Crow cars. By 1918 its members had become convinced that only desegregation of transportation would solve the problems of unequal treatment. Their efforts to challenge discrimination thus combined both Washington's industrial education and Du Bois's protest for civil rights. Using the image of motherhood to claim moral superiority, however, black women established their own approach to racial uplift.

Baptists were not the only black women to use this approach. The most important of all the women's organizations was the National Association of Colored Women (NACW), founded in response to attacks on black women's morals. In the mid-1890s, as racism was on the rise, old stereotypes resurfaced about the inherent lack of virtue among black women. One particular attack motivated a call for action. In 1895 an English organization began an antilynching campaign, inspired in part by the visit of black antilynching activist Ida B. Wells. A newspaper editor from Missouri wrote a critical letter to the organization implying that blacks were all criminals and not worthy of equal treatment. Black women were little better than prostitutes, he said; of 200 blacks in his neighborhood he doubted there were even a dozen virtuous women. The letter was clearly an attempt to discredit Wells, but when the white English secretary of the organization read it, she was outraged. She forwarded it to Josephine St. Pierre Ruffin of Boston, the African American clubwoman and founder of the *Woman's Era*, a magazine for black clubwomen around the country. Ruffin was preparing to circulate a flyer calling for a national conference of representatives from all black women's clubs, and included copies of the letter with her flyers but asked the recipients not to publicize it more than necessary. Spurred by such an insult, the conference delegates formed the National Federation of Afro-American Women, which in 1896 merged with a similar group, the Colored Woman's League, to form the National Association of Colored Women. The organization's first president was Mary Church Terrell, who had been active in clubwork for most of her life. The NACW took as its slogan "Lifting as We Climb," which best embodied their perspective on how middle-class black women could improve the race.

The NACW operated as a federation of state and local organizations with a central executive cabinet to coordinate clubwork overall. Its main focus was on activities to improve the lives of women and children, particularly by forming Mother's Clubs to teach proper nutrition and child care to working-class black women. Women from all parts of the political spectrum participated actively in the NACW. Ida B. Wells served on the executive cabinet, as did Booker T. Washington's third wife, Margaret Murray Washington, who later became president. The group cooperated with other organizations, including the National Baptist Woman's Convention and the NAACP. By 1916 it claimed over 100,000 members and had moved into areas of reform such as the establishment of juvenile court systems, woman suffrage, and improvement of conditions on the railroads. The efforts of black clubwomen to protect their reputations and reclaim their femininity resulted in considerable practical reform. Although working-class women did not always share the reformers' enthusiasm for Victorian "respectability," groups such as the NACW and the Young Women's Christian Association (YWCA) did help them improve their living and working conditions. Although the clubwomen's language sometimes sounded like Washington's in its emphasis on manners and morals, they blended into it Du Bois's ideas of the Talented Tenth and open protest. But by using their identities as mothers to claim a higher moral ground from which to attack discrimination, black women created an entirely new approach to racial uplift.

While black women organized most of the work in their community, they sometimes received help from white women. In 1905, Frances Kellor, a white social worker and attorney, and Ruth Standish Baldwin, wife of the railroad president and Tuskegee board member William H. Baldwin, formed the National League for the Protection of Colored Women. Concerned that those African American women who migrated to the North were easy targets for con men who could lead them into prostitution, the NLPCW organized agencies to steer women into safe employment. Such cooperation between white and black women was rare, but Kellor would later become part of the NAACP, and Ruth Baldwin's ties to Tuskegee fostered a family interest in race matters.

In the twentieth century, new organizations that arose to address new problems did not easily fit either the Washington or the Du Bois mold. In 1906 a group of black intellectuals formed the Committee for Improving the Industrial Conditions for Negroes in New York. Worried by the increasing number of migrants to the city but also alarmed by increasing incidents of housing and employment discrimination, the CIICN served as a watchdog agency. It lobbied to have black workers included in construction projects and black students admitted to vocational schools. The organization also called for cheap, sanitary housing. Although its founders believed that blacks should have full political equality, its main tactic was not active protest but behind-the-scenes persuasion of whites to change their discriminatory policies.

In 1910 a similar organization, the Committee on Urban Conditions among Negroes in New York, came out of the recommendations of a Columbia University study. Within a year the CUCANNY merged with the CIICN and the NLPCW to create a new organization, the National Urban League, which used social science and social work as its primary tools for addressing problems. Its first executive secretary was the African American scholar George E. Haynes, who had conducted the Columbia University study. Haynes set the creation of a social work program at Fisk University as one of his first goals. His idea was to train more African Americans in social work, believing, perhaps, that they could be more sympathetic and make better progress working with poor blacks than could white workers. The Urban League, in tune with the rest of American society in the Progressive Era, placed great faith in the ability of social scientists to discover the solutions to urban problems. Its members also followed the CIICN's tactics of working with leading whites to bring about voluntary change. Although the Urban League's focus would have been well suited to a man of Du Bois's training, its board comprised mostly conservative blacks and whites, many of whom had ties to Tuskegee. Nevertheless, the biracial nature of the league and its predecessors reflected an increased awareness in the white community of black problems. This side effect of the Great Migration played a role also in the creation of the NAACP, which would finally provide Du Bois with a platform equal to Tuskegee.

While the Washington–Du Bois debate raged, blacks were working hard to change the objective conditions they faced and finding new ways of adapting their efforts to meet their needs. Although they were grateful for the help of reform-minded whites, in the Era of Jim Crow they could not always expect whites to be sympathetic. By the twentieth century, perhaps in response to the emigrationist movement of the 1890s, blacks were finding ways to improve themselves without depending on white support. That often meant accepting segregated facilities but using them to build up the race from within, following their own plans. Such was the case in the black YMCAs, for example, where black leaders instilled a sense of pride and self-worth in their members that white YMCA officials would not have encouraged. Independently controlled black institutions and businesses created a physical space for black men to run organizations and gain leadership skills they would never have achieved in a biracial group.

Within their own charitable associations, black women not only reclaimed their sense of themselves as women but also developed first-rate organizational skills. The YWCA also segregated its chapters, and the black women of the "Y" took advantage of their independence to build their leadership skills. They particularly excelled at fund-raising. Established in 1905, the Washington, DC, African American branch of the YWCA claimed 193 members at the end of its first year, including Mary Church Terrell and Anna Julia Cooper. After working from a series of temporary headquarters, the group moved to one floor of an old school and within two years was occupying the whole building. In 1910 the branch purchased a new house near Howard University to serve as its headquarters, and by 1912 the women had raised enough money to pay off the mortgage. The NACW also developed good fund-raising skills. In 1916 it began a successful two-year national campaign for funds to preserve Frederick Douglass's former home in Anacostia as a memorial. Several previous campaigns had failed, but the NACW succeeded.

The rise of independent black institutions paralleled an increase in racial pride. As blacks realized what they could accomplish on their own, they became more committed to working for the good of the race and supporting what were called race enterprises. Centers of power developed away from the white community (and away from Tuskegee). It might have hurt black businessmen to realize that whites would no longer patronize them, but dependence on all-black patronage also meant that whites could do little to hurt them financially. Black doctors and lawyers, excluded from white professional associations, created their own so that they did not have to depend on whites for a seal of approval.

It was becoming increasingly clear that no matter how many blacks lifted themselves from poverty, improved their morals, and gained an education of whatever sort, whites were not going to grant them equality. If anything, the situation was just getting worse. During World War I, when Wilson asked American citizens to fight in a war to make the world safe for democracy, the irony did not escape the black community. Poor treatment of black soldiers and the initial refusal of the government to train black officers to command them shocked African

Americans. When, at the end of World War I, black soldiers returning to the South were lynched while still in their uniforms, frustration reached an all-time high. A series of race riots spread across the country in 1919, in which, for the first time, many blacks fought back against white violence.

By 1920, America was a very different country than it had been in 1895, when Washington made his famous speech in Atlanta. In the years following the Civil War, blacks had been optimistic about the possibility of cooperation with whites; however, the rise of Jim Crow discredited the concept of gradualism and accommodation to some extent. Although blacks were still willing to work within segregated institutions on a temporary basis, they realized that it would be mostly up to them to change their conditions rather than expecting whites to offer assistance. Without protest to prod them, whites had no incentive to reform. But Washington's ideas survived in modified form, particularly his emphasis on industrial education and moral reform as the ways to help most African Americans.

The debate between Washington and Du Bois, then, influenced the approaches of other groups to solving the race's problems, but in many ways the debate reflected the influence of changing objective conditions. Many blacks did not care about the finer points of philosophy; they just wanted to escape their poverty. Others simply went about the task of practical reform and took whatever parts of both philosophies they found useful. Nonetheless, the debate marked a clear turning point in black history. African Americans used the opportunity to reevaluate traditional approaches to racial uplift and to test them in a modern, industrial society.

Both men made significant contributions to their race. Washington funneled millions of dollars into black education, which might not otherwise have drawn much support. He gained jobs and power for many African Americans through his political influence. Du Bois contributed his scientific expertise to a thorough study of racial conditions which opened many people's eyes to the true effects of racism. His essays and publications mark him as one of the most influential American intellectuals, and his sophisticated analyses of racial issues have mostly stood the test of time. As editor of *The Crisis*, Du Bois wrote honestly about discrimination and inspired blacks to demand better treatment. The conflict probably pushed both men to do more than they would have without it. In the end, however, it was their changing times that shaped the debate.

Notes

1. Meier, *Negro Thought in America*, 213–18.
2. Anna Julia Cooper, *A Voice from the South: By a Black Woman of the South* (1892; Reprint, New York: Oxford University Press, 1988), 31.
3. For more discussion on this topic, see Evelyn Brooks Higgenbotham, *Righteous Discontent* (Cambridge: Harvard University Press, 1993).

EPILOGUE

The Tuskegee machine died with Washington, for his successor did not command the same power. Du Bois would later joke that most people thought he died when Washington did, so tied was he to his dispute with the man. In reality, Du Bois would live almost another fifty years; he had a long career and more controversy ahead of him. He died on August 27, 1963, one day before the March on Washington at which Martin Luther King Jr. gave his famous "I Have a Dream" speech. In the years between Washington's death and his own, Du Bois underwent many transformations and became even more disillusioned with American society. During World War I, when many blacks opposed fighting for a country that denied them basic civil rights, Du Bois had advised them to "close ranks" behind the American government. The unequal treatment of black soldiers during the war, the continued segregation at home, and the riots of 1919 convinced him that he had been mistaken. His editorials in *The Crisis* became increasingly militant in their call for fairness. One, on the treatment of returning soldiers, led the U.S. Justice Department to investigate *The Crisis* and the Post Office to delay the mailing of that issue. Some whites blamed Du Bois for the violence with which blacks met whites in the riots that year.

As Du Bois began to lose faith in the idea of an integrated American society, he turned toward the ideals of the black nationalists, especially Pan-Africanism. Between 1919 and 1927 he organized four international Pan-African congresses. In 1923 he visited Africa himself for the first time and, like Bishop Turner before him, came away with glowing reviews of the continent. Although Du Bois never supported emigration as a solution to racial problems, he believed that African Americans could gain strength from knowing their African heritage. Like Crummell, he believed in the greatness of an "Ethiopian empire," even though he still thought that Africans were far behind on the scale of civilization. His early images of Africa were largely romantic ones.

During the 1920s, Du Bois clashed with another prominent black leader, Marcus Garvey, who claimed that Booker T. Washington had been a major influence in his life. Garvey founded the United Negro Improvement Association (UNIA) in Jamaica in 1914. He moved to New York in 1916, bringing the same message as Blyden and Turner in the 1890s: blacks should be proud of their racial heritage, scorn anything white, move back to Africa, and establish a colony where they could have control over their lives. Garvey started a subscription effort for his own steamship line to transport African Americans to Africa. Like similar efforts in the 1890s, it failed because of mismanagement and a lack of funds. But Garvey's UNIA had tremendous appeal among the poorer blacks, especially new migrants to the North, including fellow West Indians.

Du Bois, however, was concerned that Garvey's approach was too emotional and would stir up the working class without providing any real leadership. He also worried that it would detract from the Pan-African movement, which was less militant in outlook. Consequently, Du Bois encouraged a cultural alternative to Garvey's UNIA. He was a major promoter of the Harlem Renaissance, a movement of writers, intellectuals, artists, and musicians who focused on two basic themes: pride in racial heritage and protest against racial injustices. Du Bois hoped that most blacks, led by the cultural Talented Tenth, would channel their energies into constructive and creative projects emphasizing what he believed were the special contributions of the race to civilization. He supported the work of writers in *The Crisis*, which he used also as a platform for his criticism of Garvey. Furthermore, he began to advocate the idea of black capitalism, that blacks should attempt to create a separate economy, circulating their money within the community and depending on whites as little as possible.

Garvey was arrested for fraud and convicted in 1923. Calvin Coolidge pardoned him in 1927 but deported him to Jamaica. The UNIA continued, however, and sentiment for emigration was at its peak throughout the decade. Many preachers spread the message of Garveyism in the small towns and urban areas of the North. One such preacher, Earl Little, took his son Malcolm with him to some UNIA rallies, and most likely his outspokenness led to his murder by white supremacists. Later, when Malcolm Little—the future Malcolm X—first heard members of the Nation of Islam speak about black separation from whites, he probably remembered his father's sermons and found it easier to support.

Throughout the 1920s, Du Bois became increasingly attracted to the ideas of socialism, and a visit to the Soviet Union in 1927 converted him. Throughout the 1930s he advocated producer cooperatives as a solution to the Great Depression. He began to argue that the true solution to racial problems in the United States was economic rather than social. Increasingly, he came into conflict with the board of the NAACP, which felt that his editorials in *The Crisis* no longer reflected the organization's outlook. In 1934, asserting that the NAACP represented only the interests of the black bourgeoisie and not those of the masses, Du Bois resigned from *The Crisis* and returned to Atlanta University. Ironically, he now attacked the very Talented Tenth he had championed in the past and advocated the separate black economic advancement that Booker T. Washington had cultivated. Du Bois went back to research and writing. In addition, he organized the Pan-African Congress of 1945, which brought together most of the future leaders of African independence movements.

He returned to the NAACP in 1944 but left it again in 1948 after another argument. He began to join increasingly radical groups, including the Peace Information Center, which the government identified as a Soviet agency. In the anti-Communist witch-hunt atmosphere, Du Bois came under attack and faced indictment in 1951 for failing to register as an agent of a foreign power. He was acquitted, but suffered continued persecution including the revocation of his passport. Upon its restoration in 1961, Du Bois emigrated to Ghana. Completely disillusioned with America, he joined the Communist Party and renounced his U.S. citizenship. He died two years later, at the age of ninety-five.

When we look at the legacy of Washington and Du Bois, it is difficult to make clear comparisons between their ideas and those of later black leaders. Washington acted so differently in public and in private that it is difficult to say which actions best reflected his beliefs. Du Bois changed his ideas so drastically in his later years that it is hard to pinpoint which view to compare. Moreover, changing objective conditions add to the difficulty of making a comparison. Post–World War II America differed greatly from Progressive Era America, socially, economically, and politically. World events such as the Cold War and the independence of African colonies in the 1960s had a tremendous impact on race issues and attitudes in the United States.

Still, it is possible to see elements of the debate between Washington and Du Bois in the Civil Rights Movement of the 1950s and 1960s. In part, that continuity also reflected traditional divisions in the black community. Rather than divide leaders into Washington and Du Bois camps, it is probably more effective to focus on the larger issues they addressed, the outlines of which had developed by the mid-nineteenth century: gradualism versus immediacy, accommodation versus protest, separatism versus integration, grassroots change versus top-down leadership, and economic solutions versus political solutions. During the main period of the debate, 1903 to 1915, Washington publicly favored gradualism, accommodation, eventual integration, grassroots change, and economic solutions; Du Bois increasingly favored immediacy, protest, complete integration, top-down leadership, and political solutions. Nevertheless, as we have seen, the line separating the two camps was not always clear. Washington later engaged in protest, and Du Bois supported economic advancement.

Civil rights activists debated all the larger issues that Washington and Du Bois had covered. Sometimes they came up with the same answers; at other times they developed their own alternatives. On the surface it would be simple to say that the more conservative elements of the Civil Rights Movement owed their style to Washington and the more outspoken ones to Du Bois. More militant activists, such as the members of the Student Nonviolent Coordinating Committee (SNCC) and Malcolm X, argued that Martin Luther King Jr. was simply accommodating to white people and was not willing to demand immediate change. They called him an Uncle Tom and compared him to Washington, whom they characterized in the same way. King's commitment to nonviolence convinced many militant blacks that he was backing away from confrontations. Nonetheless, his firm commitment to denouncing injustice as it occurred and his insistence that protest in Birmingham not wait for a better time showed that he was as much committed to immediacy and protest as Du Bois.

Mainstream activists, including Martin Luther King Jr., upheld the ideal of integration and the formation of a "Beloved Community" in which blacks and whites would value each other as human beings.

Like Washington and Du Bois, they saw integration as the best solution to racial problems. Many militant activists, however, came to believe in the need for separation rather than integration. Much of the rhetoric of the Nation of Islam and SNCC sounded like the language of nationalists such as Crummell, Turner, and Garvey. On this issue they chose an alternative method of racial uplift.

Like Du Bois's faith in a Talented Tenth, King believed that the existing leadership of ministers and professionals in the black community could best organize a protest movement. He created the Southern Christian Leadership Conference (SCLC) on this top-down model. Most radicals, however, favored grassroots change, as did Washington. The Nation of Islam recruited in poor inner-city neighborhoods and worked to empower the downtrodden. The Black Panthers grew out of the frustration of these same neighborhoods and ridiculed established leaders, both black and white. SNCC criticized King's SCLC for imposing itself on communities and trying to dictate to everyone in the movement.

On the issue of political versus economic solutions it is hard to trace a clear line to either Washington or Du Bois. Civil rights groups that once favored political solutions often turned to economic ones when they became discouraged with the limits of political action. Jesse Jackson's Operation Breadbasket in Chicago focused on building up black businesses, just as both Washington and Du Bois had advocated the creation of a black business league. The Nation of Islam opened stores and restaurants to circulate money within their own community. Job-training programs became a major demand of civil rights groups in northern cities after 1965, echoing Washington's call for industrial education. The Black Panthers advocated economic reform as an essential part of their ten-point platform and turned to economic interpretations of race issues, as did both Du Bois in the 1920s and Martin Luther King Jr. after 1965.

It is probably best to see the modern movement as influenced by both men but also an extension of their debate. Rosa Parks, the seamstress and activist whose arrest in 1955 started the Montgomery bus boycott, grew up in Tuskegee, Alabama. Like most black schoolchildren of the 1940s and 1950s, she thought that Booker T. Washington was a hero and heard that Du Bois was a subversive. Yet Rosa Parks was also an active member of the NAACP and trained at the Highlander Folk School to participate in civil disobedience. Indeed, as civil rights protests increased in the early 1960s, Du Bois's ideas of open protest gained more recognition. As the movement became more militant in the mid- to late 1960s, Washington's reputation actually declined. Nonetheless, both men, although they themselves were not the sole sources of the ideas, contributed to the ideological debate that surrounded the movement.

As objective conditions change, so do people's views of the best method of improving them. The tremendous progress that African Americans have made in this country since the beginning of the Civil Rights Movement has once again reshaped the responses to the traditional issues. Not surprisingly, views of Du Bois and Washington have evolved with these changes. Following the lead of later civil rights activists, some academics now challenge Du Bois's top-down model of leadership. They portray turn-of-the-century Du Bois as an elitist, out of touch with the real conditions of the masses. They denounce his intellectual beliefs as simple reflections of white concepts of race and racial characteristics. They accuse him of trying to impose Victorian standards of morality on the black community. This interpretation does not reflect Du Bois's whole legacy, however; for the most part his reputation is still intact. Few would challenge his dedication to open protest against racism and his later devotion to Pan-Africanism, which most academics and leaders agree were his unique contributions.

Booker T. Washington's ideas are regaining popularity, too. In the 1980s his focus on racial uplift through hard work and morality seemed to many conservatives to be a solution to inner-city poverty, which the Civil Rights Movement had not addressed. In the backlash to the Civil Rights Movement and particularly criticism of Affirmative Action policies, many people in both black and white communities believed that blacks had become too dependent on government programs and needed to take the initiative themselves if they were going to succeed. Blacks had always turned to self-help programs in times when whites turned away from reform. Increasing racial hostilities, police brutality, and lack of economic progress in poor black communities, however, led many blacks to believe that there was little point in trying to succeed within a system that denied them opportunities. In the wake of the Los Angeles riots in 1992, almost a century after Washington's Atlanta address, African American leaders once again asked whites to give blacks economic opportunities, while advising blacks to be patient.

The turn of the twenty-first century is not the same as the turn of the twentieth, however. Although the dragging death of James Byrd in Jasper, Texas, in 1998 reminded people of the Sam Hose lynching in 1899, most Americans condemned such racially motivated violence. Blacks now hold political office in almost every state and have seats in Congress and the judiciary. The Supreme Court has ruled segregation unconstitutional, and anyone who faces racial discrimination can sue for restitution. As blacks break down barriers in all areas of society, the change in objective conditions alters the issues they face. Undoubtedly, the issues that Washington and Du Bois debated will arise again as conditions continue to change. How the debate will manifest itself we shall have to wait and see.

DOCUMENTS IN
THE CASE

W.E.B. Du Bois to Rutherford B. Hayes, president of the John F. Slater Fund, May 25, 1891

From an early age, Du Bois had firm convictions that he was destined for greater things. He also had a low tolerance for racial discrimination. When he read a news clipping that the president of the Slater Fund, Rutherford B. Hayes, had made disparaging remarks about blacks, he was determined to respond. Hayes had stated that the Slater Fund, which was mostly financing industrial schools such as Tuskegee Institute, would gladly fund any black student who wished to study in Europe but had so far not found any qualified applicants. The tone implied that Hayes did not expect to find any, either. Du Bois, about to take his master's degree from Harvard and with his sights on a European doctorate, begged to differ. This letter is one of many that he sent to the Slater Fund demanding that Hayes honor his word. It is surprising to discover how outspoken Du Bois was for his time, especially when one considers that he was addressing a former president of the United States.

Your favor of the 2nd. is at hand. I thank you for your kind wishes. You will pardon me if I add a few words of explanation as to my application. The outcome of the matter is as I expected it would be. The announcement that any agency of the American people was willing to

give a Negro a thoroughly liberal education and that it had been looking in vain for men to educate was to say the least rather startling.
When the newspaper clipping was handed me in a company of friends,
my first impulse was to make in some public way a categorical statement denying that such an offer had ever been made known to colored
students. I saw this would be injudicious and fruitless, and I therefore
determined on the plan of applying myself. I did so and have been
refused along with a number of cases besides mine.

As to my case I personally care little. I am perfectly capable of
fighting alone for an education if the trustees do not see fit to help me.
On the other hand the injury you have—unwittingly I trust—done the
race I represent, and am not ashamed of, is almost irreparable. You
went before a number of keenly observant men who looked upon you
as an authority in the matter, and told them in substance that the Negroes of the United States either couldn't or wouldn't embrace a most
liberal opportunity for advancement. That statement went all over the
country. When now finally you receive three or four applications for
the fulfillment of that offer, the offer is suddenly withdrawn, while
the impression still remains.

If the offer was an experiment, you ought to have had at least one
case before withdrawing it; if you have given aid before (and I mean
here toward liberal education—not toward training plowmen) then
your statement at Johns Hopkins was partial. From the above facts I
think you owe an apology to the Negro people. We are ready to furnish
competent men for every European scholarship furnished us off paper. But we can't educate ourselves on nothing and we can't have the
moral courage to try, if in the midst of our work our friends turn public sentiment against us by making statements which injure us and
which they cannot stand by.

That you have been looking for men to liberally educate in the
past may be so but it is certainly strange so few have heard it. It was
never mentioned during my three years stay at Fisk University. President J. C. Price of Livingstone has told me that he never heard of it,
and students from various other Southern schools have expressed great
surprise at the offer. The fact is that when I was wanting to come to
Harvard, while yet in the South, I wrote to Dr. Haygood for a loan
merely, and he never even answered my letter. I find men willing to
help me thro' cheap theological schools, I find men willing to help me
use my hands before I have got my brains in working order, I have an

abundance of good wishes on hand, but I never found a man willing to help me get a Harvard Ph.D.

W.E.B. Du Bois

Source: *The Correspondence of W.E.B. Du Bois*, ed. Herbert Aptheker (Amherst: University of Massachusetts Press, 1973), vol. 1, *Selections, 1877–1934*.

Booker T. Washington, Atlanta Exposition Address, September 18, 1895

This speech, which opponents often referred to as "The Atlanta Compromise," is one of the most famous ever made by an African American. Washington was speaking at the opening ceremonies of the Atlanta Cotton States and International Exposition from the same platform as white dignitaries and before a primarily white audience. Critics focus on the fact that Washington seemed to give up all claims to social equality and accept many white stereotypes of blacks. Contemporaries, however, including Du Bois, praised Washington for asking whites to give blacks job opportunities and for his linkage of black and white progress in the South. The two most famous parts of the speech are the statement "In all things that are purely social we can be as separate as the fingers, yet one as the hand in all things essential to mutual progress" and the advice to blacks and whites to "Cast down your bucket where you are!" It is easy to criticize this speech today and think that Washington catered to white opinions too much. What readers should ask, however, is what response he would have received had he been more outspoken. It is also important to realize that although he seemed to compromise on black social and political rights, he made demands on southern whites in return.

Mr. President and Gentlemen of the Board of Directors and Citizens: One-third of the population of the South is of the Negro race. No enterprise seeking the material, civil, or moral welfare of this section can disregard this element of our population and reach the highest success. I but convey to you, Mr. President and Directors, the sentiment of the masses of my race when I say that in no way have the value and manhood of the American Negro been more fittingly and generously recognized than by the managers of this magnificent Exposition at every stage of its progress. It is a recognition that will do more to cement the friendship of the two races than any occurrence since the dawn of our freedom.

Not only this, but the opportunity here afforded will awaken among us a new era of industrial progress. Ignorant and inexperienced, it is not strange that in the first years of our new life we began at the top instead of at the bottom; that a seat in Congress or the state legislature was more sought than real estate or industrial skill; that the political convention of stump speaking had more attractions than starting a dairy farm or truck garden.

A ship lost at sea for many days suddenly sighted a friendly vessel. From the mast of the unfortunate vessel was seen a signal, "Water, water; we die of thirst!" The answer from the friendly vessel at once came back, "Cast down your bucket where you are." A second time the signal, "Water, water; send us water!" ran up from the distressed vessel, and was answered, "Cast down your bucket where you are." And a third and fourth signal for water was answered, "Cast down your bucket where you are." The captain of the distressed vessel, at last heeding the injunction, cast down his bucket, and it came up full of fresh, sparkling water from the mouth of the Amazon River. To those of my race who depend on bettering their condition in a foreign land or who underestimate the importance of cultivating friendly relations with the Southern white man, who is their next-door neighbour, I would say: "Cast down your bucket where you are" —cast it down in making friends in every manly way of the people of all races by whom we are surrounded. Cast it down in agriculture, mechanics, in commerce, in domestic service, and in the professions. And in this connection it is well to bear in mind that whatever other sins the South may be called to bear, when it comes to business, pure and simple, it is in the South that the Negro is given a man's chance in the commercial world, and in nothing is this Exposition more eloquent than in emphasizing this chance. Our greatest danger is that in the great leap from slavery to freedom we may overlook the fact that the masses of us are to live by the productions of our hands, and fail to keep in mind that we shall prosper in proportion as we learn to dignify and glorify common labour and put brains and skill into the common occupations of life; shall prosper in proportion as we learn to draw the line between the superficial and the substantial, the ornamental gewgaws of life and the useful. No race can prosper till it learns that there is as much dignity in tilling a field as in writing a poem. It is at the bottom of life we must begin, and not at the top. Nor should we permit our grievances to overshadow our opportunities.

To those of the white race who look to the incoming of those of foreign birth and strange tongue and habits for the prosperity of the South, were I permitted I would repeat what I say to my own race, "Cast down your bucket where you are." Cast it down among the eight millions of Negroes whose habits you know, whose fidelity and love you have tested in days when to have proved treacherous meant the ruin of your firesides. Cast down your bucket among these people who have, without strikes and labour wars, tilled your fields, cleared your forests, builded your railroads and cities, and brought forth treasures from the bowels of the earth, and helped make possible this magnificent representation of the progress of the South. Casting down your bucket among my people, helping and encouraging them as you are doing on these grounds, and to education of head, hand, and heart, you will find that they will buy your surplus land, make blossom the waste places in your fields, and run your factories. While doing this, you can be sure in the future, as in the past, that you and your families will be surrounded by the most patient, faithful, law-abiding, and unresentful people that the world has seen. As we have proved our loyalty to you in the past, in nursing your children, watching by the sickbed of your mothers and fathers, and often following them with tear-dimmed eyes to their graves, so in the future, in our humble way, we shall stand by you with a devotion that no foreigner can approach, ready to lay down our lives, if need be, in defense of yours, interlacing our industrial, commercial, civil, and religious life with yours in a way that shall make the interests of both races one. In all things that are purely social we can be as separate as the fingers, yet one as the hand in all things essential to mutual progress.

There is no defence or security for any of us except in the highest intelligence and development of all. If anywhere there are efforts tending to curtail the fullest growth of the Negro, let these efforts be turned into stimulating, encouraging, and making him the most useful and intelligent citizen. Effort or means so invested will pay a thousand per cent interest. These efforts will be twice blessed—"blessing him that gives and him that takes."

> There is no escape through law of man or God from the inevitable:—
> The laws of changeless justice bind
> Oppressor with oppressed;
> And close as sin and suffering joined
> We march to fate abreast.

Nearly sixteen millions of hands will aid you in pulling the load upward, or they will pull against you the load downward. We shall constitute one-third and more of the ignorance and crime of the South, or one-third its intelligence and progress; we shall contribute one-third to the business and industrial prosperity of the South, or we shall prove a veritable body of death, stagnating, depressing, retarding every effort to advance the body politic.

Gentlemen of the Exposition, as we present to you our humble effort at an exhibition of our progress, you must not expect overmuch. Starting thirty years ago with ownership here and there in a few quilts and pumpkins and chickens (gathered from miscellaneous sources), remember the path that has led from these to the inventions and production of agricultural implements, buggies, steam-engines, newspapers, books, statuary, carving, paintings, the management of drug-stores and banks, has not been trodden without contact with thorns and thistles. While we take pride in what we exhibit as a result of our independent efforts, we do not for a moment forget that our part in this exhibition would fall far short of your expectations but for the constant help that has come to our educational life, not only from the Southern states, but especially from Northern philanthropists, who have made their gifts a constant stream of blessing and encouragement.

The wisest among my race understand that the agitation of questions of social equality is the extremest folly, and that progress in the enjoyment of all the privileges that will come to us must be the result of severe and constant struggle rather than of artificial forcing. No race that has anything to contribute to the markets of the world is long in any degree ostracized. It is important and right that all privileges of the law be ours, but it is vastly more important that we be prepared for the exercise of these privileges. The opportunity to earn a dollar in a factory just now is worth infinitely more than the opportunity to spend a dollar in an opera-house.

In conclusion, may I repeat that nothing in thirty years has given us more hope and encouragement, and drawn us so near to you of the white race, as this opportunity offered by the Exposition; and here bending, as it were, over the altar that represents the results of the struggles of your race and mine, both starting practically empty-handed three decades ago. I pledge that in your effort to work out the great and intricate problem which God has laid at the doors of the South, you shall have at all times the patient, sympathetic help of my race; only let this be constantly in mind, that, while from representations in these buildings of the product of field, of forest, of mine, of factory, letters, and art, much good will come, yet far above and beyond material benefits will be that higher good, that, let us pray God, will come, in a blotting out of sectional differences and racial animosities and suspicions, in a determination to administer absolute justice, in a willing obedience among all classes to the mandates of law. This, then, coupled with our material prosperity, will bring into our beloved South a new heaven and a new earth.

Source: Booker T. Washington, *Up from Slavery* (New York: Doubleday, Page and Company, 1901).

W.E.B. Du Bois, "Of the Ruling of Men," 1920

Like his Souls of Black Folk, *Du Bois's* Darkwater *is a series of essays and poems on race issues and includes autobiographical information. In this excerpt from the essay "Of the Ruling of Men," Du Bois gives a masterful defense of universal voting rights. After Emancipation, many whites argued that blacks should not vote for a variety of reasons. Some argued that blacks were not intelligent enough to choose suitable politicians. Others believed that they lacked the experience in politics necessary to responsible voting. Many claimed that it was better if paternalistic whites voted for them, since blacks could not possibly understand their own best interests and were too swayed by emotions to vote rationally. Finally, whites argued that blacks simply did not want to vote—an argument still common even in the 1960s to explain the scarcity of black voters in the South. As Du Bois points out, opponents of woman suffrage used many of these same arguments. His support of women's rights was quite unusual for the time, but he strongly believed in women's equality under the law and saw a clear comparison between sexism and racism.*

Who may be excluded from a share in the ruling of men? Time and time again the world has answered:

The Ignorant
The Inexperienced
The Guarded
The Unwilling

That is, we have assumed that only the intelligent should vote, or those who know how to rule men, or those who are not under benevolent guardianship, or those who ardently desire the right.

These restrictions are not arguments for the wide distribution of the ballot—they are rather reasons for restriction addressed to the self-interest of the present real rulers. We say easily, for instance, "The ignorant ought not to vote." We would say, "No civilized state should have citizens too ignorant to participate in government," and this statement is but a step to the fact: that no state is civilized which has citizens too ignorant to help rule it. Or, in other words, education is not a prerequisite to political control—political control is the cause of popular education.

Again, to make experience a qualification for the franchise is absurd: it would stop the spread of democracy and make political power hereditary, a prerequisite of a class, caste, race, or sex. It has of course been soberly argued that only white folk or Englishmen, or men, are really capable of exercising sovereign power in a modern state. The statement proves too much: only yesterday it was Englishmen of high descent, or men of "blood," or sovereigns "by divine right" who could rule. Today the civilized world is being ruled by the descendants of persons who a century ago were pronounced incapable of ever developing a self-ruling people. In every modern state there must come to the polls every generation, and indeed every year, men who are inexperienced in the solutions of the political problems that confront them and who must experiment in methods of ruling men. Thus and thus only will civilization grow.

Again, what is this theory of benevolent guardianship for women, for the masses, for Negroes—for "lesser breeds without the law"? It is simply the old cry of privilege, the old assumption that there are those in the world who know better what is best for others than those others know themselves, and who can be trusted to do this best.

In fact no one knows himself but that self's own soul. The vast and wonderful knowledge of this marvelous universe is locked in the bosoms of its individual souls. To tap this mighty reservoir of experience, knowledge, beauty, love, and deed we must appeal not to the few, not to some souls, but to all. The narrower the appeal, the poorer the culture; the wider the appeal, the more magnificent are the possibilities. Infinite is human nature. We make it finite by choking back the mass of men, by attempting to speak for others, to interpret and act for them, and we end by acting for ourselves and using the world as our private property. If this were all, it were crime enough—but it is not all: by our ignorance we make the creation of the greater world impossible; we beat back a world built of the playing of dogs and laughter of children, the song of Black Folk and worship of Yellow, the love of women and strength of men, and try to express by a group of doddering ancients the Will of the World.

Du Bois attends a meeting for woman suffrage. He was a strong supporter of women's rights. *Courtesy of the Library of Congress*

There are people who insist upon regarding the franchise, not as a necessity for the many, but as a privilege for the few. They say of persons and classes: "They do not need the ballot." This is often said of women. It is argued that everything which women with the ballot might do for themselves can be done for them; that they have influence and friends "at court," and that their enfranchisement would simply double the number of ballots. So, too, we are told that American Negroes can have done for them by other voters all that they could possibly do for themselves with the ballot and much more because the white voters are more intelligent.

Further than this, it is argued that many of the disfranchised people recognize these facts. "Women do not want the ballot" has been a very effective counter war-cry, so much so that many men have taken refuge in the declaration: "When they want to vote, why, then—" So, too, we are continually told that the "best" Negroes stay out of politics.

Such arguments show so curious a misapprehension of the foundation of the argument for democracy that the argument must be continually restated and emphasized. We must remember that if the theory of democracy is correct, the right to vote is not merely a privilege, not simply a method of meeting the needs of a particular group, and least of all a matter of recognized want or desire. Democracy is a method of realizing the broadest measure of justice to all human beings. . . .

The real argument for democracy is, then, that in the people we have the source of that endless life and unbounded wisdom which the rulers of men must have. A given people today may not be intelligent, but through a democratic government that recognizes, not only the worth of the individual to himself, but the worth of his feelings and experiences to all, they can educate, not only the individual unit, but generation after generation, until they accumulate vast stores of wisdom. Democracy alone is the method of showing the whole experience of the race for the benefit of the future and if democracy tries to exclude women or Negroes or the poor or any class because of innate characteristics which do not interfere with intelligence, then that democracy cripples itself and belies its name.

From this point of view we can easily see the weakness and strength of current criticism of extension of the ballot. It is the business of a modern government to see to it, first, that the number of ignorant within its bounds is reduced to the very smallest number. Again, it is the duty of every such government to extend as quickly as possible the number of persons of mature age who can vote. Such possible voters must be regarded, not as sharers of a limited treasure, but as sources of new national wisdom and strength.

Source: W.E.B. Du Bois, *Darkwater: Voices from within the Veil* (New York: Harcourt, Brace and Howe, 1920).

Booker T. Washington, Speech at the Brooklyn Institute of Arts and Sciences, September 30, 1896

In this speech, Washington expounded on his standard theme that blacks needed industrial training rather than higher education. He frequently used images of poor black sharecroppers reading classical literature in the midst of poverty as a way to highlight what he saw as the impracticality of a classical education for most Afri-

*can Americans. This speech is a good example of his rhetorical
style. Washington typically seemed to agree with white stereotypes
of blacks in order to reassure whites that he did not want to challenge the existing social relations between the races, yet in the same
breath he strongly criticized the effects of racism. Here, before an
audience of white northerners, he disparaged ignorant black voters and seemed to imply that blacks had benefited from slavery.
Yet in typical Washington fashion he also launched a devastating
attack on the state of education for blacks in the South, made white
northerners feel guilty for having so much more, and undoubtedly
raised a tidy sum from his audience.*

Democracy and Education

Mr. Chairman, Ladies and Gentlemen: . . . I know
that, whether we are increasing or decreasing, whether we are growing better or worse, whether we are valuable or valueless, a few years
ago fourteen of us were brought into this country and now there are
eight million of us. I know that, whether in slavery or freedom, we
have always been loyal to the Stars and Stripes, that no schoolhouse
has been opened for us that has not been filled; that 1,500,000 ballots
that we have the right to cast are as potent for weal and woe as the
ballot cast by the whitest and most influential man in your common-
wealth. I know that wherever our life touches yours we help or hinder;
that wherever your life touches ours you make us stronger or weaker.
Further I know that almost every other race that tried to look the white
man in the face has disappeared. With all the conflicting opinions,
and with the full knowledge of all our weaknesses, I know that only a
few centuries ago in this country we went into slavery pagans: we
came out Christians; we went into slavery pieces of property: we came
out American citizens; we went into slavery without a language: we
came out speaking the proud Anglo-Saxon tongue; we went into slavery with the slave chains clanking about our wrists: we came out
with the American ballot in our hands. My friends, I submit it to your
sober and candid judgment, if a race that is capable of such a test, such
a transformation, is not worth saving and making a part, in reality as
well as name, of our democratic government. It is with an ignorant
race, as it is with a child: it craves at first the superficial, the ornamental, the signs of progress rather than the reality. The ignorant race is
tempted to jump, at one bound, to the position that it has required
years of hard struggle for others to reach. It seems to me that the temp-
tation in education and missionary work is to do for a people a thousand miles away without always making a careful study of the needs

and conditions of the people whom we are trying to help. . . . Unfortunately for us as a race, our education was begun, just after the war, too nearly where New England education ended. We seemed to overlook the fact that we were dealing with a race that has little love for labor in their native land and consequently brought little love for labor with them to America. Added to this was the fact that they had been forced for two hundred and fifty years to labor without compensation under circumstances that were calculated to do anything but teach them the dignity, beauty, and civilizing power of intelligent labor. . . .

Notwithstanding in this instance we have a whole race depending upon agriculture, and notwithstanding thirty years have passed since our freedom, aside from what we have done at Hampton and Tuskegee and one or two other institutions, not a thing has been attempted by state or philanthropy in the way of educating the race in this industry on which their very existence depends. Boys have been taken from the farms and educated in law, theology, Hebrew, and Greek—educated in everything else but the very subject they should know the most about. . . .

Some time ago when we decided to make tailoring a part of our training at the Tuskegee Institute, I was amazed to find that it was almost impossible to find in the whole country an educated colored man who could teach the making of clothing. I could find them by the score who could teach astronomy, theology, Greek, or Latin, but almost none who could instruct in the making of clothing, something that has to be used by every one of us every day in the year. How often has my heart been made to sink as I have gone through the South and into the homes of the people and found women who could converse intelligently on Grecian history, who had studied geometry, could analyze the most complex sentences, and yet could not analyze the poorly cooked and still more poorly served bread and fat meat that they and their families were eating three times a day. It is little trouble to find girls who can locate Pekin and the Desert of Sahara on an artificial globe; but seldom can you find one who can locate on an actual dinner table the proper place for the carving knife and fork or the meat and the vegetables. . . .

Few, I fear, realize what is to be done before the seven million of my people in the South can be made a safe, helpful, progressive part of our institutions. The South, in proportion to its ability, has done well, but this does not change facts. Let me illustrate what I mean by a single example. In spite of all that has been done, I was in a county in

Alabama a few days ago where there are some thirty thousand colored people and about seven thousand whites; in this county not a single public school for Negroes has been open this year longer than three months, not a single colored teacher has been paid more than fifteen dollars a month for his teaching. Not one of these schools was taught in a building worthy of the name of schoolhouse. In this county the

Female Tuskegee students learned practical skills such as upholstery instead of Greek or Latin. *Courtesy of the Library of Congress*

state or public authorities do not own a dollar's worth of school property—not a schoolhouse, a blackboard, or a piece of crayon. Each colored child had spent on him this year for his education about fifty cents, while one of your children had spent on him this year for education not far from twenty dollars. And yet each citizen of this county is expected to share the burdens and privileges of our democratic form of government just as intelligently and conscientiously as the citizens of your beloved Kings County. A vote in this county means as much to the nation as a vote in the city of Boston. . . . Do you know that a single schoolhouse built this year in a town near Boston to shelter about three hundred students has cost more for the building alone than will be spent for the education, including buildings, apparatus, teachers, of the whole colored school population of Alabama? . . .

I have referred to industrial education as a means of fitting the millions of my people in the South for the duties of citizenship. Until there is industrial independence it is hardly possible to have a pure ballot. . . .

Source: *Booker T. Washington Papers*, ed. Louis R. Harlan and Raymond Smock (Urbana: University of Illinois Press, 1972–83).

W.E.B. Du Bois, "The Conservation of the Races," 1897

In 1897, Du Bois took part in discussions with Alexander Crummell that resulted in the creation of the American Negro Academy, a group of black intellectuals dedicated to the scientific study of race conditions. In this essay, he outlined what he believed the academy should accomplish. He also revealed his acceptance of the social scientific assumptions of the day about race. Although Du Bois did not believe that blacks were innately inferior, he did accept at face value many of the assertions that whites made about them: that slavery and racism had degraded blacks and that they were prone to immorality, crime, and laziness. Nonetheless, he argued, blacks had unique contributions to offer civilization. He called on whites to help in the effort to uplift the race.

The American Negro has always felt an intense personal interest in discussions as to the origins and destinies of races: primarily because back of most discussions of race with which he is familiar, have lurked certain assumptions as to his natural abilities, as to his political, intellectual and moral status, which he felt were wrong. He has, consequently, been led to deprecate and minimize race distinctions, to believe intensely that out of one blood God created all nations, and to speak of human brotherhood as though it were the possibility of an already dawning tomorrow.

Nevertheless, in our calmer moments we must acknowledge that human beings are divided into races; that in this country the two most extreme types of the world's races have met, and the resulting problems as to the future relations of these types are not only of intense and living interest to us, but form an epoch in the history of mankind. . . .

In the field of sociology an appalling work lies before us. First, we must unflinchingly and bravely face the truth, not with apologies, but with solemn earnestness. The Negro Academy ought to sound a note of warning that would echo in every black cabin in the land: *Unless we conquer our present vices they will conquer us*; we are diseased, we are developing criminal tendencies, and an alarming large percentage of our men and women are sexually impure. The Negro Academy should stand and proclaim this over the housetops, crying with Garrison: *I will not equivocate, I will not retreat a single inch, and I will be heard.* The Academy should seek to gather about it the talented, unselfish men, the pure and nobleminded women, to fight an army of devils that disgraces our manhood and our womanhood. There does not stand today upon God's earth a race more capable in muscle, in intellect, in morals, than the American Negro, if he will bend his energies in the right direction; if he will

> Burst his birth's invidious bar
> And grasp the skirts of happy chance,
> And breast the blows of circumstance,
> And grapple with his evil star.

In science and morals, I have indicated two fields of work for the Academy. Finally, in practical policy, I wish to suggest the following *Academy Creed*:

1. We believe that the Negro people, as a race, have a contribution to make to civilization and humanity, which no other race can make.
2. We believe it the duty of the Americans of Negro descent, as a body, to maintain their race identity until this mission of the Negro People is accomplished, and the ideal of human brotherhood has become a practical possibility.
3. We believe that, unless modern civilization is a failure, it is entirely feasible and practicable for two races in such essential political, economic and religious harmony as the white and colored people of America, to develop side by side in peace and mutual happiness, the peculiar contribution which each has to make to the culture of their common country.
4. As a means to this end we advocate, not such social equality between these races as would disregard human likes and dislikes, but such social equilibrium as would, throughout all the complicated relations of life, give due and just consideration to culture, ability, and moral worth, whether they be found under white or black skins.

5. We believe that the first and greatest step toward the settlement of the present friction between the races—commonly called the Negro Problem—lies in the correction of the immorality, crime and laziness among the Negroes themselves, which still remains a heritage from slavery. We believe that only earnest and long continued efforts on our part can cure these social ills.

6. We believe that the second great step toward a better adjustment of the relations between the races, should be a more impartial selection of ability in the economic and intellectual world, and a greater respect for personal liberty and worth, regardless of race. We believe that only earnest efforts on the part of the white people of this country will bring much needed reform in these matters.

7. On the basis of the foregoing declaration, and firmly believing in our high destiny, we, as American Negroes, are resolved to strive in every honorable way for the realization of the best and highest aims, for the development of strong manhood and pure womanhood, and for the rearing of a race ideal in America and Africa, to the glory of God and the uplifting of the Negro people—1897.

Source: W.E.B. Du Bois, "The Conservation of Races." *Occasional Papers*, No. 2., American Negro Academy (Washington, DC, 1897).

Fund-Raising

Booker T. Washington controlled the flow of millions of dollars through Tuskegee, both for his school and for black education in general. He was a champion fund-raiser and had influential connections with wealthy northern whites such as John D. Rockefeller Sr. of Standard Oil, steel magnate Andrew Carnegie, and railroad president William H. Baldwin. On April 14, 1903, Washington held a fund-raising event for Tuskegee at Madison Square Garden in New York City. Carnegie made the largest donation Tuskegee had ever received. The following two letters are reminders of the wealth that Washington controlled.

Andrew Carnegie to William Henry Baldwin Jr., April 17, 1903

My dear Mr. Baldwin: I have instructed Mr. Franks, Sec'y, to deliver to you as Trustee Tuskegee, $600,000. 5% U.S. Steel Co. Bonds, to complete the Endowment Fund as per circular.

One condition only—the revenue of one hundred and fifty thousand of these bonds is to be subject to Booker Washington's order to be used by him first for his wants and those of his family during his life or the life of his widow. If any surplus [is] left he can use it for Tuskegee. I wish that great and good man to be free from pecuniary cares that he may devote himself wholly to his great mission.

To me he seems one of the foremost of living men because his work is unique. The modern Moses, who leads his race and lifts it through Education to even better and higher things than a land overflowing with milk and honey. History is to know two Washingtons, one white, the other black, both Fathers of their People. I am satisfied that the serious race question of the South is to be solved wisely, only by following Booker Washington's policy which he seems to have [been] specially born—a slave among slaves—to establish, and even in his own day, greatly to advance.

So glad to be able to assist this good work in which you and others are engaged. Truly yours,

ANDREW CARNEGIE

John Davison Rockefeller Jr. to Booker T. Washington, June 24, 1903

Dear Mr. Washington: Your favor of June 11th to my father enclosing check for $249 being the balance of his pledge authorizing the expenditure up to $34,000. for a boys dormitory, which balance you state was not required in the completion of the building, is received. My father is gratified to know that the building has been constructed so well within the estimated cost, the more so since it so frequently happens that the opposite is the case. He takes pleasure in returning the check for $249., desiring that the same be applied as you may see fit. Very truly,

JOHN D. ROCKEFELLER JR

Source: *Booker T. Washington Papers*, ed. Louis R. Harlan and Raymond Smock (Urbana: University of Illinois Press, 1972–83).

Washington's Secret Life

Washington may have opposed public protest for social and political rights, but he was very much involved behind the scenes in resisting segregation and discrimination. The following six letters reveal his private attitudes and document his secret

funding of test cases to challenge discrimination in a variety of areas. Of particular interest is his financial support of Du Bois's lawsuit against the Pullman Sleeping Car Company for refusing him a berth on a train in Georgia.

Booker T. Washington to Archibald H. Grimké, June 5, 1899

Personal

Dear Mr. Grimké: Friends in Boston have been kind enough to send me a copy of the Transcript containing your recent strong and eloquent address delivered at the mass meeting held to protest against the practice of Lynching in the South. I feel sure that your words will do good and I thank you for them. I have asked my Sec. to send you a copy of the paper containing an article which I have written to the Southern white people upon this subject. I have kept silent, because I wanted to wait until I knew the white people of the South were in that frame of mind where they were willing to listen to what I had to say. I know that there are those who have found fault with me for my utterances or lack of such, but I do not believe that I have ever said anything over my signature that you or any other friend of the race disagree with. For me to attempt to contradict many of the absurd and foolish things, which are attributed to me through the Press, would be simply a waste of time and a piece of folly.

Please remember me very kindly to your brother, and be kind enough to send him a copy of the paper which my Sec. will send you. Yours truly,

BOOKER T. WASHINGTON

William Henry Baldwin Jr. to Booker T. Washington, January 24, 1900

Personal

Dear Mr. Washington: I cannot get any answer from the Pullman people. I have written them twice and have not received reply. Therefore do not wait for me. Would it not be well when test is made of this question to have a light mulatto of good appearance, but unquestionably colored, make the test.

I don't believe that the Pullman Company will attempt to exclude the colored man from the car, but that the interpretation of the Bill will be to exclude them from the same section as the white person. I should suppose that the best place to make the test is at the Pullman ticket office in Atlanta. I wish you would let me know the developments in the case. I do hope it can be tested by someone other than yourself. Yours very truly,

W H BALDWIN JR.

Booker T. Washington to W.E.B. Du Bois, November 28, 1902

PERSONAL AND CONFIDENTIAL.

My dear Dr. Du Bois: I have your letter of recent date, and if you will let me know what the total expense will be I shall be willing to bear a portion of it provided I can hand it to you personally and not have any connection with your committee. I do not want my name to go before the committee in any shape or to be used publicly in connection with this matter. I am very glad indeed to hear that you are moving in such a sensible way. Smith is a fine and able man. Yours truly,

BOOKER T. WASHINGTON

Booker T. Washington to Wilford H. Smith, March 3, 1904

Dear Mr. Smith: I rather suspect that the law which requires that all poll taxes shall be paid by February 1st might work against any contention you should make of the kind mentioned in yours of some days ago.

I would suggest securing some such man as C. O. Harris of Montgomery, who, I understand, has been refused registration and who has been practically conducting the Montgomery Post Office for many years.

A case based upon the refusal to allow an unregistered Negro to vote for a Member of Congress, or for Presidential electors seems to me to offer another opportunity and one which I think it well for us to follow up. Very truly yours,

BOOKER T. WASHINGTON

Booker T. Washington to J. Douglas Wetmore, September 23, 1905

Personal

Dear Mr. Wetmore: One other suggestion: there are any number of opportunities in Alabama and other states, where some colored man charged with crime, might serve as a test case for not putting of colored people on the juries. That could be done without a great deal of expense, and a white lawyer could be hired to lead the way, if necessary. Very truly,

Booker T. Washington

Booker T. Washington to Oswald Garrison Villard, September 7, 1908

Personal:

My dear Mr. Villard: I know your hands are full and I hesitate to call upon you for any additional work or sympathy, or means, but there is such flagrant injustice being done to Colored people in Alabama just now, that I thought you might like to assist in the matter.

Colored people, by recent decision of the courts, are being sent to the chain gang in large numbers for violation of contracts. This simply means that any white man, who cares to charge that a Colored man has promised to work for him and has not done so, or who has gotten money from him and not paid it back, can have the Colored man sent to the chain gang. Many of the best lawyers are of the opinion that such practice is wholly unconstitutional, but it will cost about $200 or $300 *now* to have the matter attested before the courts. My own purse has been drawn upon in so many directions, that I can do nothing at present.

The enclosed memorandum was sent me, I might say to you confidentially, by one of the judges. He has done all that he could do to break up this terrible practice, but he is compelled to follow the decisions of the higher court—I mean of the State Supreme Court. Please return the memorandum. Yours very truly,

Booker T. Washington

Source: *Booker T. Washington Papers*, ed. Louis R. Harlan and Raymond Smock (Urbana: University of Illinois Press, 1972–83).

W.E.B. Du Bois, "The Evolution of Negro Leadership," July 16, 1901

The following essay is Du Bois's review of Washington's autobiography Up from Slavery, *which appeared in 1901 to great acclaim. The review did not please Washington, but Du Bois saw himself as engaged in a philosophical debate over methods of racial uplift. He claimed that he did not intend his attacks personally. Nonetheless, his disappointment in not having been appointed assistant superintendent in the Washington, DC, school district in 1900, partly because of Tuskegee's support of another candidate, undoubtedly influenced his attitude. In this essay he praised Washington for his accomplishments but criticized his approach to racial uplift as too narrow.*

In every generation of our national life, from Phillis Wheatley to Booker Washington, the Negro race in America has succeeded in bringing forth men whom the country, at times spontaneously, at times in spite of itself, has been impelled to honor and respect. Mr. Washington is one of the most striking of these cases, and his autobiography is a partial history of the steps which made him a group leader, and the one man who in the eyes of the nation typifies at present more nearly than all others the work and worth of his nine million fellows. . . .

When sticks and stones and beasts form the sole environment of a people, their attitude is ever one of determined opposition to, and conquest of, natural forces. But when to earth and brute is added an environment of men and ideas, then the attitude of the imprisoned group may take three main forms: a feeling of revolt and revenge; an attempt to adjust all thought and action to the will of the greater group; or, finally, a determined attempt at self-development, self-realization, in spite of environing discouragements and prejudice. The influence of all three of these attitudes is plainly to be traced in the evolution of race leaders among American Negroes. . . .

Mr. Washington came with a clear simple programme, at the psychological moment; at a time when the nation was a little ashamed of having bestowed so much sentiment on Negroes and was concentrating its energies on Dollars. The industrial training of Negro youth was not an idea originating with Mr. Washington, nor was the policy of conciliating the white South wholly his. But he first put life, unlimited energy, and perfect faith into this programme; he changed it from an article of belief into a whole creed; he broadened it from a by-path into a veritable Way of Life. And the method by which he accomplished this is an interesting study of human life.

Mr. Washington's narrative gives but glimpses of the real struggle which he has had for leadership. First of all, he strove to gain the sympathy and coöperation of the white South, and gained it after that epoch-making sentence spoken at Atlanta: "In all things that are purely social we can be as separate as the fingers, yet one as the hand in all things essential to mutual progress." This conquest of the South is by all odds the most notable thing in Mr. Washington's career. Next to this comes his achievement in gaining place and consideration in the North. Many others less shrewd and tactful would have fallen between these two stools; but as Mr. Washington knew the heart of the South from birth and training, so by singular insight he intuitively grasped the spirit of the age that was dominating the North. He learned so thoroughly the speech and thought of triumphant commercialism and the ideals of material prosperity that he pictures as the height of absurdity a black boy studying a French grammar in the midst of weeds and dirt. One wonders how Socrates or St. Francis of Assisi would receive this!

And yet this very singleness of vision and thorough oneness with his age is a mark of the successful man. . . . At the same time, Mr. Washington's success, North and South, with his gospel of Work and Money, raised opposition to him from widely divergent sources. The spiritual sons of the Abolitionists were not prepared to acknowledge that the schools founded before Tuskegee, by men of broad ideals and self-sacrificing souls, were wholly failures, or worthy of ridicule. On the other hand, among his own people Mr. Washington found deep suspicion and dislike for a man on such good terms with Southern whites.

Such opposition has only been silenced by Mr. Washington's very evident sincerity of purpose. . . .

Among the Negroes, Mr. Washington is still far from a popular leader. Educated and thoughtful Negroes everywhere are glad to honor him and aid him, but all cannot agree with him. He represents in Negro thought the old attitude of adjustment to environment, emphasizing the economic phase; but the two other strong currents of feeling, descended from the past, still oppose him. One is the thought of a small but not unimportant group, unfortunate in their choice of spokesman, but nevertheless of much weight, who represent the old ideas of revolt and revenge, and see in migration alone an outlet for the Negro people. The second attitude is that of the large and important group represented by Dunbar, Tanner, Chesnutt, Miller, and the Grimkes, who, without any single definite programme, and with complex aims, seek nevertheless that self-development and self-realization in all lines of human endeavor which they believe will eventually place the Negro beside the other races. While these men respect the Hampton-Tuskegee idea to a degree, they believe it falls far short of a complete programme. They believe, therefore, also in the higher education of Fisk and Atlanta Universities; they believe in self-assertion and ambition; and they believe in the right of suffrage for blacks on the same terms with whites.

Such is the complicated world of thought and action in which Mr. Booker Washington has been called of God and man to lead, and in which he has gained so rare a meed of success.

Source: *The Dial* 31 (July 16, 1901).

The Boston Riot, 1903

On July 30, 1903, Washington spoke before a local chapter of the National Negro Business League in Boston, the heart of Tuskegee opposition. Not surprisingly, the meeting degenerated into a virtual brawl between the two factions. In the aftermath, William Monroe Trotter, his sister, and two other anti-Bookerites were arrested. The Boston Riot, as it became known, gained national coverage, and many whites realized for the first time the extent of the opposition to Washington. His response was to seek revenge on all those responsible. Because Du Bois and Trotter were friends, and because Du Bois had just published The Souls of Black Folk *criticizing Washington by name, Washington assumed that Du Bois had played a part in the affair, although he was nowhere near Boston that night. Washington's heavy-handed tactics against Trotter convinced Du Bois that it was time to break from Tuskegee completely.*

Booker T. Washington to Whitefield McKinlay, August 3, 1903

Dear Mr. McKinlay: Enclosed I send you two letters from Gov. Pinchback. Please let me know what in your opinion is the wisest plan to secure without fail this position for his son, and whether there are any hindrances in the Civil Service Rules, which would prevent or make difficult his appointment.

You will be glad to know that Trotter, Forbes, Grimke, and two or three others, have by their actions completely killed themselves among all classes both white and colored, in Boston. Trotter was taken out of the church in handcuffs, yelling like a baby. They are to be tried in Court tomorrow, and every effort is being exerted by the citizens of Boston to secure their conviction. Very truly yours,

BOOKER T. WASHINGTON

Booker T. Washington to Robert C. Ogden, October 20, 1903

Dear Mr. Ogden: In connection with our conversation when I last saw you, I think I ought to say to you that I have evidence which is indisputable showing that Dr. Du Bois is very largely behind the mean and underhanded attacks that have been made upon me during the last six months. This, of course, is for your own personal information. Very truly yours,

BOOKER T. WASHINGTON

Source: *Booker T. Washington Papers*, ed. Louis R. Harlan and Raymond Smock (Urbana: University of Illinois Press, 1972–83).

W.E.B. Du Bois to George F. Peabody, December 28, 1903

My dear Mr. Peabody: —

Some time ago Mr. [Edward T.] Ware, our Chaplain, spoke to me of a letter received from you in which you spoke of certain rumors as to my connection with the disturbances over Mr. Washington in Boston last summer. Later Dr. Bumstead wrote me of a similar letter not mentioning from whom he had received it, but I took it that it was probably from you.

I want therefore to write you frankly of my position in this matter that there may be no misapprehension, and I want you to feel at liberty to use the letter as you may wish.

Mrs. Trotter the wife of the editor of the Guardian is an old friend of mine of school days. Mr. Trotter I have not known so long or so well but met him in college. I had then and afterward disagreed with him rather sharply over many questions of policy and particularly over Mr. Washington. But nevertheless both then and now I saw in him a clean-hearted utterly unselfish man whom I admired despite his dogged and unreasoning prejudices. Last summer while Mrs. Du Bois and I were looking for a boarding place, Mrs. Trotter offered to share her home with us and we gladly accepted. I went first to Tuskegee and then made a trip on a coast steamer. I did not arrive in Boston until after the Zion Church disturbance. Before seeing the account in the morning papers, I had no inkling or suspicion in any way of the matter. I did not know Mr. Washington was in Boston or intending to go there as I had just left him at Tuskegee. I had had no correspondence with Mr. Trotter for six months save in regard to a boarding place. When I arrived in Boston and heard of the meeting I told Mr. Trotter and Mr. Forbes in plain terms my decided disapproval of the unfortunate occurrence and my conviction that it would do harm. Although I was unable at that time to defend Mr. Washington's position as I once had, I nevertheless took occasion to address a meeting of men at Mr. Trotter's home and remind them of the vast difference between criticizing Mr. Washington's policy and attacking him personally.

Nevertheless, brought into close contact with Mr. Trotter for the first time my admiration for his unselfishness, pureness of heart and indomitable energy even when misguided, grew. . . . There were a great many other things not generally known that made me pity and admire Mr. Trotter as well as condemn his lack of judgment and there were also things that made me have less and less faith in Mr. Washington. . . .

While then I had absolutely no knowledge of the Washington meeting before hand and no part, active or passive, in the disturbance and while I did then and do now condemn the disturbance, I nevertheless admire Mr. Trotter as a man and agree with him in his main contentions. When I think him in the right I shall help him; when his methods or opinions go beyond law and right, I shall condemn them.

As between him and Mr. Washington I unhesitatingly believe Mr. Trotter to be far nearer the right in his contentions and I only pray for such restraint and judgment on Mr. Trotter's part as will save to our cause his sincerity and unpurchasable soul in these days when every energy is being used to put black men back into slavery and when Mr. Washington is leading the way backward.

I am sorry that I was not at the University when you called to welcome your party.

Very sincerely yours,

W.E.B. Du Bois

Source: *The Correspondence of W.E.B. Du Bois*, ed. Herbert Aptheker (Amherst: University of Massachusetts Press, 1973), vol. 1, *Selections, 1877–1934.*

Planning the Carnegie Hall Conference, 1903–04

After the Boston Riot, Washington made a last attempt to bring his allies and opponents into one organization. He had already proposed a conference where the two factions could iron out their differences in private and secured funds for such a meeting from Andrew Carnegie. Because of the disturbance, the conference did not take place until January 1904, but throughout late 1903, Du Bois and Washington fought over the invitation list. Du Bois believed Washington was trying to dominate the agenda and pack the meeting with Tuskegee supporters. The following four letters give an idea of the politics involved.

W.E.B. Du Bois to Kelly Miller, February 25, 1903

(CONFIDENTIAL)

Dear Miller: —

I was asked to go to Tuskegee some time ago and at that time the Conference you have been invited [to] was cooked up. A little judicious pressure and insistence lead to your invitation and that of Morgan of Cambridge. . . .

I think this will be a chance for a heart to heart talk with Mr. Washington. I propose to stand on the following platform:

1. Full political rights on the same terms as other Americans.
2. Higher education of selected Negro youth.
3. Industrial education for the masses.
4. Common school training for every Negro child.
5. A stoppage to the campaign of self-depreciation.
6. A careful study of the real condition of the Negro.
7. A National Negro periodical.
8. A thorough and efficient federation of Negro societies and activities.
9. The raising of a defense fund.
10. A judicious fight in the court for Civil rights.

Finally the general watch word must be, not to put further dependence on the help of the whites but to organize for self help, encouraging "manliness without defiance, conciliation without servility."

This program is hardly thought out—what is your opinion?

By the by, Washington wants to invite Fortune to the conference. I wrote him that I thought it would be a very unwise thing. I've not had an answer yet. . . .

Sincerely yours,

W.E.B. Du Bois

Source: *The Correspondence of W.E.B. Du Bois*, ed. Herbert Aptheker (Amherst: University of Massachusetts Press, 1973), vol. 1, *Selections, 1877–1934*.

Kelly Miller to W.E.B. Du Bois, November 4, 1903

Dear Du Bois: Yours received this day—Of course Prof Booker T. has notified you of the date for the New York Conference (Jan. 6th, 7th, 8th). . . . I am glad that Mr. W. will be present. It will give weight and currency to the movement. I do not think that the conference can be stampeded by his presence. I shall stand uncompromisingly opposed to the endorsement of any individual or his platform.

Roscoe will also be here. You should come by all means. Will you come if free transportation can be procured?

I was both glad and sorry to see your Guardian letter—glad for the sympathy expressed for as sincere a man as there is in the race; but sorry in that I feel sure your expression will be misjudged.

I am sending you a list of my fugitive articles—also list topics suggested for conference. Yours truly,

Kelly Miller

Source: *Booker T. Washington Papers*, ed. Louis R. Harlan and Raymond Smock (Urbana: University of Illinois Press, 1972–83).

Booker T. Washington to W.E.B. Du Bois, November 8, 1903

Dear Dr. DuBois: —

Please be kind enough to let me have your opinion of the following matters just as early as possible as time is pressing: Of course the main object of our New York Conference is to try to agree upon certain fundamental principles and to see in what way we understand or misunderstand each other and correct mistakes as far as possible. I agree with your suggestion that . . . we ought to have, as far as possible, all shades of opinion represented. I have no objection to inviting either Dr. Bentley or Mr. Morris. Which one do you prefer? Of course we could not invite them both. In this same connection I think that we ought to have W. H. Lewis from Boston as we could only get at both sides of New England thought by having him or some such man, as well as Mr. Morgan. The more I think of it, the more I feel convinced that Dr. J. W. E. Bowen ought to be present He represents a very large constituency and I have found him on all questions a pretty sane man. I have already written you as to your opinion about either Bishop Turner or Bishop Holsey. Of course we must avoid having the conference too large and too expensive. Do you really think that Dr. Grimké would represent some idea or element that would not be represented by somebody else already invited? Please think of this and write me. As to Fortune; we may or may not agree with a great many things that he does, but I think there is no question but that he influences public opinion in a very large degree. We must make an especial effort to drop out of consideration all personal feelings, otherwise the conference will be a failure from the beginning.

So far in making up the conference, I fear it has one especially weak point which should be strengthened if possible. We should bear in mind that the bulk of our people are in the South and that the problems relating to their future very largely surround the Southern colored people, and we should be very sure that there is a large element in the conference who actually know Southern conditions by experience and who can speak with authority, and we should not have to depend too much on mere theory and untried schemes of Northern colored people.

Yours truly,

BOOKER T. WASHINGTON

W.E.B. Du Bois to Booker T. Washington [1903]

Dear Mr. Washington:

I do not think it will be profitable for me to give further advice which will not be followed. The conference is yours and you will naturally constitute it as you choose. I must of course reserve the right to see the final list of those invited and to decide then whether my own presence is worth while.

W.E.B. Du Bois

Source: *The Correspondence of W.E.B. Du Bois*, ed. Herbert Aptheker (Amherst: University of Massachusetts Press, 1973), vol. 1, *Selections, 1877–1934*.

The Credo

The Credo was Du Bois's attempt to outline a clear philosophy for himself in opposition to Booker T. Washington. He also wanted to rally supporters and inspire them to do battle. First published in 1904, the Credo became one of Du Bois's most popular writings. He reprinted it in Darkwater *in 1920, and a publishing company distributed it widely on wallet-sized cards. Many African American families hung the text on their walls for inspiration.*

W.E.B. Du Bois, "Credo," 1904

I believe in God, who made of one blood all nations that on earth do dwell. I believe that all men, black and brown and white, are brothers, varying through time and opportunity, in form and gift and feature, but differing in no essential particular, and alike in soul and the possibility of infinite development.

Especially do I believe in the Negro Race: in the beauty of its genius, the sweetness of its soul, and its strength in that meekness which shall yet inherit this turbulent earth.

I believe in Pride of race and lineage and self: in pride of self so deep as to scorn injustice to other selves; in pride of lineage so great as to despise no man's father; in pride of race so chivalrous as neither to offer bastardy to the weak nor beg wedlock of the strong, knowing that men may be brothers in Christ, even though they may not be brothers-in-law.

I believe in Service—humble, reverent service, from the blackening of boots to the whitening of souls; for Work is Heaven, Idleness Hell, and Wage is the "Well done!" of the Master, who summoned all them that labor and are heavy laden, making no distinction between the black, sweating cotton hands of Georgia and the first families of Virginia, since all distinction not based on deed is devilish and not divine.

I believe in the Devil and his angels, who wantonly work to narrow the opportunity of struggling human beings, especially if they be black; who spit in the faces of the fallen, strike them that cannot strike again, believe the worst and work to prove it, hating the image which their Maker stamped on a brother's soul.

I believe in the Prince of Peace. I believe that War is Murder. I believe that armies and navies are at bottom the tinsel and braggadocio of oppression and wrong, and I believe that the wicked conquest of weaker and darker nations by nations whiter and stronger but foreshadows the death of that strength.

I believe in Liberty for all men: the space to stretch their arms and their souls, the right to breathe and the right to vote, the freedom to choose their friends, enjoy the sunshine, and ride on the railroads, uncursed by color; thinking, dreaming, working as they will in a kingdom of beauty and love.

I believe in the Training of Children, black even as white; the leading out of little souls into the green pastures and beside the still waters, not for pelf or peace, but for life lit by some large vision of beauty and goodness and truth; lest we forget, and the sons of the fathers, like Esau, for mere meat barter their birthright in a mighty nation.

Finally, I believe in Patience—patience with the weakness of the Weak and the strength of the Strong, the prejudice of the Ignorant and the ignorance of the Blind; patience with the tardy triumph of Joy and the mad chastening of Sorrow.

Source: *Independent*, October 6, 1904.

W.E.B. Du Bois, The Niagara Movement, "Declaration of Principles," 1905

Du Bois formed the Niagara Movement in response to the failure of the Committee of Twelve and Washington's increasingly heavy-handed tactics. The Niagara Movement was the first black organization to place its main emphasis on protest. Close reading of its "Declaration" also reveals some subtle stabs at Washington's unwillingness to speak out publicly against discrimination.

Progress: The members of the conference, known as the Niagara Movement, assembled in annual meeting at Buffalo, July 11th, 12th and 13th, 1905, congratulate the Negro-Americans on certain undoubted evidences of progress in the last decade, particularly the increase of intelligence, the buying of property, the checking of crime, the uplift in home life, the advance in literature and art, and the demonstration of constructive and executive ability in the conduct of great religious, economic and educational institutions.

Suffrage: At the same time, we believe that this class of American citizens should protest emphatically and continually against the cur-

Group of Niagara Movement founders in 1905. Du Bois is in the middle row, second from the right. *Courtesy of the Special Collections and Archives, W.E.B. Du Bois Library, University of Massachusetts, Amherst*

tailment of their political rights. We believe in manhood suffrage; we believe that no man is so good, intelligent or wealthy as to be entrusted wholly with the welfare of his neighbor.

Civil Liberty: We believe also in protest against the curtailment of our civil rights. All American citizens have the right to equal treatment in places of public entertainment according to their behavior and deserts.

Economic Opportunity: We especially complain against the denial of equal opportunities to us in economic life; in the rural districts of the South this amounts to peonage and virtual slavery; all over the South it tends to crush labor and small business enterprises; and everywhere American prejudice, helped often by iniquitous laws, is making it more difficult for Negro-Americans to earn a decent living.

Education: Common school education should be free to all American children and compulsory. High school training should be adequately provided for all, and college training should be the monopoly of no class or race in any section of our common country. We believe that, in defense of our own institutions, the United States should aid common school education, particularly in the South, and we especially recommend concerted agitation to this end. We urge an increase in public high school facilities in the South, where the Negro-Americans are almost wholly without such provisions. We favor well-equipped trade and technical schools for the training of artisans, and the need of adequate and liberal endowment for a few institutions of higher education must be patent to sincere well-wishers of the race.

Courts: We demand upright judges in courts, juries selected without discrimination on account of color and the same measure of punishment and the same efforts at reformation for black as for white offenders. We need orphanages and farm schools for dependent children, juvenile reformatories for delinquents, and the abolition of the dehumanizing convict-lease system.

Public Opinion: We note with alarm the evident retrogression in this land of sound public opinion on the subject of manhood rights, republican government and human brotherhood, and we pray God that this nation will not degenerate into a mob of boasters and oppressors, but rather will return to the faith of the fathers, that all men were created free and equal, with certain unalienable rights.

Health: We plead for health—for an opportunity to live in decent houses and localities, for a chance to rear our children in physical and moral cleanliness.

Employers and Labor Unions: We hold up for public execration the conduct of two opposite classes of men: The practice among employers of importing ignorant Negro-American laborers in emergencies, and then affording them neither protection nor permanent employment; and the practice of labor unions in proscribing and boycotting and oppressing thousands of their fellow-toilers, simply because they are black. These methods have accentuated and will accentuate the war of labor and capital, and they are disgraceful to both sides.

Protest: We refuse to allow the impression to remain that the Negro-American assents to inferiority, is submissive under oppression and apologetic before insults. Through helplessness we may submit, but the voice of protest of ten million Americans must never cease to assail the ears of their fellows, so long as America is unjust.

Color-Line: Any discrimination based simply on race or color is barbarous, we care not how hallowed it be by custom, expediency or prejudice. Differences made on account of ignorance, immorality, or disease are legitimate methods of fighting evil, and against them we have no word of protest; but discriminations based simply and solely on physical peculiarities, place of birth, color of skin, are relics of that unreasoning human savagery of which the world is and ought to be thoroughly ashamed.

"Jim Crow" Cars: We protest against the "Jim Crow" car, since its effect is and must be to make us pay first-class fare for third-class accommodations, render us open to insults and discomfort and to crucify wantonly our manhood, womanhood and self-respect.

Soldiers: We regret that this nation has never seen fit adequately to reward the black soldiers who, in its five wars, have defended their country with their blood, and yet have been systematically denied the promotions which their abilities deserve. And we regard as unjust, the exclusion of black boys from the military and naval training schools.

War Amendments: We urge upon Congress the enactment of appropriate legislation for securing the proper enforcement of those articles of freedom, the thirteenth, fourteenth and fifteenth amendments of the Constitution of the United States.

Oppression: We repudiate the monstrous doctrine that the oppressor should be the sole authority as to the rights of the oppressed. The negro race in America stolen, ravished and degraded, struggling up through difficulties and oppression, needs sympathy and receives criticism, needs help and is given hindrance, needs protection and is given mob-violence, needs justice and is given charity, needs leadership and is given cowardice and apology, needs bread and is given a stone. This nation will never stand justified before God until these things are changed.

The Church: Especially are we surprised and astonished at the recent attitude of the church of Christ—of an increase of a desire to bow to racial prejudice, to narrow the bounds of human brotherhood, and to segregate black men to some outer sanctuary. This is wrong, unchristian and disgraceful to the twentieth century civilization.

Agitation: Of the above grievances we do not hesitate to complain, and to complain loudly and insistently. To ignore, overlook, or apologize for these wrongs is to prove ourselves unworthy of freedom. Persistent manly agitation is the way to liberty, and toward this goal the Niagara Movement has started and asks the cooperation of all men of all races.

Help: At the same time we want to acknowledge with deep thankfulness the help of our fellowmen from the Abolitionist down to those who today still stand for equal opportunity and who have given and still give of their wealth and of their poverty for our advancement.

Duties: And while we are demanding, and ought to demand, and will continue to demand the rights enumerated above, God forbid that we should ever forget to urge corresponding duties upon our people:

The duty to vote.
The duty to respect the rights of others.
The duty to work.
The duty to obey the laws.
The duty to be clean and orderly.
The duty to send our children to school.
The duty to respect ourselves, even as we respect others.

This statement, complaint and prayer we submit to the American people, and Almighty God.

Source: *Afro-American History: Primary Sources*, ed. Thomas R. Frazier (New York: Harcourt, Brace and World, 1970).

Tuskegee Reacts I: Press Subsidies, 1905–1912

Booker T. Washington made a strong effort to present himself as the spokesman for the race in order to gain concessions from whites. When public opposition from Du Bois and the anti-Bookerites showed that he did not have the full support of the black community, Washington turned to financial support of black newspapers to ensure their loyalty to him. Many supported Washington's ideas already, but since most black papers survived on advertising and operated under constant financial pressure, regular subsidies ensured their continued support and in some cases changed editorial policy. The following seven documents relate to Washington's efforts to control the press and stifle coverage of the opposition. In 1905, Du Bois charged in The Voice of the Negro *that Washington had spent more than $3,000 on press subsidies in the previous year. The charges were undoubtedly true, but without solid evidence, Du Bois could not substantiate them and faced possible charges of libel. It was one more reason for the break between the two men. Washington's private papers reveal that Du Bois was right but also show that controlling the press was not always easy.*

W.E.B. Du Bois to Oswald Garrison Villard, March 24, 1905

(CONFIDENTIAL)

My dear Villard: In reply to your letter of the 13th inst, I am going to burden you with considerable matter. I do this reluctantly because it seems like imposing on a busy man. At the same time I want to say frankly that I have been sorry to feel in your two letters a note of impatience and disbelief which seems to me unfortunate and calling for a clear, even, if long, statement.

In the *Voice of the Negro* for January, I made the charge that $3000 of hush money had been used to subsidize the Negro press in five leading cities. The bases upon which that charge was made were in part as follows:

The offer of $3000 to the editor of the Chicago *Conservator* on 2 separate occasions to change its editorial policy, and the final ousting of the editor by the board of management, and the installing of an editor with the required policy; with the understanding that financial benefit would result. (Exhibit A.) The statement of the former editor of the Washington *Record* that he was given to understand that the *Record* received $40 a month from the outside to maintain its policy. (Exhibit B.)

The statement of one of the assistant editors of the Washington *Colored American* that it was worth to them $500 a year to maintain its policy. (Exhibit C.) There is similar testimony in regard to papers in other cities particularly the *Freeman* of Indianapolis, the *Age* of New York and the *Citizen* of Boston. All these papers follow the same editorial policy, print the same syndicated news, praise the same persons and attack the same persons. Besides the more definite testimony there is a mass (Exhibit D) of corrob[or]ative circumstantial evidence, and all this leads me to estimate that $3000 is certainly the lowest possible estimate of the sums given these 6 papers in the year 1904; I firmly believe that the real sum expended was nearer $5000 and perhaps more than that.

The object of this distribution of money and other favors was, I believe, to stop the attacks being made on the policy of Mr. B. T. Washington. The reason for this belief is as follows:

1. The fact that these papers praise all that Mr. Washington does with suspicious unanimity.
2. The existence of a literary bureau at Tuskegee under Mr. Washington's private secretary, Emmett Scott. (cf. Exhibit B and F. No.2.)
3. The sending out of syndicated matter from the bureau to appear simultaneously in the above mentioned papers and several others. This appears often in the form of editorials. (Exhibit E.)
4. The change of policy toward Mr. Washington of such papers as the *Age*, which formerly bitterly opposed his policy.
[5.] The creation of new papers and buying up of old papers by Mr. Washington's friends or former employees. (Exhibit F.)
[6.] The rewarding of favorable newspapers by Mr. Washington. (Exhibit G.)
[7.] The abuse and warning of enemies through the syndicated papers, sending out of cartoons, etc. (Exhibit H.)
[8.] The use of political patronage to reward and punish.

Finally I was not the first to make this charge. It was common property among colored people, spoken and laughed about and repeatedly charged in the newspapers. (Exhibit J.)

What now ought to be the attitude of thinking Negroes toward this situation, assuming the facts alleged to be substantially true? Two things seem certain:

1. There was some time ago a strong opposition to Mr. Washington's policy developed among Negroes. In many cases this opposition became violent and abusive and in one case even riotous.

2. Since that time by the methods above described and also as the result of conference and statements by Mr. Washington, this opposition has been partially stopped.

Now personally I strongly oppose Mr. Washington's positions: those positions have been considerably modified for the better since the time of my first public dissent from them; but they are still in my mind dangerous and unsatisfactory in many particulars.

At the same time I have been very sorry to see the extremes to which criticism has gone. I anticipated this mud-slinging in my book and deprecated it, although I knew it would come. My rule of criticism has been (a) to impute no bad motives (b) to make no purely personal attack. This has I think been adhered to in every single public utterance of mine on the subject hitherto. And when others have not adhered to it I have not hesitated to criticise them.

Moreover most of the criticism of Mr. Washington by Negro papers has not been violent. The *Conservator* was insistent but courteous; the *Record* under Cromwell was always moderate and saw things both to praise and condemn; The *Freeman* and *American* were open to the highest bidder on either side; the *Guardian* was at times violent although more moderate now than formerly, and has gained in standing as it has become less bitter. All this was a good sign. The air was clearing itself, the demand of the people known, and a healthy democratic out-come of the controversy seemed possible. It seemed at one time indeed possible that even the *Guardian* would see the situation in a better light. Then gradually a change came in. Criticism suddenly stopped in many quarters and fulsome adulation succeeded. Violent attacks on all opposers were printed in a certain set of papers. National organizations of Negroes were "captured" by indefensible methods. (Exhibit K.)

It thus became clearer and clearer to me and to others that the methods of Mr. Washington and his friends to stop violent attack had become a policy for wholesale hushing of all criticism and the crushing out of men who dared to criticise in any way. I felt it time to speak at least a word of warning.

I could not however make this warning as definite as I would have liked for three reasons.

1st. I did not want to drag Atlanta University into the controversy since the proceeding was altogether of my own initiative.

2nd. I did not want to ask those who privately gave me information to do so publicly. They are poor men and if, for instance, Mr. Cromwell, a teacher in the Washington Colored schools, were to testify as to the facts in public he might lose his position.

3rd. I uttered the warning to a Negro audience and it was addressed particularly to them; so far as possible I want to keep the internal struggles of the race in its own ranks. Our dirty linen ought not to be exhibited too much in public.

For this latter reason many of my friends do not agree with me in the policy of speaking out. Kelly Miller, A. H. Grimke and others have repeatedly expressed to me that they are perfectly satisfied that Mr. Washington is furnishing money to Negro newspapers in return for their [the newspapers'] support. But they say: What are you going to do about it? He has the support of the nation, he has the political patronage of the administration, he has apparently unlimited cash, he has the ear of the white press and he is following exactly the methods of that press; and moreover his attitude on the race question is changing for the better. These are powerful arguments, but they do not satisfy me. I am however constrained by such representations to take up the matter cautiously and to see what warnings and aroused conscience in the race will do toward stopping this shameful condition of affairs.

On the other hand when I am convinced that the time has come, that bribery is still going on and gag law manifest, and political bossism saddled on a people advised to let politics alone, I will speak again in no uncertain words and I will prove every statement I make.

I regret to say that honest endeavors on my part in the past to understand and cooperate with Mr. Washington have not been successful. 'I recognize as clearly as anyone the necessity of race unity against a common enemy—but it must be unity against the enemy and not veiled surrender to them.' My attitude is not actuated by my sympathy with Mr. Trotter, editor of the Guardian. There was once a rumor that I was acting jointly with him. My reply to that was made in a letter to George F. Peabody, which I venture to enclose as Exhibit L. I went into conference last winter with Mr. Washington and his friends. Mr. Washington selected the personnel of the conference and it did not altogether please me but I attended and urged such of my friends as were invited to come also. In that conference I did not beat around the bush but told Mr. Washington plainly and frankly the causes of our differences of opinion with him.

Mr. Washington replied in a very satisfactory speech and his friends asked me to draw up a plan of a central committee of 12. This I did. The resulting committee which I helped select was good save in two cases where I was overruled by Mr. Washington and his friend. I was taken ill during the summer and the meeting of the committee was postponed; finally the committee was organized at a meeting to which I was not invited, and of which I knew nothing till 2 weeks afterward. Whether this was by accident or design I do not know. At any rate the committee was so organized as to put the whole power virtually in the hands of an executive committee and the appointment of that committee was left to Mr. Washington. Upon hearing this some two weeks after, I resigned my membership. I could not conscientiously deliver my freedom of thought and action into the hands of Mr. Washington and his special abettors like Fortune.

I am still uncertain as to how Mr. Washington himself ought to be judged in the bribery matter. I especially condemn the bribe-takers and despise men like Fortune, Cooper, Alexander, Manly and Knox who are selling their papers. If they agree with Mr. Washington and he wishes to help them, the contributions ought to be open and above board; and if the contrary is the case and it is, to my unwavering belief, in 3 or 4 of the above instances, these men are scamps. Mr. Washington probably would defend himself by saying that he is unifying the Negro press, that his contributions are investments not bribes, and that the Tuskegee press bureau is a sort of Associated Negro Press. The reply to this is that the transactions do not appear to be thus honorable, that the character of the matter sent out is fulsome in praise of every deed of Mr. Washington's and abusive toward every critic, and that the men who are conducting the enterprises are not the better type of Negroes but in many cases the worst, as in the case of Fortune, Cooper, Knox and Thompson. (Exhibit M.)

In the trying situation in which we Negroes find ourselves today we especially need the aid and countenance of men like you. This may look to outsiders as a petty squabble of thoughtless self-seekers. It is in fact the life and death struggle of nine million men. It is easy of course to dismiss my contentions as the result of petty jealousy or short-sighted criticism—but the ease of the charge does not prove its truth. I know something of the Negro race and its condition and dangers, and while I am sure, and am glad to say, that Mr. Washington has done and is doing much to help the Negro, I just as firmly believe that he represents today in much of his work and policy the greatest of the hindering forces in the line of our true development and uplift. I beg to remain, Very respectfully yours,

W.E.B. Du Bois

Emmett J. Scott to Frederick Randolph Moore, [February 1905]

Personal

Dear Mr. Moore: Dr. Washington has suggested that I write you rather freely as I am sure you would like to have me do, in regard to the February number of the Colored American Magazine. He does not feel that the treatment of the Du Bois matter, page 67, is dignified, and in fact thinks there is altogether too much of Tuskegee in this number, giving vindication to the impression that a great many enemies of the magazine have endeavored to foist on the general public.

Tuskegee appreciates most sincerely all that you and your magazine have done toward helping our work, but we would not for one minute have the magazine interfered with by any too general impression that it is a Tuskegee publication. As a whole, I think the magazine for this month is rather satisfactory. . . .

Emmett J. Scott

Booker T. Washington to Emmett J. Scott, July 17, 1905

Telegraph Thompson and other newspaper men that you can absolutely trust to ignore Niag[a]ra movement Fortune, Anderson and I think this best white papers in the north leave [have] practically ignored it all together.

B.T.W.

Booker T. Washington to Lyman Abbott, September 2, 1906

Personal

My dear Dr. Abbott: . . .

In the last issue of the Outlook I fear you gave too much serious attention to Dr. Du Bois and his movement. I have watched it closely from the beginning. All told I do not believe there are more than two or three hundred colored people of any prominence or influence who are inclined to follow such folly as he is the leader of. The actual attendance at the Harpers Ferry meeting was less than 50. There were at least 600 delegates present at our [National Negro Business League] Atlanta meeting. Yours truly,

BOOKER T. WASHINGTON

Melvin Jack Chisum to Booker T. Washington, February 19, 1906

My dear Dr Washington: Have accomplished my best days work. Mr. Chase [editor of the Washington *Bee*] is printing your Manassas meeting speech, the Business Leag[u]e speech and writing a favorable editorial, such an one as will bring the break we want.

After all, I find him a rather tame—though dangerous I'm sure—proposition. I have found a way to stave off any probable loss of his confidence to a most remote date.

Now! The Bee will be a surprise to everybody that knows it the forthcoming week and the war is on between his highness bub Trotter and bub Chase. Are you willing that I remain here for a couple of weeks and make shure of Chase's broadsides being properly directed so as to part them beyond the point of repair, or reconnection? I know Trotter will fire on the Bee, and I think I ought to be in the con[n]ing tower with Chase when he does. . . .

Faithfully your humble servant,

CHISUM

Booker T. Washington to Melvin Jack Chisum, February 24, 1906

My dear Mr. Chisum: I have received both of your letters and am most grateful to you for what you have done. It seems that you have accomplished good results. I shall be in New York in March and shall see you. Yours truly,

BOOKER T. WASHINGTON

William Calvin Chase to Booker T. Washington, April 17, 1912

My dear Dr. Washington: Some months ago, I suggested to you the importance of your friends in office, in this city, assisting "The Bee" financially. You stated that you would see Mr. Tyler, and have them to make such contributions that would keep the paper from being embarrassed financially. This has been about two years ago. Mr. Tyler himself had been contributing twenty-dollars per month, out of his own pocket, and the paper was being used for the defense of everybody connected with you, as well as your self. Mr. Cobb, however informed me, that seven persons including himself, were contributing a prorato [*sic*] share of the twenty dollars which was not a drop in the bucket, considering their salaries, and the expense I have to under go to run "The Bee."

About a month ago Mr. Tyler informed me that the twenty-dollars, which he was contributing had to be discontinued.

Now while I appreciate what you have endeavored to do for me, and what your friends, have done, I want to be frank, by informing you that I, cannot allow "The Bee" to be used any longer for their personal use without receiving some benefits. When I informed Mr. Tyler what I thought of it, he stated: "Well you know they have to live," as if to say it makes no difference whether I live or not. You will remember that I asked for a place for my son in school or elsewhere, and a small place for the manager of "The Bee" both have been promised a year ago. With assistance in this direction, I could have been of great benefit to you and your friends. Places can be made for everybody else except your loyal friend, and those who could be serviceable to you. Mr. Tyler is about the only person that has made any kind of disposition to help you or me. Cobb would do if he could.

I thought it best to inform you, because you are no doubt of the opinion, or have been of the opinion that your friends were contributing liberally to the paper. I cannot continue to be used for the benefit of others, and receive no consideration. With but "ONE EXCEPTION" you have the weakest set of supporters in office that I would want to meet. All they think about is SELF and don't give a continental whether others sink or swim.

I know you will appreciate this frank and honest statement because, you know I have been loyal and true to you, but under the circumstances, I shall be constrained to seek assistance from other sources. Gratefully yours,

WM. CALVIN CHASE

Source: *Booker T. Washington Papers*, ed. Louis R. Harlan and Raymond Smock (Urbana: University of Illinois Press, 1972–83).

Tuskegee Reacts II: Spies and Patronage, 1904–1907

Although Washington's dealings with the black press were far from aboveboard, they were not the worst of his tactics. His network of supporters across the country, of whom many shared his political views and others owed their political careers to his influence, were often overeager in their willingness to serve the Wizard of Tuskegee. Nonetheless, they usually had Washington's blessing. By far the most powerful of these lieutenants was Charles W. Anderson, whom Theodore Roosevelt had appointed Collector of Internal Revenue for the Wall Street District of New York because of Washington's support. Anderson made it his priority to ensure that anyone who opposed Washington regretted his choice; Niagarites lost their reputations and their jobs as a result of his activities. Melvin Jack Chisum, who arranged press subsidies for the Washington Bee, *was a different kind of ally: an ardent admirer of Washington and short on cash, he set himself the task of spying on the opposition for Tuskegee. Chisum loved secrecy and the sense of importance he gained from his contact with Washington. The following six letters reveal the extent to which Tuskegee supporters would go to help the Wizard beat the opposition.*

Charles W. Anderson to Booker T. Washington, January 26, 1904

My dear Dr. Washington: I beg leave to hand you herewith a clipping from the Boston Guardian relative to Industrialism. . . . I think you will ultimately conclude to come around to my proposition of "smoking out" these fellows. I may be wrong, but I am strongly of the opinion that there are but two ways of meeting opposition; one is by submission, and the other is by resistance. Now, resistance does not necessarily mean violence or force. *It far more frequently means the display of that spirit which satisfies your opponent that opposition is not safe.* My experience in politics is, that, he is whipped oftenest who is whipped easiest, and I long ago made up my mind to give my opponent the very best I have in my shop, when he sets himself the task of fighting me. The opposition to you and your work, is confined to a little coterie of men who have graduated from some of the best Universities of the country,—*and have done nothing else.* A good thrashing would convince these young upstarts, with their painful assumption of superior intellectuality, that they had better spend their time in some less dangerous occupation. This is merely my opinion, and I pass it on for what it is worth.

I want to thank you again for that nice box of cheese, and assure you that I shall enjoy it with much gratitude to you. Perhaps after all, you had better burn this letter, that you may the more surely remember its tenor. By and by, you may think it more sensible than it now appears to be. Let me hear from you, when you have time, and advise me definitely when you conclude to make another visit to the North. Yours faithfully,

CHARLES W. ANDERSON

Melvin J. Chisum to Booker T. Washington, October 1, 1904

Dear Dr. Washington: . . . This much I beg you, if ever you *need* a real genuine piece of steel send for me, *I am not a recent convert to the principles of the Wizard of Tuskegee*, I am an original Booker Washingtonite; was born reared and raised in *Texas*, and may I be pardoned for saying, that nature in putting me together forgot to put in fear.

I have accomplished a long line of failures for my self but *never once*, have I *failed* in an undertaking for a friend.

You have proven to be the only man the race has, who is actually working for the race, and millions of us love you, worship your name and accept your counsel in the fullest measure.

The few unfortunates who do not are weaklings, half crazy or something, and we pitty them. . . .

From your obedient humble servant,

MELVIN J. CHISUM

Charles W. Anderson to Booker T. Washington, March 5, 1906

My dear Doctor: . . . Relative to our man Chisum, I want to advise you that you have left an awful load on my hands. He has been to me for money five times since you left the city, and got it four times. On the fifth visit I informed him that I could not meet his wishes. The trouble with him is that he has made up his mind not to work, and expects to live by borrowing. I think I shall have to fall out with him before you come back, so be prepared to hear of a break. He is a much too expensive luxury for me. I will, however, try to grin and bear it, but if I break down before you return here, don't be surprised.

Please let me know just when you expect to be in this city again. Yours truly,

CHARLES W. ANDERSON

Booker T. Washington to Charles W. Anderson, March 8, 1906

PERSONAL

My dear Mr. Anderson: . . . I hope you will not worry with Brother Chisum. I hope that he will be fat and with a full purse by the time I reach New York City. Seriously, I had to telegraph him to leave Washington because I found him entirely too expensive.

It is my present plan to be in New York on the 14th to stay a few days. Don't tell Chisum. . . . Yours very truly,

[BOOKER T. WASHINGTON]

Melvin J. Chisum to Booker T. Washington, March 21, 1906

Dear Dr. Washington: I have been thinking of a plan that will give me the freest possible movement and yet keep the name Chisum out of the papers, in case you decide to send me to do the Chicago work.

My plan: I will assume an other name; get about with all the people; give my business as a waiter and get a *dinner job* to prove the claim.

Dinner men, in the large restaurants and cafes work from 11 to 3 p.m. each day and some work from 3 p.m. to 12 midnight—I will get on the 11 a.m. to 3 p.m. job for that will allow me sufficient time to do my work.

I am certain I can do this work in that way for I am not known in Chicago.

No one would have any interest in Jack Cameron a waiter, just doing what he could to move in decent society and keep soul and body together with the aid of a pan.

I will observe your instruction and keep my name out of the papers and will, I assure you, get all the information you need. I remain Faithfully yours

Melvin Chisum

X

Jack Cameron

Unless you suggest a different name, which I will be glad to have you do if you like.

Charles W. Anderson to Booker T. Washington, May 27, 1907

(Personal) *Private & Confidential*

My dear Doctor: Following up my telegram of last Saturday, I beg to say, that I told "our friend" [Theodore Roosevelt] that, in my judgment, it was time we took some action against the people who are inspiring these newspaper attacks, and informed him that the man in the Interior Department [Lafayette M. Hershaw] was the leading spirit among them. I said that I felt that he would come to his senses if a reduction in rank should happen to take place, or if that was impossible, a transfer to some very hard and disagreeable service. I then asked him to give me a letter to Secretary Garfield, whereupon he sat down and penned the following note with his own hand:

"Dear Garfield:

Mr. Anderson is one of our very best friends. You can talk absolutely, freely to him, as he is a safe man to follow.

Signed."

I took the note over to Mr. Garfield, who received me most cordially and agreed with me, that the course I suggested ought to be pursued. He sent for his Secretary and had him look up the exact position occupied by the man in question and made a note of it. . . . He promised to find some way to do exactly what I requested. If reduction could not be accomplished, then a transfer to something hard and disagreeable is the plan. I think the thing will be clinched if you will write him at once, assuring him that *there is no doubt that this particular man is the head devil.* Of course I said nothing about the man's attitude toward you, but contented myself with showing up his attitude toward the present administration. . . . I may add that the Secretary treated me with much consideration.

"Our friend" asked me to see Secretary Taft and talk over the artillery matter. I called at the War Department and sent in your letter and was immediately shown into the Secretary's private office. . . . I then told him that I had noticed an advertisement of a mass meeting . . . to protest against the consideration of Taft's name for the Presidency. The Secretary at once set up and began to take notice. Seeing that he was concerned about the protestants, I then told him that this thing would go on as long as men in the government service secretly aided and inspired this opposition. I told him all about the man in the Interior Department, and then reminded him that he had one such in his own Department—by the name of [F.H.M.] Murray. I told him what I thought his friends ought to do with people of this sort, and how quickly this thing would end, if once the kickers were convinced that it was unsafe to be engaged in this sort of work. I would not be surprised to learn in the near future that Murray was having a hard row to hoe. From this you will see that I had rather a successful day of it. . . . Yours truly,

CHARLES W. ANDERSON

Source: *Booker T. Washington Papers*, ed. Louis R. Harlan and Raymond Smock (Urbana: University of Illinois Press, 1972–83).

Washington and Du Bois React to the Atlanta Riot, 1906

In the wake of the Atlanta race riot of September 22, 1906, Washington issued an editorial asking blacks to be patient and to create a committee of the "best" blacks and whites in the city to discuss race relations. By then, however, blacks were too frustrated by continuing discrimination and too convinced that whites would never grant them equality to listen. When northern whites blamed the riots on black crime, many African Americans felt betrayed. Washington's continued call for moderation seemed increasingly out of touch with reality; Du Bois's moving poem, "A Litany to Atlanta," captured the emotions of many blacks far better. In it, he sought justice from God and lamented the many outrages committed against blacks. He also expressed his anguish about the fate of Atlanta itself, the city he had called home since 1898. Like his "Credo," Du Bois's "Litany" was distributed widely and went through multiple reprints.

Booker T. Washington to the Editor of the
New York World, September 25, 1906

BOOKER T. WASHINGTON ADVISES
COLORED RACE NOT TO RETALIATE
HE URGES THE BEST WHITE PEOPLE
AND THE BEST COLORED PEOPLE TO
MEET IN COUNCIL AND ENDEAVOR TO
STOP DISORDER

To the Editor of The World: As a rule I never discuss the matter of mob violence except when I am in the South, but in this case I make an exception.

In answer to your request, I will state that in my address in Atlanta to the National Negro Business League, a few days ago, I spoke plainly against the crime of assaulting women and of resorting to lynching and mob law as a remedy for any evil. I feel the present situation too deeply to give any extended utterance at this time, except to say that I would strongly urge that the best white people and the best colored people come together in council and use their united efforts to stop the present disorder.

I would especially urge the colored people in Atlanta and elsewhere to exercise self-control and not make the fatal mistake of attempting to retaliate, but to rely upon the efforts of the proper authorities to bring order and security out of confusion. If they do this they will have the sympathy of good people the world over.

Let me repeat that wherever I have met them, without exception, I have found the leading colored people as much opposed to crime as the leading white people; but what is needed now is to get the best element of both races together and try to change the present deplorable condition of affairs. We of both races must learn that the inflexible enforcement of the laws against all criminals is indispensable, and in this I will do my utmost to have my race co-operate.

The Atlanta outbreak should not discourage our people, but should teach a lesson from which all can profit. And we should bear in mind also that while there is disorder in one community there is peace and harmony in thousands of others. As a colored man I cannot refrain from expressing a feeling of very deep grief on account of the death of so many innocent men of both races because of the deeds of a few despicable criminals.

BOOKER T. WASHINGTON

Source: *Booker T. Washington Papers*, ed. Louis R. Harlan and Raymond Smock (Urbana: University of Illinois Press, 1972–83).

A Litany of Atlanta, by W. E. Burghardt Du Bois. Done at Atlanta, in the Day of Death, 1906

O Silent God, Thou whose voice afar in mist and mystery hath left our ears a-hungered in these fearful days —

Hear us, good Lord!

Listen to us, Thy children: our faces dark with doubt are made a mockery in Thy Sanctuary. With uplifted hands we front Thy Heaven, O God, crying:

We beseech Thee to hear us, good Lord!

We are not better than our fellows, Lord; we are but weak and human men. When our devils do deviltry, curse Thou the doer and the deed,—curse them as we curse them, do to them all and more than ever they have done to innocence and weakness, to womanhood and home.

Have mercy upon us, miserable sinners!

And yet, whose is the deeper guilt? Who made these devils? Who nursed them in crime and fed them on injustice? Who ravished and debauched their mothers and their grandmothers? Who bought and sold their crime and waxed fat and rich on public iniquity?

Thou knowest, good God!

Is this Thy Justice, O Father, that guile be easier than innocence and the innocent be crucified for the guilt of the untouched guilty?

Justice, O Judge of men!

Wherefore do we pray? Is not the God of the Fathers dead? Have not seers seen in Heaven's halls Thine hearsed and lifeless form stark amidst the black and rolling smoke of sin, where all along bow bitter forms of endless dead?

Awake, Thou that sleepest!

Thou art not dead, but flown afar, up hills of endless light, through blazing corridors of suns, where worlds do swing of good and gentle men, of women strong and free—far from the cozenage, black hypocrisy and chaste prostitution of this shameful speck of dust!

Turn again, O Lord; leave us not to perish in our sin!
From lust of body and lust of blood,—
Great God, deliver us!
From lust of power and lust of gold,—
Great God, deliver us!
From the leagued lying of despot and of brute,—
Great God, deliver us!

A city lay in travail, God our Lord, and from her loins sprang twin Murder and Black Hate. Red was the midnight; clang, crack, and cry of death and fury filled the air and trembled underneath the stars where church spires pointed silently to Thee. And all this was to sate the greed of greedy men who hide behind the veil of vengeance!

Bend us Thine ear, O Lord!

In the pale, still morning we looked upon the deed. We stopped our ears and held our leaping hands, but they—did they not wag their heads and leer and cry with bloody jaws: *Cease from Crime!* The word was mockery, for thus they train a hundred crimes while we do cure one.

Turn again our captivity, O Lord!

Behold this maimed and broken thing, dear God; it was an humble black man, who toiled and sweat to save a bit from the pittance paid him. They told him: *Work and Rise!* He worked. Did this man sin? Nay, but someone told how someone said another did—one whom he had never seen nor known. Yet for that man's crime this man lieth maimed and murdered, his wife naked to shame, his children to poverty and evil.

Hear us, O heavenly Father!

Doth not this justice of hell stink in Thy nostrils, O God? How long shall the mounting flood of innocent blood roar in Thine ears and pound in our hearts for vengeance? Pile the pale frenzy of blood-crazed brutes, who do such deeds, high on Thine altar, Jehovah Jireh, and burn it in hell forever and forever!

Forgive us, good Lord; we know not what we say!

Bewildered we are and passion-tossed, mad with the madness of a mobbed and mocked and murdered people; straining at the armposts of Thy throne, we raise our shackled hands and charge Thee, God, by the bones of our stolen fathers, by the tears of our dead mothers, by the very blood of Thy crucified Christ: *What meaneth this?* Tell us the plan; give us the sign!

Keep not thou silent, O God!

Sit not longer blind, Lord God, deaf to our prayer and dumb to our dumb suffering. Surely Thou, too, art not white, O Lord, a pale, bloodless, heartless thing!

Ah! Christ of all the Pities!

Forgive the thought! Forgive these wild, blasphemous words! Thou art still the God of our black fathers and in Thy Soul's Soul sit some soft darkenings of the evening, some shadowings of the velvet night.

But whisper—speak—call, great God, for Thy silence is white terror to our hearts! The way, O God, show us the way and point us the path!

Whither? North is greed and South is blood; within, the coward, and without, the liar. Whither? To death?

Amen! Welcome, dark sleep!

Whither? To life? But not this life, dear God, not this. Let the cup pass from us, tempt us not beyond our strength, for there is that clamoring and clawing within, to whose voice we would not listen, yet shudder lest we must,—and it is red. Ah! God! It is a red and awful shape.

Selah!

In yonder East trembles a star.

Vengeance is mine; I will repay, saith the Lord!

Thy will, O Lord, be done!

Kyrie Eleison!

Lord, we have done these pleading, wavering words.

We beseech Thee to hear us, good Lord!

We bow our heads and hearken soft to the sobbing of women and little children.

We beseech Thee to hear us, good Lord!

Our voices sink in silence and in night.

Hear us, good Lord!

In night, O God of a godless land!

Amen!

In silence, O Silent God.

Selah!

Source: *Independent*, October 11, 1906.

An Open Letter

In 1910 wealthy patrons arranged a European tour for Washington, who was overworked and in poor health. He visited farms and gave lectures repeating his old message that there were no fundamental race problems in America. In response, Du Bois wrote this letter for circulation in Europe, and he and twenty-two other prominent African Americans signed it, including Archibald Grimké and William Monroe Trotter. But Du Bois wrote the letter on the National Negro Committee letterhead (the NAACP first organized in 1910 under that name), which caused friction between him and the board members, who felt that his statements were not representative of the organization's beliefs. In the aftermath of this incident, he had to issue another public letter to emphasize that the views in the first letter were those of private citizens, not of the NAACP. The dispute foreshadowed Du Bois's later problems with the board while he was editor of The Crisis.

W.E.B. Du Bois et al., An Open Letter to the People of Great Britain and Europe, October 26, 1910

To the People of Great Britain and Europe: The undersigned Negro-Americans have heard, with great regret, the recent attempt to assure England and Europe that their condition in America is satisfactory. They sincerely wish that such were the case, but it becomes their plain duty to say that if Mr. Booker T. Washington, or any other person, is giving the impression abroad that the Negro problem in America is in process of satisfactory solution, he is giving an impression which is not true. We say this without personal bitterness toward Mr. Washington. He is a distinguished American and has a perfect right to his opinions. But we are compelled to point out that Mr. Washington's large financial responsibilities have made him dependent on the rich charitable public and that, for this reason, he has for years been compelled to tell, not the whole truth, but that part of it which certain powerful interests in America wish to appear as the whole truth. In flat contradiction, however, to the pleasant pictures thus pointed out, let us not forget that the consensus of opinion among eminent European scholars who know the race problem in America. . . . is that it forms the gravest of American problems. We black men who live and suffer under present conditions, and who have no reason, and refuse to accept reasons, for silence, can substantiate this unanimous testimony. . . .

Today in eight states where the bulk of the Negroes live, black men of property and university training can be, and usually are, by law denied the ballot, while the most ignorant white man votes. . . . Along with this has gone a systematic attempt to curtail the education

Du Bois at work in the office of *The Crisis*, the NAACP's official journal, around 1910. *Courtesy of the Schomburg Center for Research in Black Culture, The New York Public Library*

of the black race. Under a widely advertised system of "universal" education, not one black boy in three today has in the United States a chance to learn to read and write. . . . In every walk of life we meet discrimination based solely on race and color, but continually and persistently misrepresented to the world as the natural difference due to condition. We are, for instance, usually forced to live in the worst quarters, and our consequent death-rate is noted as a race trait, and reason for further discrimination. . . . We are forced to take lower wages for equal work, and our standard of living is then criticised. Fully half the labor unions refuse us admittance, and then claim that as "scabs" we lower the price of labor. . . . Our women in the South are without protection in law and custom, and are then derided as lewd. . . . Against this dominant tendency strong and brave Americans, white and black are fighting, but they need, and need sadly, the moral support of England and of Europe in this crusade for the recognition of manhood, despite adventitious differences of race, and it is like a blow in the face to have one, who himself suffers daily insult and humiliation in America, give the impression that all is well. It is one thing to be optimistic, self-forgetful and forgiving, but it is quite a different thing, consciously or unconsciously, to misrepresent the truth.

Source: *Booker T. Washington Papers*, ed. Louis R. Harlan and Raymond Smock (Urbana: University of Illinois Press, 1972–83).

BIBLIOGRAPHICAL ESSAY

The purpose of this bibliography is to outline the major sources that I have used in writing this account and to provide students with an idea of where to go first to find out more information. I have tried to include sources that are both representative of different perspectives and easily understood. Some of these books are classics, some are less famous, but all provide additional information about subjects I could touch upon only briefly in this work.

The major sources on Washington and Du Bois are undoubtedly their most thorough biographies. Louis R. Harlan's two volumes, *Booker T. Washington: The Making of a Black Leader, 1856–1901* (1972) and *Booker T. Washington: The Wizard of Tuskegee, 1901–1915* (1983), are classics as well as Bancroft and Pulitzer Prize–winning books. David Levering Lewis's two volumes, *W.E.B. Du Bois: Biography of a Race, 1868–1919* (1993) and *W.E.B. Du Bois: The Fight for Equality and the American Century, 1919–1963* (2000), which also won the Pulitzer, are destined to become classics. Both Lewis and Harlan have written definitive biographies based on exhaustive research. More important, they both explain the context of their subjects' lives.

Washington and Du Bois each wrote several important autobiographical accounts. Booker T. Washington's *Story of My Life and Work* (1900) is badly flawed; he had little to do with the writing of the book until it was too late to change the many errors. He hired a more reliable ghostwriter to assist with his second autobiography, *Up from Slavery* (1901), and wrote most of the work himself. This book is one of the few sources of information we have on Washington's childhood and early life, although, as Harlan points out, he may have distorted some of the truth in order to please his white audience or to conform to standard criteria for autobiography. His third autobiography, *Working with the Hands* (1904), was largely a sequel to *Up from Slavery*. None of Washington's autobiographies discusses his behind-the-scenes fight against segregation and disfranchisement, his treatment of his enemies, or the battle with Du Bois.

Du Bois's autobiographical accounts begin in *The Souls of Black Folk* (1903) with chapters on his childhood and his experiences teaching in Tennessee. They continue in slightly more detail in *Darkwater: Voices from within the Veil* (1920) with hints of events in his later life. His first full autobiography was *Dusk of Dawn: An Essay toward an Autobiography of a Race Concept* (1940), in which he discusses the details of the debate with Washington. In his final years, Du Bois felt a need to set the record straight again with *The Autobiography of W.E.B. Du Bois: A Soliloquy on Viewing My Life from the Last Decade of Its First Century* (written in 1958–59 but first published in the United States in 1968, after his death). In part, he wished to add more details of his later life; in part, he had become willing to admit more personal indiscretions from his youth. Probably his most important reason for writing this final autobiography was that some of his old views on Africa and imperialism as well as race relations were not compatible with his newer socialist ideals, and he wanted to comment on how wrong he had been in his earlier beliefs. It was his way of recanting the "heresies" for which Marxists had criticized him over the years.

Aside from the autobiographies, probably the best way to understand the real men is to read their published correspondence. Marxist historian Herbert Aptheker, friend of Du Bois, collected and published most of the previously unpublished essays and letters in a three-volume set, *The Correspondence of W.E.B. Du Bois* (1973–78), which provides valuable background for each letter; volume 1 covers the years 1877–1934. Louis R. Harlan and Raymond W. Smock took on the mammoth task of editing Washington's correspondence for publication as *The Booker T. Washington Papers* in fourteen volumes (1972–1987). His papers had lain for years in disarray in the Library of Congress, and before Harlan began work on them, very few people knew about Washington's secret life. I highlight the significance of this work by contrasting it with a 1955 biography of Washington by Samuel R. Spencer Jr., who had only begun to skim through some of the nearly 2,000 boxes and commented, "Even so, the Papers are rewarding . . . for the glimpses of Washington as he was when, in rare instances, he let down his guard; they indicate that Washington . . . was essentially the same man he was believed to be on the basis of public knowledge."* Without the efforts of Harlan and Smock, we might still take Washington at his public word.

Several earlier biographies of Washington are interesting, although incomplete. His former personal secretary, Emmett J. Scott, with the aid of Lyman Beecher Stowe, wrote one of the first: *Booker T. Washington: Builder of a Civilization*, published in 1916. Not surprisingly, it is a highly flattering account. Others that came out at the time of his death are not particularly useful. Probably the first biography to be based on substantial research is Basil Mathews, *Booker T. Washington, Educator and Interpreter* (1948), but as a Tuskegee-authorized work it is mostly uncritical. Samuel Spencer's 1955 biography, quoted above, is likewise far from the complete story and largely positive, although Spencer does objectively evaluate Washington's philosophies and is willing to criticize some of his faults. The only other full-length biography to appear before Harlan's is Bernard Weisberger's *Booker T. Washington* (1972).

Post-Harlan, a series of essays have placed Washington in the larger context of black leaders and racial uplift philosophy, including John White, *Black Leadership in America: From Booker T. Washington to Jesse Jackson* (1985; 2d ed. 1990); and Manning Marable, *Black Leadership: Four Great American Leaders and the Struggle for Civil Rights* (1998); both devote essays also to Du Bois. Adam Fairclough's *Better Day Coming: Blacks and Equality* (2001) dedicates a chapter to each man. In 1995, the one hundredth anniversary of the Atlanta Compromise speech, there were many events at which scholars attempted to reevaluate Washington's image, as there were in 2001, the one hundredth anniversary of *Up from Slavery*. These discussions may lead to new scholarship.

Several valuable biographies of Du Bois were published before Lewis's work. Unlike Washington's, Du Bois's secrets were generally personal (such as the nature of his relationships with women) and

---

*Samuel R. Spencer Jr., *Booker T. Washington and the Negro's Place in American Life* (Boston: Little, Brown and Company, 1955), 205.

have not substantially affected the way scholars interpret his views and actions. In addition, Du Bois's extensive autobiographical writing left little to hide. The first full-length biography, Francis L. Broderick's *W.E.B. Du Bois: Negro Leader in a Time of Crisis* (1959), in fact, takes him to task for trying to tell scholars too much. Broderick argues that although the man does deserve respect for his public insistence on civil rights when few others spoke out, Du Bois's image is largely a myth of his own creation. He claims that Du Bois's philosophies were far from original, that he was simply "the first among equals" of the anti-Bookerites, but that his outliving all the rest—combined with Du Bois's assertions of his own importance—strengthened his claim to leadership. Elliott Rudwick's *W.E.B. Du Bois: Voice of the Black Protest Movement* (1960) paints Du Bois as in conflict not only with other leaders but also within his own philosophies, both integrationist and nationalist. According to Rudwick, Du Bois claimed race leadership, much like Washington, and yet never tried to understand what the race really wanted.

Four other biographical studies of Du Bois deserve attention. In 1970 the editors of *Freedomways*, a magazine devoted to civil rights issues, published an anthology of essays titled *Black Titan: W.E.B. Du Bois*. It includes both scholarly and personal interpretations as well as tributes from such notables as Kwame Nkrumah, president of the Republic of Ghana; Harlem Renaissance poet Langston Hughes; NAACP leader Roy Wilkins; and Martin Luther King Jr. The second study is Shirley Graham Du Bois's *His Day Is Marching On: A Memoir of W.E.B. Du Bois* (1971), written by his second wife. Third, Arnold Rampersad's *The Art and Imagination of W.E.B. Du Bois* (1976) focuses largely on Du Bois's writings, especially his novels and poetry, and concludes that he was a visionary who had to spend most of his time dealing with conflict rather than pursuing his visions. Finally, Manning Marable's *W.E.B. Du Bois: Black Radical Democrat* (1986), using such terms as "Stern Prophet, Flaming Angel," sees Du Bois as a leader later in life when he turned to socialist visions for solutions, and regards his identification with the oppressed as his key contribution to the race. More recently, Raymond Wolter, *Du Bois and His Rivals* (2002), addresses his disputes throughout his life.

Several scholars have focused on Du Bois's intellectual development rather than on biographical details. Shamoon Zamir, *Dark Voices: W.E.B. Du Bois and American Thought, 1888–1903* (1995), studies him in the larger context of American and European social science and traces his move into sociology. Two collections of essays address Du Bois's sociological work and its impact. First, *W.E.B. Du Bois, Race, and the City: "The Philadelphia Negro" and Its Legacy*, ed. Michael B. Katz and Thomas J Sugrue (1998), provides background and discusses Du Bois's work in its intellectual and Philadelphia contexts, then follows up on black Philadelphia since the study was published. A special issue of *Boundary 2: An International Journal of Literature and Culture* (Fall 2000), titled "Sociology Hesitant: Thinking with W.E.B. Du Bois," examines a series of Du Bois's writings between 1887 and 1910 that deal with the practice of sociology, its theory and methodology. With the hundredth anniversary of the publication of *The Souls of Black Folk* in 2003, scholars have begun to reexamine Du Bois's writings. Chester J. Fontenot Jr. and Mary Alice Morgan have edited *W.E.B. Du Bois and Race: Essays Celebrating the Centennial Publication of the Souls of Black Folk* (2002) based on papers given at a symposium on the subject; Stanley Crouch and Playthell Benjamin have coauthored *Reconsidering the Souls of Black Folk: Thoughts on the Groundbreaking Classic Work* (2002); and Dolan Hubbard has edited *The Souls of Black Folk: One Hundred Years Later* (2003), a collection of essays from a variety of disciplines that show how the book has influenced teaching practices and intellectual discourse.

    Placing Washington and Du Bois in their larger context requires more than just an examination of the autobiographical and biographical literature. Aside from textbooks that give an overview of American and African American history in this period, there are several important works that give more specific context for the debate between the two men. The oldest but probably most influential in shaping scholars' interpretations is C. Vann Woodward's *The Strange Career of Jim Crow* (1955), which was the first to examine the rise of segregation in the South in the late 1890s. He originally concluded that Jim Crow was not an outgrowth of slavery but something new, arguing that from Reconstruction to the 1890s, blacks and whites mingled freely. In light of subsequent scholarship, as it became clear that in fact there had been customary segregation long before legal segregation, Woodward revised his conclusions. The third edition (1974), therefore, remains the best statement of his views and is still a classic. One of those scholars who challenged Woodward's earlier interpretation is Howard N. Rabinowitz, whose *Race Relations in the Urban South, 1865–1890* (1978) has itself become a standard work on urban race relations and provides a good context for understanding Washington's philosophies.

Rabinowitz suggests that a younger generation of blacks who had not known slavery and who pushed for more social and political equality may, in fact, have prompted southerners to legalize what older blacks understood to be the rules.

Leon Litwack's *Trouble in Mind: Black Southerners in the Age of Jim Crow* (1998) focuses on increased violence against blacks, particularly lynchings, and examines changing racial attitudes. For more on lynchings, see the collection of essays edited by W. Fitzhugh Brundage, *Under Sentence of Death: Lynching in the South* (1997); Jacqueline Jones Royster, *Southern Horrors and Other Writings: The Anti-Lynching Campaign of Ida B. Wells, 1892–1900* (1997); and Stewart Emory Tolnay and E. M. Beck, *A Festival of Violence: An Analysis of the Lynching of African-Americans in the American South, 1882–1930* (1995).

The standard for examining racial philosophies at the turn of the century remains August Meier's *Negro Thought in America, 1880–1915* (1963), which surprisingly, while setting up the fundamental issues of the era, anticipates more recent scholarship on alternative methods of racial uplift. Although most historians have not disagreed with Meier's interpretations, scholars have begun to place more emphasis on the idea that black leaders practiced racial uplift largely as a way to boost their own social status, rather than out of real concern for the plight of the masses. Kevin K. Gaines, in particular, in *Uplifting the Race: Black Leadership, Politics, and Culture in the Twentieth Century* (1996), takes to task the black elite—including Du Bois—for imposing white Victorian standards of morality on the black working classes and essentially accepting middle-class white society's views of African Americans. The article "W.E.B. Du Bois, German Social Thought, and the Racial Divide in American Progressivism, 1892–1909" by Axel R. Schäfer, in the December 2001 issue of the *Journal of American History*, argues that Du Bois's views on race basically reflected German social scientists' views, which he absorbed at the University of Berlin. Scholars such as Schäfer and Gaines argue that Du Bois's insistence on the special contributions of blacks to civilization was no more accurate than white's insistence that blacks were inferior.

That argument is not new, however, as is particularly evident in the scholarship on the black nationalist movement of the late nineteenth and early twentieth centuries. The major sources are Edwin S. Redkey, *Black Exodus: Black Nationalist and Back-to-Africa Movements, 1890–1910* (1969); and Wilson Jeremiah Moses, *The Golden*

Age of Black Nationalism, 1850–1925 (1978). Redkey provides a chronology of the movement, and Moses analyzes the ideology of nationalist leaders. Both emphasize that few African American or white emigrationists had any real understanding of Africa and that their attempts to "civilize" the continent were more about their own problems than about the Africans. Among more specialized books on nationalism, Hollis R. Lynch, *Edward Wilmot Blyden: Pan-Negro Patriot, 1832–1912* (1967); a second book by Moses, *Alexander Crummell: A Study of Civilization and Discontent* (1989); and Stephen Ward Angell, *Henry McNeal Turner and African-American Religion in the South* (1992), give more details on the lives of nationalist leaders. William E. Bittle and Gilbert Geis, *The Longest Way Home: Chief Alfred C. Sam's Back-to-Africa Movement* (1964), focuses on the emigration movement among blacks in Oklahoma and Arkansas.

A number of biographies of other black leaders offer good alternative perspectives on black life at the turn of the century. Among these are William S. McFeely, *Frederick Douglass* (1991); Dickson D. Bruce Jr., *Archibald Grimké: Portrait of a Black Independent* (1993); Stephen R. Fox, *The Guardian of Boston: William Monroe Trotter* (1970); Emma Lou Thornbrough, *T. Thomas Fortune: Militant Journalist* (1972); Jacqueline Goggins, *Carter G. Woodson: A Life in Black History* (1993); Louise Daniel Hutchinson, *Anna J. Cooper: A Voice from the South* (1981); Patricia Ann Schechter, *Ida B. Wells-Barnett and American Reform, 1880–1930* (2001); and Beverly Washington Jones, *Quest for Equality: The Life and Writings of Mary Eliza Church Terrell, 1863–1954* (1990). Wells-Barnett and Terrell also wrote autobiographies: *Crusade for Justice: The Autobiography of Ida B. Wells*, ed. Alfreda M. Duster (1970), and Terrell's *A Colored Woman in a White World* (1940). For information on Blanche K. Bruce and P.B.S. Pinchback, see Howard N. Rabinowitz's edited collection, *Southern Black Leaders of the Reconstruction Era* (1982). In addition, John Hope Franklin and August Meier's edited collection of essays in *Black Leaders of the Twentieth Century* (1982) covers Washington, Du Bois, Fortune, Wells-Barnett, and Marcus Garvey.

In the 1990s there was a resurgence of interest in the black elite and their involvement in racial uplift debates. Willard Gatewood was the first to publish a broad analysis in *Aristocrats of Color: The Black Elite, 1880–1920* (1990). Local studies that followed include Fon Louise Gordon's *Caste and Class: The Black Experience in Arkansas, 1880–1920* (1995); Jacqueline M. Moore's *Leading the Race: The Black Elite* in the Nation's Capital, 1880–1920 (1999); and Lynne B. Feldman's *A Sense of Place: Birmingham's Black Middle-Class Community, 1890–1930* (1999). These books examine the social distinctions within the black community and the ways in which black leaders first tried to assimilate to white culture and then protested discrimination.

The literature on alternative methods of uplift is expanding each year. Paula Giddings paved the way for scholarship concerning the women's club movement with *When and Where I Enter: The Impact of Black Women on Race and Sex in America* (1984). That book was followed by Cynthia Neverdon-Morton, *Afro-American Women of the South and the Advancement of the Race, 1895–1925* (1989); Dorothy Salem, *To Better Our World: Black Women in Organized Reform, 1890–1920* (1990); Rosalyn Terborg-Penn, *African American Women in the Struggle for the Vote, 1850–1920* (1998); and Evelyn Brooks-Higgenbotham, *Righteous Discontent: The Women's Movement in the Black Baptist Church, 1880–1920* (1993). For more on the black church, see William E. Montgomery, *Under Their Own Vine and Fig Tree: The African-American Church in the South, 1865–1900* (1993).

The Great Migration is the topic of much scholarship, including general sources such as Florette Henri's *Black Migration: Movement North, 1900–1920* (1975); Carole Marks's *Farewell—We're Good and Gone: The Great Black Migration* (1989); and Milton C. Sernett's *Bound for the Promised Land: African American Religion and the Great Migration* (1997). Most of the books, however, focus on the effects of the migration on specific destinations: Gilbert Osofsky, *Harlem: The Making of a Ghetto, 1890–1930* (1963); Kenneth Kusmer, *A Ghetto Takes Shape: Black Cleveland, 1870–1930* (1976); James R. Grossman, *Land of Hope: Chicago, Black Southerners, and the Great Migration* (1989); and Lillian Serece Williams, *The Development of a Black Community: Buffalo, New York, 1900–1940* (1999). Jacqueline Jones's pioneering work on black women, *Labor of Love, Labor of Sorrow: Black Women, Work, and the Family, from Slavery to the Present* (1985), discusses how the Great Migration changed the nature of women's work and gender relationships. New organizations that helped the migrants are the subject of Nina Mjagkij, *Light in the Darkness: African Americans and the YMCA, 1852–1946* (1994); Charles Harris Wesley, *The History of the National Association of Colored Women's Clubs: A Legacy of Service* (1984); and Jesse T. Moore, *A Search for Equality: The National Urban League, 1910–1960* (1981). A good beginning reference source for any of the black associations is *Organizing Black America:*

An Encyclopedia of African American Associations, ed. Nina Mjagkij (2001).

Black education has received excellent coverage in James D. Anderson, *The Education of Blacks in the South, 1860–1935* (1988); and Henry Allen Bullock, *A History of Negro Education in the South: From 1619 to the Present* (1967). William P. Vaughn addresses the origins of black public schools during Reconstruction in *Schools for All: The Blacks and Public Education in the South, 1865–1875* (1974), as do Robert C. Morris in *Reading, 'Riting, and Reconstruction: The Education of Freedmen in the South, 1861–1870* (1981), and Ronald E. Butchart in *Northern Schools, Southern Blacks, and Reconstruction: Freedmen's Education, 1862–1875* (1980). On black universities, see Rayford W. Logan's *Howard University, 1867–1967* (1969) and Joe M. Richardson's *History of Fisk University, 1865–1946* (1980).

General discussions of blacks during Reconstruction include Leon F. Litwack's *Been in the Storm So Long: The Aftermath of Slavery* (1979); and Eric Foner's *Reconstruction: America's Unfinished Revolution, 1863–1877* (1988).

INDEX

Abbott, Lyman, 162–63
Abbott, Robert S., 22
Abolitionism, 5, 7, 43, 46, 47, 96, 102, 144
Accommodationism, 5, 23–24, 24–25, 27–28, 30, 32–33, 34–35, 81, 118, 143–45, 169–71
Adams, Henry, 10
Adams, Lewis, 11, 26
Addams, Jane, 53, 54, 83
African Methodist Episcopal Church (AME), 6, 50, 97, 98
African Methodist Episcopal Zion Church (AME Zion), 6, 26, 40
Afro-American Council, 29, 63–64, 69, 74
American Colonization Society (ACS), 96, 98, 99, 100
American Missionary Association, 22, 41
American Negro Academy, 52–53, 65, 90, 136–38
Anderson, Charles W., 81, 165–66, 166–67, 168–69
Armstrong, Samuel Chapman, 30, 35, 102; advises BTW, 26; background, 21–22; founds Hampton, 19; at Lake

Mohonk, 31; principal of Hampton, 22–24; recommends BTW, 25–26; views on protest, 24–25
Assimilation, 3–4, 43–44, 118–19
Atlanta Cotton States and International Exposition (1895), 32–33, 52, 125–29
Atlanta Riot (1906), 79–80, 169–73
Atlanta University, 53, 64, 91, 159; annual conferences, 58, 71; Atlanta University Studies, 57–58, 83, 84; curriculum, 32; Du Bois hired, 56; Du Bois returns, 117; loses philanthropists' support, 70, 75; student values, 43
Atlantic Monthly, 34, 56

Baldwin, Ruth Standish, 109
Baldwin, William H., 66, 74, 109, 138–39, 140–41
Baptists, 106–8
Barber, J. Max, 77, 78, 81, 84
Barnett, Ida B. Wells. *See* Wells-Barnett, Ida B.
Birth of a Nation (film), 86–87

Black nationalism, 7–8, 94–95,
  95–100, 110–11, 116–17,
  118–19. *See also* Emigration
Black soldiers, 111–12, 115,
  155
Black Panthers, 119
Blyden, Edward Wilmot, 98, 116
Boas, Franz, 83
Boston Guardian, 68, 69, 75,
  159, 160, 165
Boston Literary and Historical
  Association, 68
Boston Riot (1903), 74–75, 90,
  145–48
Brown, Henry Edwards, 102
Brownsville Affair (1906), 79,
  80, 83, 94
Bruce, Blanche K., 5, 8, 29, 33,
  69, 81
Bruce, Roscoe Conkling, 69, 82,
  149
Bullock, Rufus Brown, 33
Bumstead, Horace, 56, 71
Burghardt, Adelbert (half
  brother of Du Bois), 39
Burghardt family, 37–39, 41
Burroughs, James, 15, 17
Burroughs, Nannie Helen, 107
Burroughs family, 15, 17
Byrd, James, 121

Calloway, Thomas J., 42
Carnegie, Andrew, 2, 34, 76,
  138–39, 148
Carnegie Conference (1904), 76,
  90–91, 148–51, 160–61
Chase, W. Calvin, 61, 82, 163,
  164–65
Chisum, Melvin Jack, 163, 166–
  68
Church, Robert, 91
Civil Rights Act (1875), 11
Civil Rights Movement, 118–20
Clark University, 52
Cleveland, Grover, 46
Clubwomen, 93, 105–9, 111
Committee for Improving the
  Industrial Conditions for
  Negroes (CIICN), 109, 110
Committee of Twelve, 76, 91,
  152

Committee on Urban Condi-
  tions among Negroes in New
  York (CUCANNY), 110
Constitution League, 83
Convention movement, 6–7
Cook, George F. T., 65
Cook family, 5
Coolidge, Calvin, 116
Cooper, Anna Julia, 105, 111
The Crisis, 84, 85, 86, 91, 112,
  115, 116, 117, 174, 175
Crogman, William H., 52
Cromwell, John W., 159, 160
Crop-lien system, 10, 94
Crummell, Alexander, 52–53,
  71, 96–97, 100, 116, 119
Cuney, Norris Wright, 5

Darwin, Charles, 3
Davidson, Olivia A. *See* Wash-
  ington, Olivia A. Davidson
Disfranchisement, 9, 11, 12, 54,
  62, 63–64, 86–87, 129–32.
  See also Voting rights
Douglass, Frederick, 8, 29, 33,
  111
Du Bois, Alexander (grandfather), 37, 40–41, 52, 96
Du Bois, Alfred (father), 37, 39,
  40
Du Bois, Burghardt Gomer
  (son), 55, 58–59, 71
Du Bois, Mary Burghardt
  (mother), 37, 38–39
Du Bois, Nina Gomer (wife), 52,
  55, 58, 147
Du Bois, William Edward
  Burghardt, 7, 13, 34, 93, 94,
  100, 101, 108, 109, 110;
  accused as subversive, 115,
  117, 119; Afro-American
  Council, 63–64; applies for
  Tuskegee job, 29–30, 50;
  applies to Slater Fund, 47–
  48, 123–25; at Wilberforce,
  50–52; Atlanta University,
  56, 57–58, 117; attends Fisk,
  41–44; attends Harvard, 45–
  46, 47; becomes socialist,
  117; born, 37; Boston Riot,
  75, 145–48; BTW press

subsidies, 76–77, 156–63; Carnegie Conference, 76, 90–91, 148–51, 160–61; comparison with BTW views, 61–62; congratulates BTW on Atlanta Exposition address, 33; cooperates with BTW, 61, 63, 64–65, 66–67, 74, 140–41; *Credo*, 151–52; critiques BTW, 71–73; dies, 118; early childhood, 39–40; emigrates to Ghana, 8, 118; European circular (1910), 173–76; faith in integration, 43–44, 136–38; and Garvey, 116–17; in Europe, 48–49; in Philadelphia, 54–55; legacy of, 117–21; life after BTW, 115–17; marries, 52; master's degree, 47; mixes with Boston elite, 45–47; modern criticism of, 120; and NAACP, 84–85, 117, 173–74; Niagara Movement, 77–78, 79, 80, 81–83, 91, 152–56; on education, 57; on impact of racism, 56; on lynching, 58; on protest, 40, 57; on racial characteristics, 136; on woman suffrage, 129, 130, 131–32, 131; on YMCA, 105; Pan-Africanism, 67, 97, 115–16, 117; Paris Universal Exposition, 38, 67; Ph.D. degree, 50; *Philadelphia Negro* (1899), 55–56; Pullman lawsuit, 66–67, 71, 140–41; reaction to Atlanta Riot, 79, 169, 171–73; relationship with Crummell, 52–53, 96; relationship with Trotter, 69, 70, 75; reviews *Up from Slavery*, 69, 143–45; seeks DC position, 65–66; sociological research, 55–56, 57–58; son dies, 58–59; summer teaching, 42–43; teaches at Tuskegee, 74; tensions with BTW, 71–74; *The Crisis*, 84, 85, 86, 116, 117; *The Souls of Black Folk* (1903), 40, 52, 56, 71–74, 76, 145; *Suppres-sion of the African Slave Trade* (1895), 50; visits grandfather, 40–41; voting, 79, 82, 85; voting rights, 129–32, 153; works as waiter, 44–45; writes BTW obituary, 87

Du Bois family, 37, 41

Eastman, George, 35
Economic advancement, 5, 91, 118, 119, 120, 128, 154
Education, 7, 12, 26, 30, 102–3. *See also* Industrial education
Emigration: back-to-Africa movements, 95–100, 110, 116–17; con artists, 98, 99; Crummell advocates, 52; Du Bois to Ghana, 8, 118; earlier movements, 7–8; Garvey and, 116–17
Exodusters, 10

Farmers' Alliance, 10–11
Feminism, 101, 105–9
Ferguson, Amanda (BTW half sister), 15, 24
Ferguson, Jane (BTW mother), 15, 16, 24
Ferguson, Washington (BTW stepfather), 15, 17, 18
Fisk University, 41–42, 43, 44, 50, 110, 124
Forbes, George, 46, 68, 69, 75, 147
Forten, James, 5, 47, 53
Forten family, 5
Fortune, T. Thomas, 40; Afro-American Council, 29, 63–64; becomes unreliable, 77; Boston Riot, 74–75; BTW press subsidies, 160, 161; Carnegie Conference, 150; introduces Roosevelt to BTW, 35; meets BTW, 29; *New York Age*, 29, 35, 40, 68, 77, 157, 158
Fraternal organizations, 6, 82
Free blacks, 5, 6, 102
Freedmen's Bureau, 8, 22

Freeman, Elizabeth (Du Bois great-grandmother), 37
Frissell, Hollis, 30–31, 32

Garrison, Francis, 70
Garrison, William Lloyd, 5, 70, 77
Garvey, Marcus, 116–17, 119
Gradualism, 7, 118, 120; BTW's views, 5, 23–24, 24–25, 27–28, 30, 32–33, 34–35, 125–29, 133–36; discredited, 112; Du Bois advocates, 117; Du Bois criticizes, 143–45; Kelly Miller's views, 90
Great Migration, 100–101, 103, 109–10. See also Migration
Grimké, Angelina Weld, 47
Grimké, Archibald H., 46–47, 53, 65, 76, 84, 140, 145, 160, 174
Grimké, Charlotte Forten, 47
Grimké, Francis J., 47, 65, 140, 145, 150
Grimké, Sarah, 46

Hampton Normal and Agricultural Institute, 31, 50, 57, 61, 145; BTW admitted, 19–20; founding of, 21–22; life at, 22–23; noted graduates, 22, 27
Harlan, Robert, 5, 12
Harlem Renaissance, 116
Harrison, Benjamin, 98
Hart, Albert Bushnell, 47, 50, 57
Hart, William H., 77
Harvard University, 41, 45–46, 47, 49, 57
Hatcher, Benjamin, 15
Hayes, Rutherford B., 31, 48, 123–25
Haynes, George E., 110
Hershaw, Lafayette M., 77, 81, 82, 169
The Horizon, 81, 82
Hose, Sam, 58, 64, 94
Howard University, 43, 50, 64, 65, 82, 90, 91, 93, 103, 111
Hunton, William A., 103

Immigration, 2–3, 4, 24, 39–40, 127
Imperialism, 2
Indians. See Native Americans
Industrial education: at Hampton, 21; BTW advocates, 30, 61, 119, 132–36; disadvantages of, 21; Du Bois criticizes, 57, 61–62, 71; evolution of, 20–21; in college curriculums, 54; Kelly Miller supports, 90; Lake Mohonk conferences, 31–32; Slater Fund supports, 123–25
Industrialization, 2, 20–21
Integration, 4, 42, 43–44, 118–19
International Migration Society, 99–100

Jackson, Jesse, 119
James, William, 47, 49
Jeanes, Anna T., 30
Jim Crow, 3, 48, 57, 73, 101, 110, 112; challenged, 108; Du Bois's first experience, 42; in government, 86; origins of term, 1–2; rise of, 11–12, 43, 63. See also Segregation

Kellor, Frances, 109
King, Martin Luther, Jr., 118–19

Lake Mohonk conferences, 31–32, 48
Lewis, William H., 46, 82, 150
Liberia, 96, 98–99, 100
Lindsay, Samuel McCune, 53, 54, 55
Little, Earl, 117
Locke, Alain, 53
Lynchings: BTW on, 64, 140; Ida Wells campaigns against, 12, 108; in Leland, 100; in Waco, 100; NAACP campaigns against, 85; rise of, 2, 12, 57, 63; Sam Hose, 58, 64, 94, 121

Malcolm X, 117, 118
Masculinity, 101, 102, 105
Massachusetts Racial Protective
    Association, 68
McCabe, Edwin, 95
McKinlay, Whitefield, 145–46
Migration: Great Migration,
    100–101, 103, 109–10; to
    North, 95; to West, 10, 95, 98
Milholland, John, 83
Miller, Kelly: American Negro
    Academy, 53; as indepen-
    dent, 90–91, 94, 145;
    Carnegie Conference, 148–
    49; Committee of Twelve, 76;
    in Washington, DC, 65;
    NAACP, 84; on BTW press
    subsidies, 160
Minstrel shows, 1–2
Montgomery, William S., 65
The Moon, 78, 81
Moore, Frederick Randolph,
    162
Moorland, Jesse, 103
Morgan, Clement G., 45, 77, 82,
    148, 150
M Street High School (Washing-
    ton, DC), 44, 65, 66, 81, 93
Murray, F.H.M., 77, 81, 82, 168

National Association for the
    Advancement of Colored
    People (NAACP), 6, 76, 83–
    85, 86–87, 91, 93, 117, 119,
    174
National Association of Colored
    Women, 108–9, 111
National Baptist Woman's
    Convention, 106–8, 109
National Equal Rights League
    (1864), 7
National Equal Rights League
    (1908), 82
Nationalism. See Black nation-
    alism
National League for the Protec-
    tion of Colored Women
    (NLPCW), 109–10
National Negro Business League
    (NNBL), 34, 36, 63, 68, 74,
    79, 82, 85, 145, 163

National Negro Committee. See
    National Association for the
    Advancement of Colored
    People
National Training School for
    Women and Girls, 107
National Urban League, 6, 91,
    110
Nation of Islam, 117, 119
Native Americans, 3–4, 21, 25
New York Age, 29, 35, 40, 68,
    77, 157, 158
Niagara Movement, 77–78, 79,
    80, 81, 82–83, 91, 93, 152–56

Ogden, Robert C., 70–71, 75, 146
Ovington, Mary White, 83–84

Pan-Africanism, 67, 97, 115–16,
    117
Parks, Rosa, 119
Payne, Daniel, 51
Peabody, George, 30, 71, 146–
    47, 160
Peabody Education Fund, 30
Peace Information Center, 117
Phelps, Olivia, 30
Philadelphia Settlement, 53–54,
    55
Pinchback, Pinckney Benton
    Stewart, 8, 29, 65, 145
Pittman, William Sidney, 105
Plessy v. Ferguson (1896), 11–
    12, 32
Populism, 10–11
Progressivism, 2, 3–4, 53, 54,
    85, 110

Racial solidarity, 6, 12–13, 102–
    5, 110–11
Racial uplift: BTW v. Du Bois,
    62; feminism, 101, 105–9;
    Kelly Miller's approach, 91;
    masculinity, 101, 102, 105;
    morals, 102; NACW, 108–9;
    noblesse oblige, 42
Racism: changing nature of, 2–
    3; Du Bois's first experience,
    40; in North, 101; as political
    tactic, 10–11; scientific, 3,
    12, 56, 63

Radical Reconstruction, 7, 8–9,
    24–25, 43, 106
Rice, Thomas Dartmouth, 1–2
Rockefeller, John D., Jr., 103, 139
Rockefeller, John D., Sr., 2, 34,
    138
Roosevelt, Theodore, 35, 68, 80,
    81, 85, 165, 168
Rosenwald, Julius, 103
Ruffin, Josephine St. Pierre, 45,
    46, 108
Ruffin family, 5
Ruffner, Lewis, 18
Ruffner, Viola, 18–19, 20

Santayana, George, 47, 49
Scott, Emmett J., 34, 77, 78,
    158, 162
Segregation: at Tuskegee, 35;
    BTW's views on, 33, 125–29;
    challenges to, 108; Du Bois's
    first experiences, 42; in
    government, 86; in YMCA,
    103; justification for, 2; rise
    of, 9, 11–12, 43, 89. See also
    Jim Crow
Self-help, 6, 12–13, 120
Separatism. See Black
    nationalism
Settlement houses, 6, 53–54, 55
Sharecroppers, 9–10, 23, 43, 71,
    94, 132
Singleton, Benjamin "Pap," 10
Slater, John F., 30
Slater Fund, 30, 31, 48, 49,
    123–25
Slavery, 4–5, 15–17, 50, 102,
    127, 133
Smith, Wilford H., 141
Social Darwinism, 3
Southern Christian Leadership
    Conference (SCLC), 119
Stereotypes: black on black, 5,
    101; BTW acceptance of, 125,
    133; Du Bois works to
    counter, 48, 56; in North, 54–
    55; of black women, 105–6,
    107; of blacks, 4–5; of
    immigrants, 40; of Native
    Americans, 21; origins of,
    1–2

Stokes, Caroline Phelps, 30
Student Nonviolent Coordinat-
    ing Committee (SNCC), 118

Taft, William Howard, 80, 81,
    82, 85, 93, 169
Talented Tenth, 62, 84, 100,
    103, 109, 117, 119
Taliaferro family, 15
Terrell, Mary Church, 65, 80,
    84, 91–94, 108, 111
Terrell, Robert H., 65, 81–82,
    93
Trotter, Maude, 75, 145
Trotter, William Monroe, 61, 70,
    163, 174; at Harvard, 46;
    Boston Riot, 74–75, 145–48;
    founds Guardian, 68; Niagara
    Movement, 77, 82; opposes
    BTW, 69, 74–75, 85, 145–48;
    relationship with Du Bois,
    47, 160, 145–48
Turner, Henry McNeal, 97–98,
    99–100, 116, 119, 150
Tuskegee, Ala., 11, 26, 119
Tuskegee Normal and Industrial
    Institute, 31, 61, 65, 103,
    109, 111, 123, 134, 145;
    classes at, 31, 135; clearing-
    house for race issues, 34, 53,
    57, 58, 71, 161; Du Bois
    applies for job, 29–30; Du
    Bois teaches at, 61; early
    years, 26–29; fundraising, 27,
    28, 29, 30, 33, 138–39;
    origins of, 11, 25–26; rela-
    tionship with Africa, 67;
    segregates visitors, 35;
    Tuskegee machine, 36, 61,
    73, 86, 93, 115

United Negro Improvement
    Association (UNIA), 116–
    17
University of Berlin, 48–49
Urban problems, 101, 109–10

Villard, Oswald Garrison, 77,
    80, 83, 84, 85, 142, 157–62
Voice of the Negro, 76, 77, 78,
    157

Voting rights: BTW on 30, 141; Du Bois on, 129–32; protection of, 8; restrictions of, 9, 11. *See also* Disfranchisement

Walters, Alexander, 69, 86
Washington, Booker Taliaferro, 7, 13, 22, 43, 46, 55, 94, 94, 100, 101, 106, 108, 109, 110, 112, 116; accommodationist views, 5, 23–24, 24–25, 27–28, 30, 32–33, 34–35, 81, 125–29, 133–36, 169–71; and Afro-American Council, 63–64; assimilation, 5; and Atlanta Riot, 79, 80, 169–71; attacks opposition, 68, 69–70, 75–76, 78–79, 81–82, 145–48, 168–69; attends Hampton, 19–20, 22–24; beaten in street, 85; born, 15; and Boston Riot, 74–76, 145–48; career options, 23–24; Carnegie Conference, 76, 90–91, 148–51, 160–61; challenges segregation, 62, 66–67, 140–42; and cleanliness, 18–19, 23; comparison with Du Bois, 61–62; cooperates with Du Bois, 61, 63, 64–65, 66–67, 74, 140–41; death, 87, 115; differs with Du Bois on education, 57; dines at White House, 35; early teaching career, 24; early years of Tuskegee, 26–29; economic advancement, 5; experiences in slavery, 15–17; founds Tuskegee, 25–26; gives Atlanta Exposition address, 32–33, 51–52, 125–29; and Howard University, 82; influence on philanthropy, 48, 69–70, 82, 133, 138–39; journey to Hampton, 19; learns to read, 18; legacy, 117–21; loses power, 80, 86; modern views of, 120; and NAACP, 84; need for secrecy, 62–63; offers Du Bois a job, 50, 64, 74; on lynching, 64, 140; on YMCA, 105; opposes disfranchisement, 62, 141; opposition develops, 63, 64, 68; opposition in Boston, 47, 145; and Pan-Africanism, 67; press subsidies, 68, 69, 75, 76–77, 78, 156–65; relationship with Armstrong, 23; relationship with Carnegie, 34; relationship with Roosevelt, 35, 62, 168–69; relationship with whites, 18–19, 23, 34; rises to national leadership, 33–36; rising tensions with Du Bois, 71–74; secret life, 139–42; stifles Niagara Movement, 162–63; teaches at Hampton, 25; Tuskegee "lieutenants," 165–69; *Up from Slavery* (1901), 16, 34–35, 69, 143–45; views of Malden, 17–18; views on segregation, 33, 139–42; "Wizard of Tuskegee," 36, 70; works as waiter, 24, 44–45; works for Ruffners, 18–19; works in salt mines, 18
Washington, John (brother), 15, 16, 18, 24, 34
Washington, Margaret Murray (third wife), 42, 109
Washington, Olivia A. Davidson (second wife), 27, 28, 29, 42
Washington, Portia (daughter), 61, 105
Washington Bee, 61, 82, 163, 164–65
Washington Record, 157, 159
Weld, Angelina Grimké, 46
Wells-Barnett, Ida B., 12, 68, 69, 84, 108, 109
Wetmore, J. Douglas, 142
Wharton, Susan, 54
Wharton School, 53, 54
Wilberforce, William, 50
Wilberforce University, 50–51, 52, 53, 93, 96
Wilson, Woodrow, 85–86, 111
Woman suffrage, 129–32

Women's organizations. *See* Clubwomen
World War I, 111–12, 116
Wormley, James A., 9

Young Men's Christian Association (YMCA), 6, 101–5
Young Women's Christian Association (YWCA), 109, 111